SONIC
ALCHEMY

VISIONARY MUSIC PRODUCERS AND
THEIR MAVERICK RECORDINGS

SONIC
ALCHEMY

VISIONARY MUSIC PRODUCERS AND
THEIR MAVERICK RECORDINGS

Sonic Alchemy
Visionary Music Producers and their Maverick Recordings

Copyright © 2004 David N. Howard

Published by Hal Leonard Corporation
7777 Bluemound Road
P.O. Box 13819
Milwaukee, WI 53213

Trade Book Division Editorial Offices
151 West 46th Street, 8th Floor
New York, NY 10036

Library of Congress Cataloging-in-Publication Data
Howard, David N., 1969-
  Sonic alchemy : visionary music producers and their maverick
recordings / by David N. Howard.— 1st ed.
      p. cm.
Includes bibliographical references.
  ISBN 0-634-05560-7 (pbk.)
  1. Sound recording executives and producers—Biography. I. Title.
ML406.H69 2004
781.49'092'2—dc22
                          2003025451

Printed in the United States of America
First Edition
Book Designed by Hal Leonard Creative Services

Visit Hal Leonard online at **www.halleonard.com**

• *For Lauren* •

CONTENTS

ACKNOWLEDGMENTS

I would like to thank the following people who all directly contributed to the writing of this book: My parents, Cheryl and Richard, for all their support and letting me steal their copy of *Revolver*; my agent, Andrew Stuart, for his tireless work and sage advice; John Kovacich, Jon Strickland, and Brian Hirsh, whose feedback and keen suggestions were invaluable; Gene Farkas and Janice Laureen, for always being there; David Axelrod, Shel Talmy, and Carol Kaye, for sharing their stories, Stephen McParland, for his photo assistance; Aidan Wylde, for the skinny on Mr. Jimmy; and all the people at Hal Leonard.

INTRODUCTION

"Don't you wonder sometimes 'bout sound and vision?"
—David Bowie 1977

• • • • •

For everyone who ever picked up the back of an album cover, spied a producer's name, and wondered what the hell he did, this book is for you. It all started for me with a Beatles record copped from my parents' collection. Nearly everyone born in the last 40 odd years has had a similar experience. I was lucky; my first Beatles record was one of their finest, *Revolver*. I still clearly recall pulling it out of the family record collection; its black-and-white collage cover called to me from the dusty pile of vinyl in the closet. I was five years old, and my life would never be the same again.

Of course, I hadn't the faintest idea that this was "psychedelic" music, but I instantly connected with its intrinsic childlike sense of discovery. Playfully surreal, brimming with ingenious recording studio tricks, it seemed like nothing less than a vibrant musical cartoon. It was the wondrous little elements that first hooked me—the comical count-off before "Taxman," the mysterious electronic seagull sounds that swirl around "Tomorrow Never Knows," the 3-D backwards guitar of "She Said She Said," the stark violins that surround all the lonely people of "Eleanor Rigby," and, of course, the mirthful sailor sound effects of "Yellow Submarine."

I had one of those self-contained stereo record players, with two tiny speakers, a volume knob, and a balance knob. This wasn't one of those colorfully cool Peter Max–like portable units that were so prevalent around the late '60s and early '70s; rather, mine was gray, almost industrial in its practical utilitarianism—but who needed a Day-Glo record player when the sounds wafting out of my speakers spewed so many vivid hues?

One day, while playing my one and only adult record, I had a stereophonic epiphany. As the needle circled its usual trip around "Yellow Submarine," for some reason I started messing around with the speaker balance knob. Suddenly, I made a fascinating discovery: by turning the knob all the way to the left speaker, all I heard were the vocals. Then I turned it as far as it could go to the right side, and the only thing audible was the music! Joyfully unraveling the mysteries of stereo production at age five, I have not stopped since.

A few years later, I began accumulating more Beatles records, and I starting detecting a pattern. Contained on the back of each of their covers appeared the same credit: "produced by George Martin." Although I had no idea what a producer did, or who George Martin was, I figured that, since he was credited on every album that existed in my tiny universe, whatever he did must be important. As I got older, I realized that I was by no means the only one who pondered the question "what does a music producer *really* do?" For many, the question never was really answered, and that is where this book comes in. There are as many answers as there are producers, but ultimately these shadowy studio gurus all share one simple goal: to make a record sound as good as it possibly can.

Naturally, when dealing with the expansive scope of the subject, there will be those with gripes and cries of "why wasn't he in here?" And that is the way it should be. This book is about "visionary producers," Oz-like men who pulled the levers from behind the curtain and created a legacy of sound that is woven into the fabric of daily life. Whether serenaded while pushing a shopping cart down a supermarket aisle, watching the millionth television commercial co-opted from a classic song, booting up a computer, or even listening to the radio, the odds are good that somebody in this book had something to do with it.

—David N. Howard
Los Angeles, 2004

THE PIONEERS: PHIL SPECTOR AND GEORGE MARTIN

In February 1966, Phil Spector, the anointed "Tycoon of Teen" is at a career crossroads. Mortally afraid time has passed him by, the man who transformed the role of record producer from shadowy studio dweller into star-making celebrity through an unparalleled string of early 1960s hits was working desperately against irrelevance. The rock 'n' roll generation was growing up and away from the carefree teenaged symphonies that characterized Spector's meteoric ascension to the top of the music world. Now the Svengali producer was trying to squeeze one last hit from his defiantly inflexible formula before it was rendered completely obsolete by an onslaught of self-contained, new breed rock bands.

Residing in a seedy part of Hollywood, Gold Star Studios was Phil Spector's home away from home. Its cracker-box-sized Studio "A" was stuffed with sweaty and exhausted session musicians packed into

"The Tycoon of Teen,"
Phil Spector

the claustrophobic room like hipster sardines. Working without the luxury of breaks, the dark shades–clad producer continued to crack the proverbial whip as he searched for the right sound. The overflowing assemblage of two-dozen musicians had been working around the clock, so cramped in the tiny studio they barely have enough space to scratch an itch. Mercifully, the robust rhythm tracks were finally completed and the sessioneers were sprung from their studio cell. Now, the last daunting responsibility rode on the petite, brown-skinned shoulders of a weary, bedraggled singer named Tina Turner.

Spector had wrung nearly every ounce of Turner's considerable soul into countless takes of an unusually constructed song, but he remained unsatisfied. Suddenly, the studio lights were doused; it was pitch black, dead silent. Turner shed her sweat-soaked blouse and sidled up to the microphone. Standing in her bra, she unleashed an untapped reservoir of raw adrenaline so sexually charged she held her crotch as she delivered the spine-tingling high notes. Turner managed to plumb expressive depths lower than she thought existed within herself to cut the definitive take of Spector's magnum opus and most spectacular flop, "River Deep (Mountain High)." The obtuse, densely constructed song was the very essence of the producer's unrelenting vision—muddy, grandiose, and exhilarating. This was Phil Spector's Wall of Sound.

Simultaneously, as "River Deep" was becoming Spector's Waterloo, the band most responsible for driving his demise was reaching an artistic watershed. The Beatles and their producer George Martin had just begun the sessions for their genre-transforming album, Revolver. In stark contrast to Spector's distorted, over-the-top studio formula, Revolver's shape-shifting sound was predicated on crystalline clarity and tasteful restraint.

As the Revolver sessions commenced at Abbey Road recording studios, work began on a song unlike any other the band had attempted before. Influenced by a string of mind-bending acid trips, John Lennon made a rather unusual query to George Martin: "I want to sound as though I'm the Dalai Lama singing from the highest mountain top[1]," he said deadpan. Martin and his young engineer, Geoff Emerick, looked quizzically at Lennon and then stared blankly at each other. Lennon was in the habit of lobbing challenging requests at his producer, but *this confounding whim far exceeded anything that preceded it. However, Martin thrived on challenge, and his greatest strength was in his dogged determination. His lengthy list of successful productions was a direct result of an uncanny knack for studio improvising, and he digested Lennon's demand until he was suddenly struck with an idea.*

Martin called Emerick over and ordered him to break into the circuitry of a Hammond organ, and remove the revolving "Leslie" speaker component that provided the instrument with its distinctive swirling sound. Once the speaker was extracted from the casing, it was rigged to Lennon's microphone with the hope that it would produce the same swirling sound for his voice. With all systems go, it was time to give it a try, Martin crossed his fingers and switched on the speaker. Suddenly, the entire studio gasped in collective amazement as Lennon's vocal darted around the studio like a hyperactive firefly. They had succeeded—Lennon was the Dalai Lama shouting on top of the mountain! With a number of additional boldly innovative enhancements piled on (including sped-up guitars, strange tape loops, and compressed drums), the song that became known as "Tomorrow Never Knows" almost single-handedly ushered in the psychedelic age of recording studio experimentation.

With Phil Spector and George Martin's visionary achievements in sound, the recording studio was now its own instrument; record production had been elevated into art.

• • • • •

In the late 1950s, Los Angeles was home to a number of inspired R&B and jazz musicians who primarily thrived in the town's black South Central district. From tenor honker Big Jay McNeely to cool-jazz alto-saxophonist Art Pepper, the town had its stars, but, as a recording center, L.A. was most definitely the minor leagues. New York, Memphis, Nashville—that's where the real hits were crafted. Los Angeles had shoddy studios, fly-by-night promo men, and a murky, second-class sound.

Located on an unsavory stretch of Hollywood's Vine Street sat tiny Gold Star Studios. Forged from an old storefront into two miniscule studios by owners Stan Ross and Dave Gold in 1950, its low-slung fourteen-foot ceilings and 35' x 23' room dimensions were far from ideal. In order to compensate for the studio's diminutive dimensions and acoustically thin sound, Ross and Gold proceeded to construct two separate echo chambers. Where most traditional studios only utilized one echo enclosure, the additional chamber provided Gold Star with a unique allure and a competitive distinction. By the late 1950s Gold Star was among the most in-demand studios in L.A., and vocal groups such as The Four Lads and The Hi-Los enjoyed hits predicated on the resonant harmonies that the dual echo chambers afforded.

One afternoon a rail-thin teenager named Harvey Phillip Spector showed up at a Stan Ross–engineered Gold Star session and sheepishly asked Ross to cut him a deal on some studio time. Ross immediately took a shine to the young man, who answered to "Phil." However, leery of a deluge of bargain-hunting teen producers, Ross stayed steadfast to the regular studio fees—$15 an hour, and $6 for each roll of quarter-inch recording tape. Spector promised he'd be back.

After the suicide of his iron-working father in 1949, Spector's mother had moved Phil and his older sister out to Los Angeles for a fresh start. Settling in the lower-middle-class Jewish section of West Hollywood, Spector demonstrated a keen interest in music, especially the sophisticated sounds of jazz and raw emotion of blues. After receiving a guitar for his bar mitzvah, he practiced prodigiously, often through the wee hours of the night. By the time Spector was in high school, he was scheming song and production ideas in preparation for the studio time he planned to purchase at Gold Star.

Utilizing a small tape recorder, Spector and school chum Marshall Lieb would record their two voices and sing over the playback in a unique attempt to double their vocals. Instead of adhering to the traditional method of hearing the track played back through headphones and singing over it, Spector had a different idea. He wanted the first track played over the studio speakers, and then he would sing over that, in an effort to enlarge the sound to titanic proportions. Rather than the traditional, and rather limited, overdubbing afforded by the archaic recording equipment of the time, Spector's concept of "stacking" voices was entirely new, and it was specifically designed to take full advantage of the studio's possibilities.

After scrapping together the $40 needed for a two-hour session at Gold Star, Lieb and Spector, along with two classmates, Harvey

Goldstein and Annette Kleinbard, embarked on recording their coy original "Don't You Worry My Little Pet" in May 1957. Instantly Spector fell into his element and seized control of the session with an almost preternatural assurance. After contributing vocal, guitar, and piano parts to the simple Chuck-Berry-meets-do-wop ditty, Spector excitedly raced back to the control booth to hear the playback.

Trying out the stacked vocal concept that Spector had envisioned proved to be tricky. With the cacophonous din of the playback tape blaring over the studio speakers, it was difficult to hear the vocal parts clearly. Undeterred, his persistence paid off, and eventually the stacked voices worked. With his first session completed, Spector was handed a shiny acetate demo record. He held it gently in his small hands as if it were a piece of fragile china. Phil Spector had found his life's calling.

After dubbing themselves the Teddy Bears and landing a deal with a tiny independent label, the newly christened group searched for an appropriate B-side for "Little Pet." Spector decided on an original he had been massaging for some time, called "Wonderful Lovable You," but he made one crucial change to the song. Haunted by his father's suicide, Spector would frequently fixate on his gravestone epitaph, which read "Ben Spector: To Know Him Was to Love Him." With a slight change, "Wonderful Lovable You" became "To Know Him Is to Love Him." Highlighted by Kleinbard's vulnerable vocal, a repetitious chorus, and a do-wop arrangement that featured an unusual jazz chord progression, the composition was fresh and emotional.

Released with little fanfare or attention, the Teddy Bears caught a most unlikely break after a Fargo, North Dakota, DJ flipped the single and added "To Know Him Is to Love Him" to the rotation. The song sparked, and "To Know Him" began to be promoted as the A-side. Following a nerve-wracking live appearance on *American Bandstand* in late November 1957, the Teddy Bears' ballad made a final Cinderella charge to Number 1 on both *Billboard* and *Cash Box*'s singles charts.

After signing with Liberty Records, the Teddy Bears recorded a final full-length album that proved to be unsuccessful, due in large part to the fact that the album was not recorded at Gold Star. Liberty used the somewhat dilapidated Master Sound Recorders, a studio that clearly lacked the echo-laden magic of Gold Star. Nonetheless, the sessions afforded Spector the opportunity to further his singular studio vision. Intrigued by the transparent possibilities of sound, Spector began mixing instruments directly in an effort to capture the overall ambience of the room. In many ways the air around the notes was as important as the actual notes. In essence, Spector was seeking a sound far larger then the sum of its parts. Construction on the Wall of Sound was under way.

• • • • •

Across the pond in London, George Martin, a young producer for Parlophone Records was in a quandary. His boss, and label head, Oscar Preuss, abruptly retired, and Martin had been tapped as his unexpected successor. Only 29, Martin had been given the unenviable position of resuscitating the floundering record label. As part of EMI, the dominant English record label conglomerate of the 1950s and 1960s, Parlophone routinely had its top artists moved over to its better-distributed sister label, Columbia Records.

As a young man in Drayton Park, England, George Martin fell in love with the piano and quickly discovered that he possessed the gift of perfect pitch. After a four-year stint as a pilot in the Fleet Air Arm during WW II, Martin used a government grant given to ex-Navy officers to finance an education at the Guildhall School of Music. Martin studied three years at the music academy where he inhaled music theory, conducting, and orchestration and studied piano and oboe. Highly influenced by the impressionistic-influenced French modern composers Ravel and Debussy, Martin was fascinated by their lofty attempts to "paint sound." Soon, he would co-opt the concept into his own musical pursuits.

Out of school, Martin quickly realized that he lacked the talent to make it as a concert musician. Unsure of his future, he toiled as a clerk at the BBC music library, until he received a fateful break when he landed a job as the assistant to the head of Parlophone in the fall of 1950. The label had a diverse roster, and its encompassing genres included jazz, classical, dance music, light orchestral, and even comedy albums. Despite its variety, Parlophone was a very small operation, and this provided the eager Martin with a golden opportunity to learn the business from all sides.

One of Martin's earliest triumphs was in collaboration with his friend, the *enfant terrible* of British actors, Peter Ustinov. Ustinov was a gregarious, larger-than-life figure known to entertain people with a myriad of comical mouth sound effects. Inspired by his wacky gift of mouth music, Martin was struck with the adventurous idea to record "Mock Mozart," a satirical mini-opera of Ustinov's various voices blended together.

Without the luxury of multi-track recording, the young producer was forced to record each of Ustinov's four parts one by one, dub it from one tape to another, and mix it together on the fly. Unfortunately, with each subsequent dub, the recording quality markedly degenerated. Tested but undaunted by the limitations of the studio, Martin persevered. Finally, after a particularly complicated and arduous process, he succeeded, and "Mock Mozart" became an unlikely hit British single. Nowhere was its success more surprising than to the bemused EMI executives who had been perplexed by the experimental nature of the recording. Undeniably, this auspicious foray into overdubbing was a harbinger of cutting-edge techniques to come from Martin.

Martin continued to develop his editing skills with a succession of collaborations with comedic genius and fledgling actor, Peter Sellers. Sellers had attained great notoriety alongside Spike Milligan and Harry Secombe as part of the irreverent BBC radio show team, the Goons. *The Goon Show*, which featured often outrageous comedy skits, enjoyed a ten-year run, beginning in 1951, and its surreal humor paved the way for everything from *Monty Python's Flying Circus* to *Saturday Night Live*. Many of Sellers's bits were ad-libbed, and Martin and his engineer sometimes would make as many as 150 editing cuts to pare the pieces down to their most amusing moments. Several other Sellers bits hinged on hilarious musical parodies of rock "The Trumpet Volunteer," "We Need The Money," and British folk "Suddenly, It's a Folk Song."

As Parlophone became entrenched as the home of novelty recordings, Martin longed to sign a pop star on the order of Cliff Richard, who was beginning to burn up the British charts as something like an English Elvis. As a result of Martin's labor-intensive comedy records, a great deal of time and energy was going into each recording. Furthermore, a novelty act would not sell records based solely on only his or her name, and generating captivating novelty material was often an arduous task. As Martin saw it, producing a pop star was a much easier road to hoe; once successful, the artist would become "fireproof" and could sell follow-up songs based solely on established name recognition. While on the lookout for such an act, Martin received a phone call that would forever alter the cultural landscape not only of England, but of the entire world.

· · · · ·

With his ambitions swelling, Phil Spector headed east to the center of it all. Arriving in New York, the young man parlayed his wunderkind notoriety into a place on the payroll of the highly successful songwriting/producing team of Mike Stoller and Jerry Lieber as an associate songwriter and apprentice producer. After what seemed like an eternity spent observing on the sidelines, Spector finally got called into action as a session guitarist for a smattering of Leiber and Stoller recording dates. Painfully out of his league on a musicianship level, Spector constantly received the cold shoulder from the hard-bitten New York session pros.

By the summer of 1960, Spector was growing more confident in New York, and he ditched his L.A. suits for an eccentric look that included long black capes, ill-fitting pants, and galoshes. With Mike Stoller out of town, Spector received a fortunate break when Jerry Leiber gave him a shot at writing the melody for "Spanish Harlem," a new song slated for ex-Drifters vocalist Ben E. King. Under enormous pressure, Spector rose to the occasion, delivering the memorable Latin-derived "da-da-da, da-da-da" marimba hook that helped make the song a smash. With Spector's star rising, he accepted an A&R position with highly respected Atlantic Records. It was 1961 and he was not yet 20 years old.

Ultimately, Spector's Atlantic stint proved fruitless. The muddy-sounding sessions he produced were misunderstood by some and reviled by others. Atlantic had one of only two eight-track recorders in existence (the other was custom built and operated by Les Paul), and much of Spector's Atlantic failures were related to his uneasy grasp on technology. He was much more comfortable with two-track recorders, and the advanced eight-track technology left Spector confused and ill at ease. Finally, after label head Jerry Wexler discovered Spector was bilking the label out of hundreds of dollars on late-night long-distance calls that centered on his schemes of autonomy, his stint at Atlantic came to an unceremonious end.

Now splitting his time between New York and L.A., Spector forged a deal with his L.A. publisher, Lester Sill, and the duo formed Philles Records. He also began a close working relationship with arranger, Jack Nitzsche. Like Spector, the horn-rimmed bespectacled Nitzsche also possessed an outrageous personality, and the two men quickly gelled.

After auditioning several different groups for Philles, Spector finally found what he was looking for with a quintet of teen-aged black girls named the Crystals. Hailing from Brooklyn, the group already had "There's No Other (Like My Baby)" in its repertoire, and Spector was rapturous over the song and the singers. Deftly shaping their sound over a two-week period, Spector would often turn the studio lights off, leaving the girls to rehearse in the dark until their voices were left hoarse.

The first Philles Records release, "There's No Other (Like My Baby)," became a hit, and it established the Crystals along with the Shirelles and the Cookies as one of the early leading "Girl Groups"— a new genre that was marked by buoyant female harmonies, a snappy backbeat, and infectious melodies usually written by Brill Building pros such as King-Goffin and Barry-Greenwich. Making the transition from upstart to mogul, Spector abandoned his eccentric wardrobe for stylish suits and expensive close-cropped haircuts. His clout was now expanding at the same accelerated pace as his musical vision, and, with his apropos next song "He's a Rebel," the wunderkind was about to hit full stride.

• • • • •

In April 1962, George Martin received a call from Syd Coleman, a friend who ran Ardmore & Beechwood, the publishing arm of EMI. Coleman asked if Martin would take a meeting with a manager named Brian Epstein, who was shopping a demo tape of a rock group from Liverpool. Martin told Coleman he was game and asked him the name of the group. "The Beatles," Coleman answered.

For Brian Epstein, Parlophone was the final desperate stop on his tour of potential record labels for his shaggy-haired band. Beaten down and dispirited, the Beatles had suffered through two failed auditions at Decca and had been flatly rejected by both Phillips and Pye Records. Things were looking bleak for Epstein's band when Coleman managed to get hold of the demos and suggested meeting with Martin because of his success with unusual recording acts.

When Epstein arrived at Parlophone, Martin was immediately impressed by the manager's polished appearance and bountiful intelligence. Surprisingly, he was not as taken with the music. In fact, he understood why everyone in town had turned down the group. Included on the demo tape were a clutch of oldies including Fats Waller's "Your Feet's Too Big," and a handful of originals that Martin considered mediocre at best. But the producer's interest was piqued by the band's rough quality and the unusual arrangements of more than one vocalist singing at the same time. Although far from convinced, Martin heard enough promise to invite the group to EMI's Abbey Road studios for a recording test. Leery of further dashed hopes, Epstein skeptically agreed, and a date was set.

All four Beatles were fervent Peter Sellers fans, and the fact that Martin had produced the beloved comedian immediately endeared him to the band. Committed to give him their best, they began the tryout. As they tore through their live club set, Martin remained nonplussed by the band's material, especially the four originals, "Love Me Do," "Ask Me Why," "Hello Little Girl," and "P.S. I Love You." Even more troubling was their drummer, Pete Best, who Martin immediately deemed not good enough for the band. Unbeknownst to Martin, the band felt the same way towards the amiable Best. In fact, they were already courting flashy skins-man, Ringo Starr, from fellow Star Club perennials Rory Storm and the Hurricanes.

George Martin "With the Beatles"

Despite Martin's disregard of their songwriting talents, his personal affinity for the group was strong. Unable to deny their overflowing charisma and unbridled enthusiasm, he presented Epstein with a five-year Parlophone contract a month after the audition. Martin contends that he was the band's last gasp, and, had he turned them down, they quite possibly would have never had been heard from again.

With the Beatles' straightforward early songs, Martin's primary responsibilities were supervising the recording sessions and ensuring that the engineer properly captured the session on tape. He would also make arrangement suggestions so the songs ran the standard radio-friendly length of roughly two-and-a-half-minutes per single. Among the early sessions, Martin had a particular influence on "Please Please Me," which was initially conceived by John Lennon as a brooding Roy Orbison–like ballad. Originally running just over a minute long, Martin suggested Lennon pick up the tempo and called for an extra chorus. With his help, the song was transformed into one of the band's biggest early hits.

Martin also significantly bolstered "Can't Buy Me Love." Originally structured with a standard opening verse, Martin wanted to shake things up with "an introduction, something that catches the ear immediately, a hook"[2] and suggested starting with the sticky-as-superglue chorus instead. Strengthened by its unorthodox structure, the song became another mammoth hit—and a prime early example of Martin eagerness to shun convention.

With the Beatles' *Merseybeat* igniting the charts, Martin fanned the flames further with productions for a trio of additional Epstein acts: Gerry and the Pacemakers, Cilla Black, and Billy J. Kramer and the Dakotas. Kramer in particular tested Martin's skill and studio creativity. Obviously lacking the talent of the Beatles, or even the Pacemakers, Kramer was more a teen idol than a legitimate singer. Due to Kramer's singing shortcomings, Martin would often "double-track" his vocals, a technique that involved recording his voice twice and then synching them together for greater resonance. At this stage, the crude recording equipment available made double-tracking a highly laborious endeavor. Another trick Martin resorted to was loudly overlaying a piano track as camouflage for Kramer's frequent sour notes. The trickery worked, and Kramer scored a huge hit with his debut single, a cover of the Beatles' "Do You Want to Know a Secret."

With his productions occupying the top spot on the British charts for 37 out of 52 weeks in 1963, George Martin had become the hottest producer England had ever seen. Meanwhile, he tirelessly continued to helm sessions for a number of older Parlophone acts, including Britain's "King of Polka" Jimmy Shand, easy-listening orchestra leader Ron Godwin, and pop vocalist Matt Monro. Ironically, all of these artists were well on their way to commercial obsolescence, thanks to Martin's dynamic new rock acts.

• • • • •

Longing for Gold Star's acoustic magic, Phil Spector returned to Hollywood in an effort to make "He's a Rebel" a hit for the Crystals. However, due to a collective fear of flying, the Crystals refused to follow him out west. Spector (who owned the rights to the group's name) treated their absence as only a minor inconvenience and hired the Blossoms, an experienced trio of back-up singers, to record as the Crystals.

Back on the familiar turf of Gold Star, Spector began working with engineer Larry Levine. No stranger to overdub experiments, Levine's resume included Eddie Cochran's eternal rock cornerstone,

"Summertime Blues." Finally paired with a sympathetic engineer, Spector's penchant for grandiose sounds and excessive personnel began to truly take flight. For the impending "He's a Rebel" session, Spector ordered two bass players, an unheard-of request that left its participants perplexed.

Quickly, Spector's drawn-out trial-and-error methods exacted a toll on his tired session musicians, especially guitarists Howard Roberts and Tommy Tedesco. Because Spector built the other instruments around the guitars, the two were forced to repeatedly play the first four bars of "He's a Rebel" for hours on end without a break. The demands were so rigorous on Roberts that he complained of severe wrist pain, and by night's end his fingers dripped with blood.

Validating his exhausting methods, "He's a Rebel" landed at Number 1 in November 1962 and, in the process, established itself as one of the definitive Girl Group anthems. Buoyed by his chart momentum, Spector crammed the studio full of even more crack session players for his next session. This time, two bassists were not enough; he needed three. Once the unnamed session got under way, Spector demanded Levine bring the recording level of each instrument up so high that the sound verged on total distortion. With Spector's demands running contrary to everything Levine knew about engineering, the engineer had had enough. In a fit of frustration, Levine defiantly turned all the microphones off. Like an ominous calm before the storm, the control booth suddenly hushed—then Spector hit the roof, yelling at the top his lungs that he had just ruined three hours of work. Eventually the irate producer cooled from his tantrum, and Levine painstakingly rebuilt the levels to a compromising point that satisfied Spector.

With the tune-ups completed and the deafening levels set, Levine asked what the song was called. When Spector answered "Zip-a-Dee-Doo-Dah" (from Disney's 1946 film *Song of the South*) Levine thought he was being put on, but the producer was dead serious. Fueled by a ferocious vocal and a clanging groove, "Zip-a-Dee-Doo-Dah" was rendered truly special by Billy Strange's mercurial guitar solo. Without an actual microphone, Strange's amp spilled out into all the other mics in the room and resulted in, arguably, rock's first intentionally fuzz-toned guitar solo. Credited to the fictitious

Bob B. Sox and The Blue Jeans, the left-field song clawed its way to Number 8 on the singles chart in early 1963.

Additionally noteworthy was "Zip-a-Dee-Doo-Dah"'s flipside, "Flip and Nitty," which became the first in a long line of Spector's intentionally lackluster B-sides. Shrewdly, Spector figured that, by grafting formless instrumental studio jams onto the B-side, he could prevent DJs from flipping the records and deflecting attention from his laboriously constructed "plug sides." Furthermore, with the flip-sides solely credited to Spector, he could earn more royalties on each single.

While many questioned his indulgent and demanding methods, no one could argue with the unprecedented chart success of Philles Records from September 1962 to November 1963. With his finger on the pulse of young America, writer Tom Wolfe famously dubbed the producer "The Tycoon of Teen." "Phil really was the artist, and it wasn't just out of ego. Phil understood the teenage market, he related to their feelings and impulses,"[3] Jack Nitzsche said.

For all his tyrannical studio control, Spector was generous with his studio players. He would often award drummer Hal Blaine with after-session steaks and tip others, like Leon Russell, who was once written a $50 check after playing a particularly moving piano solo. Spector also began to employ Sonny Bono, an eager-to-please promo man who with Nitzsche had co-written the folk-rock hit "Needles and Pins" for Jackie DeShannon. Hired as Phil's flunky, and full-time yes man, Bono was awed by what his boss could accomplish in the studio.

By 1963 technology was changing, and stereo recordings were becoming prevalent. Eternally obstinate, Spector predictably resisted the new trend and continued to exclusively record in mono. When Gold Star installed a three-track recorder, Larry Levine earnestly tried to convince the producer to give stereo a try. Levine suggested separating some of the horn and guitars, but he was quickly rebuffed. Spector contended that the musical elements could never be brought back into the mix exactly the same way in stereo as they could in mono.

With his savage production of the Crystals' inspiring hit, "Then He Kissed Me," Spector's echo-drenched vision was reaching its full maturation. His formula now perfected, he turned his attention to the Ronettes, a young New York trio featuring sisters Estelle and Ronnie Bennett and their cousin Nedra Talley. By no means the most technically talented vocal group around, the raccoon mascara-ed Ronettes possessed an irresistible, tough-yet-vulnerable allure. Spector labored for over a year in choosing the proper song for the Ronettes to debut with. At last he decided on "Be My Baby" in July 1963.

Written by the team of Barry-Greenwich and Spector himself, the "Be My Baby" sessions were especially taxing. Finally, after more than 40 draining takes, the song scaled the joyous heights Spector was after. Plastering a machine-gun snare-drumbeat, flamenco-like clicking castanets, and tension-and-release string arrangement to Ronnie's seductive, vibrato heavy lead-vocal, "Be My Baby" is for many Spector's greatest achievement—two and half sweaty minutes of sexual pop perfection.

In an interview with the *London Evening Standard* in January 1964 Spector elaborated on his production theory:

"The records are built like a Wagnerian opera. They start simply and end with dynamic force, meaning and purpose....It's in the mind. I dreamed it up. It's like art movies. I aimed to get the record industry forward a little bit, make a sound that was universal."[4]

As "Be My Baby" rumbled up the charts, Spector schemed an unusual new project. His idea was to produce an album of traditional Christmas songs cut in a rock 'n' roll context. The concept was off-the-wall, even by Spector's standards, but as had been the case with "Zip-a-Dee-Doo-Dah," the Semitic Spector possessed genuine reverence for the Christmas songs. Emptying his entire stable of singers and musicians, Spector ran the highly rigorous Christmas sessions over a non-stop six-week period. Cots were set up in the studio for participants, who often remained hunkered down inside for days at a time. Nestled among Yuletide favorites like the Crystals' version of "Santa Claus is Coming to Town" and the Ronettes' stab at "Frosty the Snowman" was the Darlene Love–sung "Christmas (Baby Please Come Home)," a transcendentally soulful ballad that was also the album's sole original composition.

Initially considered as a curiosity upon its early November 1963 release, the album, titled *A Christmas Gift for You from Phil Spector*, was quickly doomed following the nation-traumatizing Kennedy

Phil Spector,
A Christmas Gift for You
from Phil Spector *(1963)*

assassination that occurred just days after its arrival. With the fall of Kennedy and the subsequent "British Invasion," cultural and musical change was suddenly palpable. Seeking to capitalize on the intense heat being generated by the Beatles and their scruffier counterparts, the Rolling Stones, Spector followed the Ronettes out to England in early 1964.

Dubbed a genius by the hyperbolic British press, Spector was met at Heathrow Airport by Wall of Sound worshipper and Rolling Stones manager/producer Andrew Oldham. Straightaway, Spector was seduced by the wild ways of Oldham and the Stones. Spector, who had shunned drugs previously on his trip abroad, softened his resolve and his edges as Oldham fed him a variety of pills, along with ample amounts of cannabis, throughout his stay.

While attending one particularly contentious Stones recording session, Spector watched as the adversarial bandmates nearly came to blows. Fortunately, the mood eventually lightened, thanks to help of several fifths of French cognac. Officially there as a spectator, Spector began to exert control of the session as it progressed in drunken, yet inspired, fashion through the night. At one juncture, he realized something was missing from the sound, and he suggested adding maracas. Mick Jagger was game to give it a try, but there was a problem: he didn't know how to shake them properly. Sensing the singer's confusion, Spector quietly took Jagger aside and gave him an impromptu maraca-shaking lesson. Later on, Spector called for additional percussion, and he began tapping a coin on one of the empty cognac bottles himself. The long session finally ended, and its result netted an impassioned cover of Buddy Holly's "Not Fade Away." Reaching the U.S. Top 50, it became the Rolling Stones' first American chart appearance.

Reveling in the vibrant *Swingin' London* scene, Spector and his protégés, the Ronettes, were veritable cause célèbres. After receiving an introduction to the Beatles, the admiring Liverpudlians asked Spector to fly with them to New York, where they were scheduled to make their first American television appearance on the *Ed Sullivan Show.* Arriving stateside to hysterical *Beatlemania*, Spector anonymously exited the plane and took a deep whiff of the air of change.

• • • • •

Kick-started by their ratings-shattering *Ed Sullivan Show* appearances, *Beatlemania* had moved from trend to phenomenon. By December 1964, the band's frantic recording pace had netted four albums in a mere 21 months. But that was only the tip of the iceberg for Martin. On top of the exhausting, near-continuous Beatles sessions, he produced a number of additional records for artists ranging from classy soul singer Shirley Bassey to the underrated mod band the Action.

In February 1965, the Beatles began work on the *Help!* soundtrack. A transitional time, the sessions marked a turning point in how the band and Martin recorded together. At the end of 1963 Abbey Road had acquired a stereo four-track recorder, and by the time of the *Help!* sessions Martin was becoming more adept at incorporating its capabilities with each successive session. Exploiting the new technology, Martin began to build the songs in a more layered, methodical fashion, a technique that he likened to "painting a picture in sound." First, he would record the rhythm track, and then overdub the additional elements the song required, such as the vocals, lead guitar, piano (often played by Martin himself), and additional percussion.

However, as the Beatles' musical ambitions grew exponentially throughout the year, four tracks quickly became only slightly more helpful than two. Almost immediately, Martin would find that all four tracks had already become full. To alleviate the dilemma, Martin conceived a number of ingenuous methods to free up space for additional overdubs. His most oft-utilized technique involved mixing the four tracks down to a finished two-track stereo take.

Then, he would transfer the two tracks to a backup four-track machine, which in turn created two new tracks to utilize. On the downside, this method would cause a drop off in sound quality with each new generation of tape, and as a result it would take a Herculean effort to equalize everything to the point of acceptability.

Throughout most of the *Help!* sessions, Paul McCartney labored to complete a pensive acoustic guitar ballad that he had been calling "Scrambled Eggs." Newly re-titled "Yesterday," McCartney and Martin concluded that something was lacking from the sentimental song's spare arrangement. After mulling it over, Martin suggested adding strings. But because McCartney was leery of making the song too syrupy, he was reluctant to embrace the radical idea. Cognizant of McCartney's concerns, Martin asked him to consider using a string quartet, which he contended would lend the song a distinguished sophistication without veering it too closely towards MOR (the "middle of the road" format). Finally, the Beatle agreed, and the two promptly began collaborating on the score. While McCartney came up with some very specific ideas, Martin was responsible for hammering out the majority of the delicate arrangement. The triumph of Martin's score resided in the way it never threatens to overwhelm the song's heartfelt sentiment. The revolutionary composition promptly rose to the U.S. Number 1 spot for a full month and eventually became one the most covered songs in music history.

Although Martin garnered unparalleled success for EMI, the notoriously stingy conglomerate continued to pay him a tightwad salary. Martin had a strong sense of loyalty and attempted to tamp his frustration, but eventually the exploitation was simply too much to ignore. His breaking point came at the end of 1963, after he was outrageously denied a Christmas bonus on a technicality. EMI rules stipulated that anyone making over £3,000 a year was not eligible, so instead of receiving an obviously much-deserved bonus, Martin got a note that congratulated him on his job and chided him "do better next year." Martin was finished with EMI's miserly ways, and in the middle of 1964 he gave the label a year's notice that he would be leaving. Demonstrating surprising arrogance, EMI only made a half-hearted effort to keep him employed. But it was too late; the producer was now determined to start his own company.

In August 1965, Martin was finally emancipated from EMI. Newly liberated, he founded Associated Independent Recording, better known as AIR. The company also included his assistant producer, Ron Richards, and two other EMI assistant producers, John Burgess and Peter Sullivan. Although Martin's professional stature towered high above the others, all four men became equal partners in the company.

AIR was a bold concept. It was not a record label but rather a producer's organization, and its formation was a risky proposition in 1965. While today an independent powerhouse such as AIR would be considered a home run, its unprecedented structure made securing capital challenging. Luckily, Martin had the Beatles as his trump card, and EMI was forced to negotiate his continued production involvement following his defection from the label. Negotiating as an independent, Martin was further exposed to EMI's hardball negotiating tactics and eventually agreed to an acceptable, but not entirely favorable, royalty payment rate. Nonetheless, the deal solidified AIR's existence.

Powered by the twin successes of their second film, *Help!*, and its ensuing soundtrack, the Beatles were continuing their indefatigable roll through the early fall of 1965. However, there was a problem. Faced with the burden of recording a new album in less than two months (for a mandated pre-Christmas December release), the band had a shortage of new material to record. As they scrambled to write and record a required dozen new songs, for the first time sessions stretched far past midnight. Abbey Road was still a very regimented, straight-laced operation, and the white-lab-coat-clad engineers shortly grew weary of the demanding all-night sessions.

With the deadline pressure looming, the Beatles rallied with the wistful *Rubber Soul*, their most ambitious and fully realized set of songs yet. "For the first time we began to think of albums as art on their own, as complete entities,"[5] Martin said of the folk-rock influenced triumph. One of Martin's most direct contributions came on "In My Life." Martin attempted to set a distinctively Elizabethan mood for the song, one of the album's most beautiful cuts; by performing the middle-section piano break himself. Yet, after several takes, he was unable to nail down the richly delicate harpsichord-like tone the song cried for. Frustrated, Martin continued to rack his brain for the elusive sound. Finally, he had an idea to perform the solo at half-speed, which he then played it back at double-speed. Magically, he had found the pristine sound that helped elevate the song to immortality.

Featuring sandalwood and suede-scented tracks like "Norwegian Wood," "Nowhere Man," "Girl," and "If I Needed Someone," *Rubber Soul* remains one of pop's most timelessly evocative albums. Their thirst for experimentation growing, Martin and the Beatles would obliterate recording studio conventions on their next album. Stretching conventions further than ever before, it would become one of the most revered albums ever recorded.

· · · · ·

Painfully aware that the Beatles were re-writing the rock rule-book, Spector continued to defiantly cling to his well-worn formula. Still only in his mid-twenties, he had sold more than 10 million records worldwide, but because he was totally unwilling to update his own sound in the transitional climate, his records starting flopping. As his "genius" tag increasingly became an albatross, the stress to continue his awesome winning streak was taking its toll. Spector began to immerse himself in martial arts at a West Hollywood studio and took to provoking fights around town with unsuspecting strangers, inevitably leaving his bodyguard to do the actual dirty work, as he scurried to the safety of his locked limo.

After suffering a stinging chart failure with the regal Ronettes ballad "Walking in the Rain," Spector regained his commercial footing with the *blue-eyed soul* duo, the Righteous Brothers. Consisting of Bill Medley and Bobby Hatfield, the dynamic duo's impassioned, gospel-derived style netted a few modest hits and a regular performance slot on TV's *Shindig*. However, the right material proved to be elusive. As he had done similarly with the Ronettes, Spector labored for months in selecting the proper song for his newest act to debut with. Just as had been the case with "Be My Baby," the time was well spent. Finally, Spector decided on a Mann-Weil composition called "You've Lost That Lovin' Feelin'."

Beginning with an ominously stark, near *a capella* opening stanza: "You never close your eyes anymore when I kiss your lips," the emotionally fraught song slowly built, swooning towards an apocalyptic crescendo of nearly impossible power and beauty. In a bold move to allow its full majesty to unfold, Spector allowed the song to run considerably longer than the industry standard of two and half minutes. Well aware that radio programmers would balk at its 3:50 running time, Spector surreptitiously falsified the single's label to read 3:05. The deceptive strategy worked, and the song ascended up the charts to Number 1 in February 1965.

Capitalizing on the gorgeous song, George Martin produced a Cilla Black cover of "Lovin' Feelin'" that was rushed out in England before the Righteous Brothers single was imported to England. Loyal Spector-disciple Andrew Oldham was outraged and took out a loquacious ad in music bible *Melody Maker* touting the Righteous Brothers' original version. In the ad, he called the song "Spector's greatest production, the last word in Tomorrow's Sound Today." Spector was flabbergasted by Oldham's devotion and loved the phrase so much he began using the slogan *Tomorrow's Sound Today* on his album sleeves for Philles. Oldham continued to run ads in support of Spector and aptly dubbed the sonic rush of "Lovin Feelin'" a "wall of sound," which, of course, became forever synonymous with Spector's technique.

Their collaborative triumph aside, tensions between Spector and the Righteous Brothers soon surfaced. After an early 1966 hit with the smoldering torch-ballad "Ebb Tide," the duo summarily broke free from Spector's tyrannical control. "The two of them weren't exceptional talents, but they did have a musical contribution to make. I loved them. I

The Ronettes "Appearing in the big T.N.T. show (1966)

thought they were a tremendous expression for myself. I think they resented being an expression,"[6] Spector said of Medley and Hatfield.

With the shifting musical winds of 1966 blowing with gale-force power, Spector was enlisted to serve as musical director for the concert film *The Big T.N.T. Show*. Reflective of the fluxing times, Spector assembled an eclectic slate of new- and old-school performers that included upstart folk-rockers the Byrds, Donovan, and the Lovin' Spoonful, veterans Bo Didley and Ray Charles, his own Ronettes, and the Ike and Tina Turner Revue. The energetic film was a success and provided many of its participants with valuable exposure in an age where national publicity was rare for rock acts.

As the Beatles' shadow continued to grow larger and more intimidating, Spector was rapidly becoming more disengaged and reclusive. More and more so, he retreated to the solitude of his opulent Beverly Hills mansion. For the producer the writing was on the wall. During a particularly non-productive Ronettes session, Spector turned to his arranger Jack Nitzsche and sadly proclaimed: "It's all over. It's just not here anymore."[7]

· · · · ·

By early 1966, the Beatles' songwriting innovations were occurring faster than ever, and as a result Martin was faced with the daunting task of keeping pace technically. Quite fortunately, he scored a significant breakthrough when the Abbey Road team invented a revolutionary system to easily allow for automatic double-tracking, dubbed ADT.

Up until its invention, double-tracking was a highly complicated and laborious proposition, and it would quickly monopolize the limited number of available recording tracks when utilized. With the advent of ADT, Martin was now allowed to easily create two sound images instead of one. Like photographic slides, the system enabled two sound images to overlap, and by varying the distances between the two images, the previously identical frequencies could be subtly altered to achieve greater acoustical depth. Because of its thrilling flexibility, a new world of atmospheric possibilities was suddenly available, and the breakthrough technology became a precursor to forthcoming sound-enhancing devices such as phasers, flangers, and harmonizers. The Beatles quickly became enamored of ADT's silky

The Beatles
Revolver
(1966)

luxuriousness and subsequently employed the technology on nearly every track of their brazen new album, Revolver.

The *Revolver* sessions commenced in April of 1966 with the watershed "Tomorrow Never Knows." With its recording, Martin and the Beatles' escalating studio ambitions shifted to warp speed. Inspired by John Lennon's lysergic acid sojourns, the song's sonically mysterious tone was set by Martin's swirling Leslie-speaker vocal treatment and bolstered by a visionary use of tape loops. The loops were a product of experimental recording snippets that had been edited together individually by the band members in their own crude home studios. McCartney was especially keen on bringing in sacks brimming with homemade loops, which he would proudly play for Martin and the rest of the band. The screaming seagull-like cries that characterize the opening of "Tomorrow Never Knows" originate from one of McCartney's distorted guitar loops, while sped-up guitars and treated wine-glass percussion enhanced the song's shape-shifting sound even further.

Another notable advancement of "Tomorrow Never Knows" was the recording treatment applied to Ringo's drums. To cultivate its startlingly crisp sound, engineer Geoff Emerick stuffed a woolen sweater with four neck openings (used by the band on a famous early photo shoot), into Starr's bass drum to deaden the sound. He then shunned the standard bass drum microphone placement by moving it far closer than ever previously attempted. Lastly, he ran the signal through a number of compressors and valve-limiters. "It became the sound of *Revolver* and *Pepper* really. Drums had never been heard

like that before,"[8] Emerick said. This type of unflinching studio experimentation characterized the entirety of the *Revolver* sessions.

A dizzyingly eclectic affair, *Revolver* discharged bouncy Tamla
soul ("Got to Get You Into My Life"), mystical Indian Raga ("Love
You Too"), backwards-guitar-driven psychedelic hard rock ("She
Said, She Said"), heavy-lidded surrealism ("I'm Only Sleeping"), and
Beach Boys–inspired harmony ("Here, There and Everywhere"). The
album was also home to Paul McCartney's acutely observed character study of loneliness, "Eleanor Rigby." As had been the case with
"Yesterday," Martin was called on to devise a tastefully emotional
classical score for a solitary McCartney ballad. Inspired by stalwart
film composer Bernard Hermann's rhythmic score for Francois
Truffaut's film version of *Fahrenheit 451*, Martin wrote the haunting,
meticulously arranged composition for double string quartet.

Predictably, the results were golden; "Eleanor Rigby," along
with its whimsical flip-side, "Yellow Submarine," became worldwide
Number 1 hits in the summer of 1966. Promptly, *Revolver* performed
the same feat on the album charts. Martin and the Beatles had merged
experimentalism and commercialism with startling results, but they
were just getting warmed up.

· · · · ·

As the enormous pressure of topping "Lovin' Feelin'" continued
to mount in the quicksilver moments of early 1966, Spector mustered
enough energy for another desperate push towards the top of the
charts. During the filming of *The Big T.N.T.* movie, he had been
knocked-out by the sweaty, soul-stirring performance of the Ike and
Tina Revue. Assembled by Ike Turner around his lead-singing wife
Tina, the revue included the Ikettes, a sprawling group of over 20
musicians and back-up singers. Although the group had enjoyed a
modicum of recording success, it was far more renowned for its incendiary live shows that featured frenetic dance routines and go-for-broke
vocal histrionics by spitfire singer Tina. Like many, Spector was helplessly drawn to Tina's raw sexual magnetism.

Demonstrating his usual methodical patience with selecting material, Spector spent well over a year searching for the perfect composition for Ike and Tina. In his mind, the elusive song was to be the grand

Ike and Tina Turner
"River Deep, Mountain High"
(1966)

summation of his Wall of Sound. Returning to the well of earlier triumphs, Spector enlisted his old dependable team of Jeff Barry and Ellie Greenwich. Although the couple had recently divorced, they continued their professional partnership, and Spector collaborated with the two of them over a long week in L.A. The writing sessions were fractured and resulted in a distinctly different idea from each of the writers. Spector liked all three disparate parts, and he attempted to fuse them together into one inspired whole called "River Deep (Mountain High)."

Commencing in February 1966, the "River Deep" sessions were the most grueling of Spector's career. Utilizing four guitarists, four bassists, an army of percussionists, and an unwieldy horn section, Spector was going for broke. Displaying an intense, laser-like focus, Spector worked his so-called "Wrecking Crew" of A-list studio musicians like a cruel taskmaster. Adamantly denying them union-mandated breaks, he was out to extract every last ounce of creativity from his talented battalion of session pros.

"It was amazing to watch 'River Deep' grow. Even during the cutting of the track, when (Tina) was putting on a scratch, Tina was so into it, she was holding her crotch on the high notes," Nitzsche said.[9]

Like a mad scientist, Spector toiled obsessively at the mixing board for days. Privately, many associates worried that he had finally gone too far. The collective fear was that "River Deep"'s echo-soaked orchestral cacophony was far too savage, too distorted, that the Wall of Sound had become a sloppy slab of sludge. Blatantly disregarding the concerns, the finished single was Spector's ultimate artistic statement—

a searing declaration of desperation, fueled by an orgasmic rush of sonic adrenaline.

Disappointingly, radio programmers and the record-buying public did not see it the same way. With its dissonant production and unusual lyrical imagery, the song was out of step with the prevailing hits of 1966. After a disastrous one-week run on the Top 100, where it feebly languished at an anemic Number 88, the single dropped completely off the charts by the following week. Spector was stunned but, miraculously, all was not lost for the flop single. Reprieved by strong support from a number of offshore pirate radio stations in England, the song reached Number 3 on the British charts in July 1966.

However, in the end, the overseas vindication was a little too late, and Spector declared the song his farewell. The bitter disappointment of "River Deep"'s failure lingered painfully. It would be two long years before Spector would be heard from again.

· · · · ·

By the time of the Beatles' exhausting 1966 tour, the group had grown to loathe the nightly din of pandemoniac audiences. Furthermore, it was nearly impossible to replicate the complex studio-derived songs from *Revolver* in a live setting. With the conclusion of the tour in August, the band made the unprecedented decision to retire from live performances. From this point forward, they would exist solely as a studio band. Following a mind-expanding three-month hiatus, they returned to the studio in late November. With their batteries chemically recharged and their creative juices rushing, they were ready to enter the next phase of their recording career.

With their original obligation to EMI to record two albums a year now fulfilled, for the first time, the Beatles were free to labor as long as they wanted in the studio. The first new song they tackled was a Lennon composition inspired by a Salvation Army home in Liverpool named Strawberry Fields. As was often the case with new material, Lennon debuted the hallucinatory song to the rest of the band on acoustic guitar in the studio. Martin was particularly moved by its gentle loveliness, but, once the band got their hands on it, the song quickly changed course. Working the song into a full electric version, it dramatically mutated through the night.

The Beatles
"Strawberry Fields Forever/
Penny Lane"
(1967)

Nine and a half hours later, the heavily overdubbed take was completed. Harder and heavier than anything the Beatles had ever recorded, it was only a distant cousin to the gentle acoustic ballad Lennon had debuted at the start of the evening. Immediately setting the recording apart was its use of the mellotron, a prototypical string synthesizer that utilized programmed tapes of real instruments. Previously used solely for sound effects, the recording marked the first time the mellotron had been employed in a rock context. Lennon himself owned one of the earliest models, and he requested that it be programmed to make the electronic flute sound that was used for the song's otherworldly, warbled introduction.

At the session's completion Martin privately reflected on how the song transmogrified from ruminative ballad to full-bore psychedelic rocker by night's end. While Lennon appeared satisfied with the change, he unexpectedly came back to Martin a week later and said that he would to like record the song again. Rather cryptically, Lennon asked Martin to create a score for the song using "a bit of strings, or brass or something."[10] This request marked the first time the Beatles attempted to entirely remake one of their recordings.

As the new sessions for "Strawberry Fields" continued throughout early December 1966, the song was progressively turning slower and stranger. Contributing to its peculiar sound was Martin's menacing string and trumpet arrangement, an Indian table harp-like instrument called a swarmandal (played by George Harrison), timpani, and backwards-recorded drum cymbals. Finally, the second version was completed, but Lennon was in a quandary: although he liked the beginning of the first heavy rendition, he favored the end section of the drowsier second attempt.

"Why don't we just join them together?" Lennon said naively to his producer.[11] Befuddled, Martin informed him that, because the song was in different keys and varying tempos, it would be nearly impossible to make it work. Unfazed, Lennon simply replied, "You can fix it, George," and stalked off.[12]

Never technically minded, Lennon would frequently make a request in layman's terms and expect Martin to come up with a viable solution. After mulling over possibilities, Martin hypothesized that he could match the pitches by using a variable-control tape machine to speed up one version and slow down the other. He then hoped that the two different tempos would be close enough to match pitches once edited together. A case of being lucky and good, the tempos matched, and his edit of the two versions was nearly seamless. (If you listen closely, though, you can hear the seam where the song changes from the first version to the second.)

Following the completion of "Strawberry Fields" and McCartney's contagiously optimistic "Penny Lane," EMI began clamoring for a new single. Obviously, losing the two groundbreaking songs for the intended new album would be a major setback, but Martin knew it was in everyone's best interest to couple "Strawberry Fields Forever" and "Penny Lane" together as a single. Released as a double-A-sided record, Martin contends that the single was the best the Beatles ever released. Additionally, its colorfully surreal sound became a direct touchstone for burgeoning psychedelic bands, like Pink Floyd, the Move, and the Smoke, that were beginning to mushroom around London.

As the sessions for *Revolver*'s unnamed follow-up album moved forward, the band's fearless experimentation was reaping wondrous results despite pronounced studio limitations. While eight-track recorders were starting to surface at various studios, Abbey Road stubbornly clung to its antiquated four-track technology. The band was also growing frustrated with the studio's institutional surroundings, and they began to bring in accoutrements like colored lights and lava lamps to help combat the stilted environment.

With the psychedelic culture bubbling under the surface, the interstellar influence of LSD was seeping into the band's recordings. However, the hallucinogenic inspiration was completely lost on the straight-laced Martin. While he was aware that the boys dabbled in pot and pills, the producer had no idea they were regularly dropping acid during the sessions.

A month into the sessions, the album reached a turning point with a McCartney song called "Sgt. Pepper's Lonely Hearts Club Band." Smitten by the candy-colored monikers from the emerging American West Coast psychedelic scene like Moby Grape, the Grateful Dead, and Quicksilver Messenger Service, McCartney decided it would be liberating to unshackle the Beatles burden and become a fictitious group. For the duration of the album, they were not the Beatles, but, rather, Sgt. Pepper's Lonely Hearts Club Band.

For the album's proposed centerpiece, the band attempted to write "a turn-on song" called, "A Day in the Life." Originally, it was Lennon who conceived the song to consist of three separate sections. He wanted them linked by a "tremendous build-up, from nothing up to something absolutely like the end of the world," and he requested Martin book a symphony to execute the idea.[13] Yet again, Martin was left with the challenge of translating a vague Lennon idea into a formal symphonic score.

For the planned symphony session, McCartney asked that Martin and the entire 42-piece orchestra come dressed in formal evening wear. The orchestra was understandably perplexed by the unusual request but proceeded to get into the joyous spirit as the evening wore on. Illustrating the levity, the entire orchestra put on silly hats, its leader wore paper glasses and a red false nose, one of the violinists held his bow wearing a large gorilla paw, and Martin wore a pointy Cyrano de Bergerac nose. The Beatles themselves came dressed in bright Carnaby Street garb; they donned fake glasses, plastic stick-on nipples, and baldhead-caps. Further transforming the session into an all-out happening was the presence of Mick Jagger, Marianne Faithfull, Donovan, and the Monkees' Mike Nesmith.

Before recording, Martin gave the orchestra the score and specific instructions "to start very, very quietly and end up very, very loud."[14] While Martin and McCartney conducted the orchestra together, Geoff

Emerick was left with the daunting responsibility of capturing it all on tape. Despite the stressful situation, Emerick successfully manipulated the sliding volume-faders and captured the orchestra's crashing crescendo. The orchestra was recorded four times, initially residing on each of the available four tracks. Then it was all mixed down to one track to free up the other three for remaining overdubs. The end result was the sound, not of 40 musicians blaring away, but of a spectacular 160. Miraculously, within the chaotic party atmosphere, the session was a smashing success.

Bolstered by the stupendous momentum of "A Day in the Life," the *Sgt. Pepper* sessions progressed in inspired form. Again, Lennon challenged Martin's studio acumen by explaining that he wanted to "smell the sawdust on the floor" for his carnival-flavored "Being for the Benefit of Mr. Kite."[15] By now, Martin was becoming more and more adept at translating Lennon's esoterically vague ideas, and he attempted to track down a calliope (essentially an antique steam organ) to forge a fairground hurdy-gurdy-like sound for the song's middle section. Unable to locate an old-fashioned hand-operated calliope, Martin made several unsuccessful attempts to capture the carnival vibe by using electric organs and altering the octaves.

Seemingly stumped for a solution, Martin harkened back to the resourcefulness of his novelty record days; suddenly, he had an idea and ordered one of his assistants over. Martin's instructions were to gather tapes of calliope recordings (culled from Sousa marches and other traditional songs) and then edit various different bits together into one string. Once assembled, Martin instructed Geoff Emerick to haphazardly cut the tape into foot long sections and toss them straight up in the air. After they watched the bits of tape flutter to the floor, Martin had them pick up the randomly fallen pieces and splice them back together. Then, to further enhance the hurdy-gurdy sound, they turned certain sections of the tape backwards. The idea worked perfectly; Lennon got his carnival.

After 700 grueling recording hours, the album was finally released on June 1, 1967. Deftly sequenced and lushly layered, the kaleidoscopic *Sgt. Pepper's Lonely Heart's Club Band* served as the solstice for the "summer of love." Created on only a four-track recorder, Martin and Emerick's achievements were as miraculous as they were glorious.

Instantly, nearly every band, from the Rolling Stones to the Four Seasons to the Ultimate Spinach, tried to emulate Pepper's revolutionary, multi-tracked studio techniques with their own psychedelic concept album. Dramatically emboldened with an entirely new set of recording possibilities, the role of producer had ballooned almost overnight.

• • • • •

Following the psychedelic releases of *Magical Mystery Tour* and the *Yellow Submarine* soundtrack, the Beatles abandoned the *Pepper* blueprint by the end of 1967. Devastated by the sleeping pill overdose of their troubled homosexual manager Brian Epstein earlier that summer, tensions within the band began to surface. Epstein was always a unifying presence, and without him sessions for the band's new self-titled release (a.k.a., "The White Album") were a marked contrast to the spirited Four Musketeers team approach of Pepper.

The bulk of *The Beatles* was written while the band was studying Transcendental Meditation at the foot of the Maharishi Mahesh Yogi in India during the early part of 1968. Because most of the album was essentially a collection of solo songs, the majority of the sessions were conducted with each Beatle simultaneously recording his own songs at different studios within Abbey Road. As a result, the group members now functioned more as backing session men called in to supplant each other's recordings than as a cohesive band. As a result of the fragmented situation, Martin and his new assistant producer, Chris Thomas, had to run from studio to studio to keep up with the activity.

Despite the ill feelings and fractured unity, *The Beatles* contained a panoply of wondrous songs that included quietly contemplative acoustic numbers, idiosyncratic pop, heavy-duty hard rock, and flat-out experimentalism. Despite the rewarding diversity, Martin was vehemently opposed to releasing it as a 30-track double-album, and he strongly lobbied to cut it down to what he deemed to be the fourteen or sixteen strongest tracks. But the band refused, and, soon after, their instincts were validated. The double-album shattered sales records by selling almost two million copies in the United States alone in its first week of November 1968. The phenomenal success aside, trouble loomed on the horizon for Martin and the group.

The pressures within the Beatles were continuing to mount. With peacemaker Epstein dead, the burden of their failing Apple Corps. snowballing, and the constant studio presence of Yoko Ono growing more divisive, animosity within the band plagued their follow-up to *The Beatles*. Titled *Get Back* and conceived as a return to their Hamburg-era rock 'n' roll roots, the band intended to record every song live, without any overdubs or production gimmicks. Essentially, *Get Back*'s direct simplicity was intended as the antithesis of *Pepper*'s densely layered experiments, and Martin interpreted its direction as a personal rebuke of his hard-labored studio advancements.

Insulated by the perceived snub and fed up with the band's constant bickering, Martin's involvement with *Get Back* was sporadic. Dispirited by the disharmony, he did not even attend several of the sessions, instead leaving the production reigns to the young engineer and fledgling producer, Glyn Johns. Martin wanted nothing to do with the project, and eventually Johns was given the highly unenviable task of constructing a final version of *Get Back* from the mountains of tape that had accumulated during sessions.

Although the funky "Get Back" single was another chart-topping success, the remaining performances were largely spotty and unfinished. Johns struggled to elevate the album above its frequent mediocrity, but there was only so much he could do. With Martin's hands washed of the "miserable experience," and John's inability to mix a miracle, completion of the album appeared doomed. Originally slated for an early summer 1969 release, *Get Back* was indefinitely shelved. Tragically, it seemed as though the world's greatest band was going out with a whimper instead of a bang.

• • • • •

As the not-so-secret longtime object of his affection, Spector finally married Ronettes lead-singer Ronnie Bennett in 1968. Befitting his controlling personality, once married to Ronnie, Spector was unable to share his wife with the world. Instead of focusing on re-establishing her waning career, he literally kept her locked up in their mansion day and night. Spector produced only one more song for the Ronettes after their union, the tellingly titled chart flop "You Came, You Saw, You Conquered."

With his new marriage, Spector seemed reinvigorated, and in the spring of 1969 he returned to action with the the racially mixed soul band, Checkmates Ltd. Instead of making their living in rock clubs, the Checkmates were mainstays of the Las Vegas lounges. Spector was confident that he could harness the Checkmates' sweet-soul sound into one last hit before the decade came to a close. After his first single with the group, "Love Is All I Have to Give," stalled at Number 65, Spector switched lead singers, opting for Sonny Charles instead of Bobby Stevens for the follow-up, "Black Pearl."

Inspired by the Sidney Poitier movie *For the Love of Ivy*, the single was a nostalgic throwback to an earlier 1960s style of sweet-soul balladry, far removed from the obtusely grandiose "River Deep." Credited to Sonny Charles and the Checkmates Ltd. (much to fellow vocalist Stevens' chagrin), "Black Pearl" featured a sunny and simple arrangement, warmly delivered by Charles in a lilting Motown-like style. With its uncluttered production, Spector consciously attempted to return to the direct emotionality of his early hits, and, somewhat surprisingly, he succeeded. "Black Pearl" became a moderate hit, climbing to Number 13 on the pop charts in July 1969. Unfortunately, the rivalry between vocalists Charles and Stevens soon became too much for Spector, and a planned album was unceremoniously scraped.

As the sixties came to a close, Spector made a brief but memorable cameo appearance as a cocaine dealer in the counter-culture defining film *Easy Rider*. Finally, the producer appeared ready to embrace the new rock world. All he needed now was the right project.

• • • • •

With the Beatles at seemingly career-ending odds, George Martin received an unlikely call from Paul McCartney, who asked him if he would be willing to "really produce" another album. Things had not ended particularly well between Martin and the warring group, which made McCartney's question all the more surprising. Leery of the *Get Back* debacle, Martin conditionally agreed, only if there was not a set of preconceived recording restrictions. McCartney assured him that there wasn't, and recording began in early summer 1969.

The Beatles
Abbey Road
(1969)

As the sessions for the album, initially named *Everest*, stretched out, the band managed a forced, yet improved, civility with each other. After the basic rhythm tracks were cut together, they reverted back to the practice of individually overdubbing in separate studios. Once again, Martin had to scurry between studios to keep proper tabs, but, unlike the obstinate air of *Get Back*, this time his suggestions were taken into serious consideration.

Newly re-titled *Abbey Road*, in homage to their career-spanning recording studio, the album's structure began to appear. Lennon, who felt that rock had strayed too far from its down and dirty roots, insisted that Side One house a succession of stripped-down, rock 'n' roll songs. Side Two was designated as McCartney's arty concept side, although ironically, several of its pieces were actually written by Lennon. It was Martin's suggestion to segue the various song fragments into one sidelong song suite, and, as usual, he wrote its elaborate accompanying orchestral score.

As the band took its time laboring through the completion of the Side Two suite, the recording budget of the album swelled. Forced into a cost-cutting move, Martin decided to record all of the orchestral overdubs at once during the album's final sessions, which was no easy proposition. On August 15th, the orchestra musicians assembled in two different studios within Abbey Road, ingeniously assisting in the recording coordination; the two studios were linked together by close-circuit television. In the first studio Martin conducted one set of musicians, while engineers Geoff Emerick, Phil McDonald, and Alan

Parsons supervised the other portion in the second room. The two teams then communicated back and forth via walkie-talkies to synchronize the recordings, which was high-tech stuff back in 1969.

Unfurled in the early fall 1969, the peerless *Abbey Road* marked the final time the Beatles and Martin would record together. Martin called *Abbey Road* "a kind of *Sgt. Pepper* mark two."[16] To this day, he continues to cite the album his personal favorite among all his Beatles productions.

Contrasting the tidy triumph of *Abbey Road*, the band still had unfinished business with the messy *Get Back* tapes, which had remained in limbo. With McCartney enveloped in the recording of his homespun debut album (on his way to quitting the band), Lennon and Harrison recruited a shared idol to rescue the languishing project from its perceived doom. The unlikely savior was Phil Spector.

• • • • •

As the seventies dawned hazily, Spector found himself in the ironic position of producing the band that had been most responsible for turning his sound into an anachronism. With *Get Back* re-titled *Let It Be*, Spector was well aware that the album was going to be the Beatles' swansong. Cognizant of its historical importance, he eschewed including any of the originally intended oldies covers, instead opting to feature only new material. Coating tracks such as "The Long and Winding Road" in syrupy strings and a bombastic backing choir while leaving others like "Two of Us" and "Dig a Pony" nakedly unadorned, Spector proceeded to follow his well-worn instincts.

Expectedly, a storm of criticism gathered around Spector's final version. McCartney was specifically outraged with the heavy-handed treatment given to the "The Long and Winding Road," which barely resembled his sparse original version. Spector knew he was in a no-win situation and called out the openly critical George Martin: "It was no favor to me to give me George Martin's job because I don't consider (him) in (my) league....He's an arranger, that's all," he said.[17]

Despite the outcry, "The Long and Winding Road," stretched to Number 1 on the singles chart, and *Let It Be* conquered the top album spot for over a month. The posthumous album even managed to snag a Grammy for Best Original Motion Picture Score. Collecting the award was the formerly disapproving McCartney.

During Spector's extensive remixing of *Let It Be*, John Lennon called on the producer to helm a new solo song, "Instant Karma." Featuring a barebones band of Lennon, George Harrison, bassist Klaus Voorman, and drummer Alan White, Spector dug deep into his bag of tricks in an attempt to beef up the minimalist recording. Deciding he wanted keyboard overdubs, Spector ordered Lennon to play one piano, suggested Harrison and White share a second one, and told Voorman to jam on an electric piano. Later, Spector instructed White to drape a bath towel over one of his drums, and the treatment provided the distinctively muffled-yet-punchy sound that drives the song. To provide the song with its final celebratory touch, Spector sent a few members of Lennon's entourage out to scrounge up some revelers from a local pub to help sing the spirited chorus.

Listening to the playback, Lennon was thrilled by Spector's gigantic sound and especially excited by the richness of his own vocal. Since his early Beatle days, Lennon loathed the sound of his untreated voice. Because of this, he would routinely order George Martin to try a myriad of studio different tricks and microphones to mask it. *"Do something with my voice! Smother it in tomato ketchup!"* he once pleaded to Martin.

Hearing how Spector had enlarged his voice clearly delighted the newly solo Beatle, and at the end of the end of the all-night session Lennon pronounced the song done. Predictably, Spector wanted to tinker more with the mix, and he begged Lennon to allow him to take the tapes back to L.A. for violin overdubs. When Lennon adamantly declined, Spector snuck out a copy of the master tape and had it sent back to L.A. to remix it anyway. Before it was pressed, he even had "Phil & Ronnie" scratched into the single's runoff groove. Lennon's version of "Instant Karma" was released in England, and several weeks later Spector's re-mixed version came out stateside. The two versions of the single combined to become a million-seller, and it endures as one of Spector's most sparkling productions.

Hot on the heels of his success with Lennon, Spector was enlisted to produce George Harrison's debut solo album, *All Things Must Pass*. Because Harrison had been allotted just two songs per Beatles

George Harrison
All Things Must Pass
(1970)

album, he had amassed an impressive backlog of material. Undoubtedly, the quiet Beatle felt he had something to say. Using a tight and talented backing band that included Eric Clapton, Billy Preston, Dave Mason, and Ringo Starr, the collision of Spector's Wall of Sound and Harrison's acoustic-based confessionals coalesced into an unpredictably captivating and cohesive whole.

Alternating between pounding rockers and pensive ballads, Harrison's songs were imbued with a visceral quality that owed a tremendous debt to Spector's studio techniques. The contributing studio musicians were collectively in awe as they watched Spector meticulously separate and layer each instrument and then lavishly bathe it in echo. "I still don't know how he got the echo like he did," keyboardist Billy Preston said years later.[18]

All Things Must Pass was released as a triple-album in late 1970, and, to the astonishment of many, it quickly grabbed the top spot on both sides of the Atlantic. Helping to solidify its success was the slide-guitar sweetened single "My Sweet Lord/Isn't It a Pity," which occupied the top spot for over a month. Spector's soaring production had propelled Harrison to unlikely solo stardom, and the album's merging of expansive hard rock and intimate acoustic-confessionals became a touchstone for the emerging sound of seventies rock.

Returning to his workaholic ways, Spector continued his budding partnership with Lennon on his primal-scream-influenced debut solo album, *Plastic Ono Band*. Corralling Lennon's haunting ruminations, inspired by everything from his painful childhood ("Mother") to the myth of hero worship ("God"), Spector adhered to an antithetical "less is more" axiom for perhaps the only time in his production career. While the deeply troubling, emotionally exposed album did not enjoy the runaway success of Harrison's debut, the sparsely produced *Plastic Ono Band* serves as Lennon's greatest post-Beatles achievement.

Cleansed by the cathartic *Plastic Ono Band*, Lennon and Spector began work on *Imagine*, a follow-up that was more accessible than confessional. With its pop-oriented material, Spector was allowed to comfortably return to a fuller-bodied sound, notably on the lovely "Jealous Guy" and the scathing anti-McCartney "How Do You Sleep." Also included was the expressively sung, utopia-themed title track, a song that would become Lennon's defining solo statement.

With his string of Beatles-affiliated successes, Phil Spector had miraculously resurrected his career by working with the individuals who had been most responsible for derailing it. But his personal instability was increasing. Sadly, sustaining the recaptured glory would become impossible.

• • • • •

With the breakup of the Beatles, George Martin turned his efforts towards building up his company, AIR. Originally functioning as an independent production house, AIR branched out and became a record

"A Caribbean-tanned"
George Martin, late '70s

Photo credit: St. Martin's Press

label and recording studio in the early 1970s. With the first AIR studio completed in London, Martin dreamt of constructing a "total environment studio," which would be housed on a floating ship. However, as a result of a worldwide oil crisis and an English recession, Martin was forced to abandon his unorthodox dream studio idea in 1974.

In place of the floating studio, Martin opted to build a more feasible facility on the then–British Colony Island of Montserrat, in the West Indies. Completed in 1979, the accommodations were plush; visiting recording artists stayed at nearby villas, and the studio itself sat on an idyllic 30-acre farm that overlooked the Caribbean Sea. Tragedy struck, though, when the notoriously violent Hurricane Hugo destroyed the studio ten years after its completion.

With the exception of Ringo Starr's debut, *Sentimental Journey*, a collection of Tin Pan Alley–era standards, Martin had not worked on any solo Beatle outings, until he collaborated with McCartney on the soundtrack to the James Bond film *Live and Let Die* in 1973. With the film's driving, multi-sectioned title track, Martin and McCartney crafted a fittingly cinematic, orchestrated piece of pop music. Despite the song's dramatic appeal, Martin had to fight for it to be used in the film franchise's traditionally female-sung opening credits. Bond's producers were pushing Thelma Houston, but Martin (who also supplied the film's orchestrated score) finally convinced the filmmakers to use McCartney's song in the opening sequence. Released in August 1973, the single became a worldwide hit.

Freed of the unrealistic commercial expectations of the Beatles, Martin kept a high profile throughout the 1970s. Among the highlights was guitar hero Jeff Beck's 1975 jazz-fusion classic, *Blow By Blow*, an all-instrumental album that was distinguished by Martin's trademark lush production and impeccable string arrangements. He also produced the Mahavishnu Orchestra's ambitious *Apocalypse*, a genre-bending jazz-meets-classical collaboration with the London Symphony Orchestra. His most underrated turn came with his low-key production for respected songwriter Jimmy Webb's satisfying 1977 album, *El Mirage*.

Martin's greatest post-Beatles commercial success was with the chart-topping soft-rockers America. Following an initial string of early 1970s AM radio staples, America's fortunes were on the wane until

Martin signed on for their 1974 album, *Holiday*. Martin provided an appropriate gloss for America's effortlessly breezy, honeyed pop, and the album netted two monster hits, "Tin Man" and "Lonely People." He continued to work steadily with America throughout the decade, producing their next five albums.

· · · · ·

Eternally paranoid, Spector began to take it to new levels by the early 1970s. Surrounding himself with burly bodyguards, he would not dare leave his mansion without a gun strapped to his side. When kindred spirit John Lennon relocated to L.A. for his infamous two-year "lost weekend," he came looking for his idol producer. Referring to himself as "Dr. Winston O'Boogie," the perpetually soused Lennon proceeded to drag Spector and fellow songwriter Harry Nilsson into one Brandy Alexander–soaked misadventure after another.

Lennon had recently lost a publishing lawsuit and decided to pay off the court-ordered settlement by asking Spector to produce an album of early rock 'n' roll covers. Treading on Spector's terrain of expertise, he only agreed after Lennon granted him total control of the recordings. Attempting to allay Spector's fears, Lennon insisted that he merely wanted to be the singer in the band. Seeking to avoid a repeat of the "Instant Karma" final-mix disagreement, Spector footed the bills for the sessions himself, which provided him ownership of the tapes.

The sessions for the album, simply titled *Rock 'n' Roll*, became the personification of druggy, boozy '70s L.A. decadence. Using a large and highly skilled crop of session men, including guitarists Jesse Ed Davis and Steve Cropper, pianists Leon Russell and Dr. John, and ace drummer Jim Keltner, the sessions were incredibly long, disorganized, and woefully sloppy. To complicate matters, Spector would habitually wobble in late, packing heat and usually clutching a bottle of Magen David kosher wine.

The sessions continued in chaotic fashion for weeks, with many nights monopolized by drunkenly belligerent shouting matches between Lennon and Spector. The studio parties raged so boisterously that they were eventually kicked out of A&M studios and forced to relocate to the Record Plant West. The endless sessions came to a final grinding halt after Spector punched Lennon's longtime friend Mal Evans in the nose. Before Evans could retaliate, Spector brandished his pistol in front of Lennon and shot a hole in the studio ceiling. Totally freaked out, the ex-Beatle yelled, "Phil, if you're gonna kill me, kill me. But don't fuck with me ears. I need 'em."[19]

With Spector and Lennon's creative partnership now abruptly ended, Capitol Records was left with the unenviable job of buying the master tapes back from Spector. Eventually Spector agreed to a $94,000 settlement, and Capitol got the master tapes of the sub-par sessions. Released in February 1975, *Rock 'n' Roll*'s listless arrangements of several oldies, including "Stand By Me" and "Bonie Maronie," was a low-water mark for both Spector and Lennon.

Following the *Rock 'n' Roll* debacle, Spector began an uneven, sporadically satisfying endeavor with early rock pioneer Dion DiMucci in 1975. The former leader of the Belmonts had been toiling in relative obscurity for years, and a pairing with Spector seemed to make sense. Held back at Gold Star Studios, the sessions for an album, titled *Born to Be With You*, contained all of the old Spector grandiosity but little of the joy. Although Dion was unhappy with the album's muddy, dirge-like sound, the brooding title track possessed an intriguing, mesmerizing power. Never released in the States, the album has managed to find a cult following overseas, where it has become recognized as something of a minor classic.

Soon after the commercially failed Dion project and an unsuccessful collaboration with Cher (on the regrettable prostitute tale "A Woman's Story"), Spector was coaxed back into action for a seemingly incongruous collaboration with mono-toned dark poet Leonard Cohen. Cohen had released several albums of skeletal arrangements and brittle wordplay, and a pairing with Spector seemed bizarre. However, the two quickly found common ground in their devotion to the bottle. Of course, the sessions did not run smoothly; Spector paid little attention to Cohen, who was shunted aside like just another session man. Highly paranoid, Spector took the master tapes home with him each night accompanied by an armed guard.

Titled *Death of a Ladies' Man*, the album contained eight songs, seven of which featured Spector/Cohen co-credits. Despite the presence of Bob Dylan on several of the cuts, the album was a commercial dud. Somewhat misunderstood and unfairly dismissed, the album had its merits. Cohen's lyrics, which explored the shifting nature of machismo in an increasingly politically correct world, were as good as any he had ever written. While Spector's arrangements were expectedly dense, they were often glorious, especially on the cutting "Paper Thin Hotel" and the poignant "True Love Leaves No Traces." In the end, just like Dion, Cohen was unhappy with his Spector-produced album and openly complained that the producer had "taken the guts out of the record."[20]

His sound nearly forgotten in the age of disco and arena rock, coupled with his recent string of flops, Spector was disconsolate. However, he suddenly found himself re-energized after watching punk pioneers the Ramones perform at the Whiskey-a-Go-Go in early 1977. With their street-tough New York attitude, leather jackets, and back-to-basics buzz-saw sound, Spector heard something in the band that recalled the visceral gut-level emotion of his early 1960s recordings.

After the show, Spector anxiously pushed his way backstage announced, "My bodyguards wanna fight your bodyguards," and insisted the band let him produce their next record.[21] Well aware of the producer's infamous difficult reputation, the band resisted despite lead singer Joey Ramone's personal idolization of Spector. Undeterred, Spector routinely pestered Joey with phone calls promising to make a "great record instead of just a good record."[22] Finally, the band relented and Spector was installed to produce their fifth studio album, *End of the Century*, at Gold Star in late 1979.

From day one Spector's monotonous methodology clashed with the Ramones' "knock 'em out in one take" philosophy. Trying to get a grasp on their sound, Spector made the band run through each song more than a hundred times before recording the first take. This situation got even more ridiculous after Spector made guitarist Johnny Ramone play "Rock 'N' Roll High School"'s opening chord for ten straight hours. Slowly it became evident that Spector was confused by the Ramones' brand of punk rock. After countless hours spent mixing and drinking enormous amounts of kosher wine in tiny white cups, Spector's frustration often spilled out into obscenity-laced temper tantrums that ground the sessions to a halt.

Somehow the album was completed. Released in February

The Ramones
End of the Century
(1980)

1980, at a cost of $200,000, *End of the Century* was nearly as expensive to record as the four previous Ramones albums combined. Although an uneven record, "Danny Says," with a classic Spectorian "teen symphony" arrangement, and the nostalgic "Do You Remember Rock & Roll Radio?" rank among the band's finest songs. *End of the Century* cracked the Top 50 and became the band's most commercially successful release to that date, but Spector would never work with the Ramones again.

• • • • •

George Martin continued to work steadily throughout the 1980s, including notable turns on Paul McCartney's critically lauded *Tug of War* and *Pipes of Piece* albums. He also produced diverse albums, ranging from power-popper's Cheap Trick *All Shook Up* to Ultravox's chilly synth-pop offering, *Quartet*. With the shift towards the compact disc format in the late '80s, Martin oversaw the release of the Beatles catalog for CD. While supervising the reissues, he made the mildly controversial move to release their first four albums in their original mono form, citing weaknesses in the stereo versions.

Martin was also behind the three-volume mid-nineties *Beatles Anthology* collection of rarities and outtakes. Included were the controvertibly successful "Free As a Bird" and "Real Love," collaborations of posthumous John Lennon demos and new music recorded by the remaining three members. All three volumes were unmitigated hits, proving that the band's staggering popularity had not waned since its breakup a quarter of a century earlier. Martin also helmed the platinum Broadway cast version of the Who's *Tommy* and Elton John's teary-eyed farewell to Princess Diana, "Candle in the Wind '97," the biggest-selling single in pop music history.

Knighted in 1996, Martin chose to formally end his career with a project appropriately entitled *In My Life*. Released in late 1998, *In My Life* featured a selection of handpicked Beatles songs, arranged and orchestrated by Martin and performed by a varied and somewhat curious collection of musicians and actors including Jim Carrey, Jeff Beck, Celine Dion, Phil Collins, Sean Connery, and Goldie Hawn. The album's unpredictable lineup was a fitting swansong for the well-humored Martin.

• • • • •

After aborted projects with pop singers LaToya Jackson in the late 1980s and Celine Dion in the early 1990s, *End of the Century* remains Phil Spector's last production. Finally inducted into the Rock and Roll Hall of Fame in 1989, a drunken Spector clung to one of his bodyguards as he wobbled up to accept the induction. Slouching at the podium, Spector rambled incomprehensively about Tina Turner and President George Bush Sr., then teetered offstage and disappeared into the night. It remained his last official public appearance until his arrest in connection with the shooting death of a female visitor that occurred at his Alhambra, California mansion in February 2003. Spector has since been released from custody and has not been charged with any wrongdoing in the ongoing investigation.

• • • • •

Certainly no two men elevated the role of the record producer more than Phil Spector and George Martin. For both, the recording studio became its own instrument, and they each played it with dedicated virtuosity. Through their pioneering efforts, an entirely new world of sonic possibilities was forged. However, their radically differing methods of achieving their results illuminate the fact that no two production approaches are exactly the same.

KEY RECORDINGS
George Martin

The Action –	*Ultimate Action* (Edsel 1980)
Aerosmith –	"Come Together" (Columbia 1978)
America –	*Holiday* (Warner Bros. 1974)
	Hearts (Warner Bros. 1975)
American Flyer –	*American Flyer* (United Artists 1976)
Shirley Bassey –	*EMI/UA Years 1959–1979* (EMI 2000)
The Beatles –	*Please Please Me* (Parlophone 1963)
	With the Beatles (Parlophone 1963)
	Meet the Beatles! (Capitol 1964)
	A Hard Day's Night (Capitol 1964)
	Beatles for Sale (Parlophone 1964)
	"I Feel Fine/She's a Woman" (Capitol 1964)
	Help! (Capitol 1965)
	Rubber Soul (Capitol 1965)
	"We Can Work It Out/Day Tripper" (Capitol 1965)
	"Paperback Writer/Rain" (Capitol 1966)
	Revolver (Capitol 1966)
	"Strawberry Fields Forever/Penny Lane" (Capitol 1967)
	Sgt. Pepper's Lonely Hearts Club Band (Capitol 1967)
	Magical Mystery Tour (Capitol 1967)
	"Lady Madonna/The Inner Light" (Capitol 1968)
	"Hey Jude/Revolution" (Capitol 1968)
	The Beatles (White Album) (Capitol 1968)
	Yellow Submarine (Capitol 1969)
	Abbey Road (Capitol 1969)
	Hey Jude (Capitol 1970)
Jeff Beck –	*Blow By Blow* (Epic 1975)
	Wired (Epic 1976)
Cilla Black –	*Cilla* (Parlophone 1965)
	Cilla Sings a Rainbow (Parlophone 1966)
Cheap Trick –	*All Shook Up* (Epic 1980)
Flanders and Swann –	*At the Drop of a Hat* (Angel 1960)
Gerry and the Pacemakers	*Don't Let the Sun Catch You Crying* (Laurie 1964)
	Ferry Cross the Mersey (United Artists 1965)
Elton John –	"Candle in the Wind/The Way You Look Tonight" (Rocket 1997)

45

George Martin & –   *George Martin Plays Help* (United Artists 1965)
His Orchestra

George Martin –   *Produced By George Martin* (Box Set)
(Capitol 2001)

Billy J. Kramer –   *Listen to Billy J. Kramer* (Parlophone (1963)
and the Dakotas   *Billy Boy* (Parlophone 1965)

Mahavishnu Orchestra –*Apocalypse* (Columbia 1974)

Paul McCartney –   *Tug of War* (Columbia 1982)
Pipes of Peace (CBS 1983)
Give My Regards to Broad Street (Columbia 1984)
Flaming Pie (Capitol 1997)

Paul Winter Consort –   *Icarus* (Epic 1972)

Seatrain –   *Seatrain* (Capitol 1970)

Peter Sellers –   *Songs for Swingin' Sellers* (Parlophone 1959)
Peter Sellers Collection (EMI 1990)

Ringo Starr –   *Sentimental Journey* (Capitol 1970)

Ultravox –   *Quartet* (Chrysalis 1983)

Jimmy Webb –   *El Mirage* (Atlantic 1977)

Wings –   "Live and Let Die" (Apple 1973)

Original Broadway–   *Tommy* (RCA 1993)
Cast

Original Soundtrack –   *Live and Let Die* (United Artists 1973)

Original Soundtrack –   *Sgt. Pepper* (RSO 1978)

Phil Spector

Alley Cats –   "Puddin n' Train" (Philles 1963)

The Beatles –   *Let it Be* (Apple 1970)

Bob B. Soxx –   "Why Do Lovers Break Each Other's Hearts?"
and the Blue Jeans   (Philles 1963)
"Zip-a-Dee-Doo-Dah" (Philles 1963)

Sonny Charles and –   "Black Pearl" (A&M 1969)
the Checkmates LTD "Proud Mary" (A&M 1969)
Love is All We Have to Give (A&M 1969)

Leonard Cohen –   *Death of a Ladies' Man* (Columbia 1977)

The Crystals –   "He Hit Me (and it Felt Like a Kiss)" (Philles 1962)
"He's a Rebel" (Philles 1962)
"There's No Other (Like My Baby)" (Philles 1962)
"Uptown" (Philles 1962)
"Da Doo Ron Ron" (Philles 1963)
"Then He Kissed Me" (Philles 1963)

	The Crystals Sing the Greatest Hits Vol. 1 (Philles 1963)
	"All Grown Up" (Philles 1964)
Dion –	*Born to Be With You* (Phil Spector International 1975)
George Harrison –	*All Things Must Pass* (Apple 1970)
	The Concert for Bangladesh (Apple 1972)
	Living in the Material World (Apple 1973)
Ben E. King –	"Spanish Harlem" (Atco 1960)
Curtis Lee –	"Pretty Little Angel Eyes" (Dunes 1961)
John Lennon and – Yoko Ono	*The Wedding Album* (Apple 1969)
John Lennon –	"Instant Karma" (Apple 1970)
	Plastic Ono Band (Apple 1970)
	"Power to the People" (Apple 1971)
	"Imagine" (Apple 1971)
	Imagine (Apple 1971)
	"Happy Xmas (War is Over)" (Apple 1971)
	Sometime in New York City (Apple 1972)
	Rock and Roll (Apple 1975)
Darlene Love –	"(Today I Met) the Boy I'm Gonna Marry" (Philles 1963)
	"A Fine Fine Boy" (Philles 1963)
	"Christmas (Baby Please Come Home)" (Philles 1963)
	"Stumble and Fall" (Philles 1964)
Yoko Ono –	*Season of Glass* (Geffen 1981)
Paris Sisters –	"Be My Boy" (Gregmark 1961)
	"I Love How You Love Me" (Gregmark 1961)
Ray Peterson –	"Corinna, Corinna" (Dunes 1961)
Gene Pitney –	"Every Breath I Take" (Musicor 1961)
The Ramones –	*End of the Century* (Sire 1980)
Righteous Brothers –	"You've Lost that Lovin' Feelin'" (Philles 1964)
	You've Lost that Lovin' Feelin' (Philles 1965)
	"Just Once in My Life" (Philles 1965)
	"Unchained Melody" (Philles 1965)
	Back to Back (Philles 1965)
	"Ebb Tide" (Philles 1965)
The Ronettes –	"Be My Baby" (Philles 1963)
	"(The Best Part of) Breakin' Up" (Philles 1964)
	"Do I Love You" (Philles 1964)
	"Walking in the Rain/How Does it Feel?" (Philles 1964)

The Ronettes (cont.) –	*Presenting the Fabulous Ronettes* (Philles 1964)
	"Born to Be Together" (Philles 1965)
	"Is This What I Get for Loving You?"
	(Philles 1965)
	"You Came, You Saw, You Conquered"
	(A&M 1969)
Phil Spector –	*A Christmas Gift for You* (Philles 1963)
	Back to Mono 1958–1969 (Box Set) (Abkco 1991)
Ronnie Spector –	"Try Some, Buy Some" (Apple 1971)
The Teddy Bears –	"To Know Him is to Love Him" (Dore 1958)
	"I Don't Need You Anymore" (Imperial 1959)
	The Teddy Bears Sing (Imperial 1959)
Ike and Tina Turner –	"River Deep, Mountain High" (Philles 1966)

THE CALIFORNIA SUNSHINE SOUND: BRIAN WILSON, GARY USHER, TERRY MELCHER, AND CURT BOETTCHER

Sunshine is a ubiquitous presence in Southern California. Its bright, searing yellow rays are part of the fabric of everyday life and have come to symbolize the region's seductive promise of eternal optimism, freedom, and prosperity. Beginning in the early '60s, this sunshine-stoked "California Myth" was musically translated by a small clutch of visionary producers into the California Sound.

The genesis of the California Sound can clearly be attributed to Brian Wilson and his band, the Beach Boys. Wilson harnessed the wide-eyed, sunny optimism that marked southern Californian teenage life in the late '50s and early '60s into hit songs inspired by such wholly Californian pursuits as surfing and hot rod cruising. With his envelope-pushing production techniques and brilliantly constructed songs, the Beach Boys struck a resonant, magical chord with land-locked teenagers around the world.

It was a special time in the recording world of Los Angeles; competition was genuinely friendly, and producers and artists regularly collaborated without the hindrance of nay-saying labels and lawyers. Wilson's early work was often undertaken with Gary Usher, a man who would become the most prolific producer of the early California Sound, earning the nickname "King of Surf." Another close friend of Wilson's, the tanned and handsome Terry Melcher, was the personification of the California golden boy and the youngest house producer for major label Columbia. Melcher's seminal production work with the Byrds was instrumental in transitioning the California Sound from its naïve fun-in-the-sun themes to the more sophisticated and world-weary folk-rock era.

Curly-haired pixie Curt Boettcher was a transplant from frigid Minnesota whose roots resided in traditional folk music. Moving to Los Angeles in the mid '60s, his knack for endlessly innovative harmonies, tireless enthusiasm for studio experimentation, and keen judge of talent made him a crucial figure in the further maturation of the California Sound. Along with frequent collaborator Gary Usher, Boettcher's late '60s, breezy, lush and deceptively dark studio-driven innovations gave birth to the commercially successful sunshine-pop offshoot of the California Sound. And with Usher and Melcher's pioneering latter Byrds productions, the table was set for country-rock's prevailing '70s chart dominance.

For these four intertwined visionary producers, their immensely popular and meticulously crafted California Sound was the messenger, and the sunshine-baked California Myth was their message—a message warmly received by millions of California dreamers around the world.

The late '50s were a tranquil and idyllic time in Southern California. Prosperity abounded, the public schools were good, people knew their neighbors, and residents even left their doors unlocked at night. It seemed as though every teenager had his or her own car, which inevitably took him or her to one of the endless strips of pristine beach, then off to one of the countless burger stands, and perhaps to a sock-hop later that night where one could shake and shimmy to the latest rock 'n' roll hits courtesy of radio stations KFWB or KDAY.

Located fifteen miles south of Hollywood and even closer to the beautiful beaches of the South Bay, Hawthorne, California, was the postcard-perfect picture of suburban idealism. With its close proximity to aviation and aerospace industry giant Northrop, Hawthorne became known as the "Cradle of Aviation." However, the town would soon become world famous for something else entirely.

It was in the summer of 1958 that Hawthorne teenager Brian Wilson had his world changed forever. For his sixteenth birthday he received a large, bulky, Wollensak two-reel tape recorder from his sadistically disciplinarian father Murry—a frustrated songwriter—and doting mother Audree. Brian was instantly spellbound, as he and younger brother Carl fooled around with the buttons and watched the tape spin backwards over and over again with child-like wonder.

Brian coveted the recorder, treating it like the rarest gem. Tirelessly experimenting, he recorded himself a cappella and replayed the tape, adding piano and singing live, enabling him to harmonize with himself. Then he would add Carl's voice, totally unaware that his makeshift technique was actually a crude stab at "overdubbing."

Soon after, Carl Wilson got a Rickenbacker guitar and, with help from a neighbor, learned how to play by copping licks from Chuck Berry records. Brian began to add Carl's guitar playing to his vocal tapes that consisted of his melodic Four Freshman–inspired harmonies. It was here that Brian Wilson discovered his passion and realized it coincided with rare God-given talent. It was here in that suburban middle-class neighborhood that the seeds of the mythical "California Sound" were first sewn.

• • • • •

Fast-forward to December 1961. Brian Wilson along with younger brothers Carl and Dennis, cousin Mike Love, and high-school football teammate Al Jardine just released their debut single, "Surfin'," for the tiny independent label Candix under their new name, the Beach Boys. Drummer Dennis, the only member of the group who actually surfed, proposed the idea for the song and Brian took it from there. "Surfin'," with its nasally So-Cal drawl of a lead vocal, somewhat ragged but spirited group harmonies, raw beat, and, most significantly, colorful beach imagery, was the first shot fired in the California Sound revolution. Just days after the release of "Surfin'," L.A.'s two most influential radio stations, KFWB and KDAY, began to play the Beach Boys debut record. The teenaged group from Hawthorne had scored an unlikely hit with its very first record.

Disappointed by their meager royalties from Candix, Brian Wilson decided to book time in a studio, produce a professional-sounding demo, and make a deal with one of the major labels. Soon the Beach Boys had secured a contract with Capitol Records on the strength of a new demo called "Surfin' Safari." Vigorously rehearsing in their family music room, noise from the nascent group wafted loudly out towards the peaceful suburban neighborhood. The racket managed to allure a skinny kid whose uncle lived across the street

THE BEACH BOYS

*The Beach Boys,
"The Pendleton Years"
(Brian Wilson top-center)*

from the Wilson abode; his name was Gary Usher. Wanting in on the fun, the self-assured Usher walked up to the Wilson house, knocked on the door, and asked to see Brian.

Despite the fact that Usher was five years older than Wilson, the two quickly realized they were kindred spirits. Usher was a singer and guitarist who had already recorded two independent singles, and his confidence and savvy fascinated the insecure Wilson. That first night, the two collaborated on their first song together, a beautiful and dreamy ballad called "The Lonely Sea." Wilson decided he wanted the sound of real waves on the song and convinced Usher to help him lug the cumbersome Wollensak recorder to the ocean in the middle of the night. "For the rest of his life, Usher laughed about knocking on someone's door at 1 a.m. and asking to plug in our extension cord. 'This isn't music,' Usher said as we laid the electrical cord in the sand. 'It's madness.'"[1]

The two developed a deep bond as the older Usher helped educate Wilson on the finer points of the music business. Usher told Wilson about the fiercely competitive Brill Building songwriting teams in New York such as Mann-Weil and King-Goffin, explaining how they aimed for a Number 1 song every time out. Working prolifically, Usher and Wilson averaged a song a day, although the two regarded most of the songs as mediocre at best. That would change on the day when, inspired by the sanctuary of Wilson's own music room, the two came up with "In My Room," which would become one of the Beach Boys' defining ballads.

Like any good Southern California boys, Usher and Wilson loved cars, especially hot rods. Usher drove a white 348 Chevy but dreamed of a hot rod 409. That inspired the two to write "409," which became the first in a long line of hit car songs for the Beach Boys and in turn kick-started the hot rod music craze. After Wilson decided he wanted the sound of a real car for the demo of "409," the two got an idea around 2 a.m. that night to record Usher's 348 in the middle of Wilson's slumbering Hawthorne street. Stringing together a line of extension cords, they placed the tape recorder beside the car's hood and repeatedly gunned the engine, rumbling the entire block awake. These raw, but fresh, ideas were the genesis of Wilson's desperate quest to get the songs to sound exactly the way he heard them in his head.

The Wilson brothers' tyrannical father Murry managed the Beach Boys during this early stage of their career. And with that control came his emotionally tortuous methods of holding on to it, methods that would traumatize the fragile Brian Wilson for the rest of his life. Murry's hard-line tactics included once whacking Brian in the side of the head with a 2' x 4', the result of which left Wilson virtually deaf in his right ear; amazingly, he retained perfect pitch with just one good ear. Because of Wilson's partial deafness, he favored recording in mono long after most of his peers had made the switch to stereo.

Murry and his eldest son constantly fought, and Brian never received the positive reinforcement he so needed from his extreme father. Murry felt he was responsible for the Beach Boys' success and sought to grab as much credit as he could. Sensing a rival in Gary Usher, Murry worked to eradicate his presence. The Wilson patriarch disdained Usher and loathed coming home to the sight of Brian and Gary collaborating. Things finally came to a boil one day when Murry insisted that the two "should write about something timeless, like love or beautiful flowers or a pretty day, instead of surfing and girls."[2] Usher mocked the dictatorial dad and then rudely informed him that he had no idea what was hip. Seething, Murry countered by telling Usher, "If you knew a quarter of what you thought you did, Einstein would be out of a job."[3]

The situation degenerated from there. Murry froze Usher out of any publishing royalties, and, with Brian unable to stand up to his intimidating father, Usher was forced out of the picture (although the two would continue to collaborate intermittently throughout the years). However, the Usher incident was the final straw for Brian, who had had enough of Murry's iron-fist. Brian moved out of the family house and rented an apartment in Inglewood with a friend whom he had met at a gig at USC.

Banished from working with Brian, Usher found a new collaborator in Roger Christian, a DJ on L.A.'s preeminent rock 'n' roll radio station KFWB. Seeking to further capitalize on the hot rod fad, the duo worked feverishly, writing and recording over 50 car songs in a one-month period alone. It was around this time that Usher struck up a partnership with singer Chuck Girard after meeting him at a sock-hop event. With Girard's high-registered vocals, Usher had found the perfect lead vocalist for his fictitious surf, hot rod, and novelty groups, such as the Superstocks, the Kickstands, Mr. Gasser and the Weirdos, and the Knights. Usher's biggest success of the period ironically came from a Brian Wilson penned song, "Little Honda," recorded by the Hondells, which zoomed all the way to Number 9 on the charts in October 1964.

Usher was astoundingly prolific during this period, producing over 30 albums in an eighteen-month span and an unbelievable 69 singles in 69 months between 1961 and 1966. Nearly all of his surf and hot rod output was characterized by a crisp, driving, reverb-bathed beat usually supplied by the same crop of session pros that were contributing to Wilson's Beach Boys recording dates. According to frequent Usher session contributor, bassist Carol Kaye, Usher's sessions "...grooved very strong, he seemed to know just exactly what he wanted."[4] Indeed, the similar makeup of session musicians like Kaye utilized by Usher and Wilson was a large factor in contributing to the distinctive uniformity of the sunny California Sound.

• • • • •

In May 1963, the Beach Boys scored their first Top 10 single with "Surfin' U.S.A." The group was well on its way towards becoming a phenomenon. Their fun-in-the-sun songs extolled the mythical virtues of the sunshine-drenched California ideal: beautiful tanned girls, hot rod cars, and surfing endless waves. It is not hard to comprehend the appeal of such ideals, especially if one was living somewhere bleak, frozen, and landlocked. By spring 1963, Brian Wilson knew that, in order to faithfully capture the sounds he heard in his head, he would have to become the Beach Boys sole producer. He also knew that it would be an uphill battle to acquire such unprecedented control. Wilson was adamant about achieving autonomy, and, after lobbying hard with the Capitol Records executives, he was finally granted his wish. Brian Wilson was barely 21 years old.

Vested with this unique, unprecedented power, Wilson's first decision was to eschew the Capitol Records studio. Convinced that Capitol did not have the appropriate acoustics for making real rock 'n' roll records, Wilson wanted to record at the more reverb-friendly Western Studios. Wilson was confident that could get a "ballsier sound" at Western and proceeded to explain this to the Capitol executives. Swayed by his conviction, Capitol begrudgingly agreed to let Wilson record a couple of tracks at Western; if they liked what they heard, the Beach Boys would be permitted to continue recording there.

"We set up at Western in Studio 3. I was officially listed as producer, though my dad sat at the board next to Western's engineer Chuck Britz and issued orders. We worked on a four-track, recording in mono. The vocals were done live, one at a time, then overdubbed, each of us singing into old-fashioned tube U-47 microphones as we stood in a single-file line. In the booth, there might be four or five instruments plugged directly into the board," Wilson recalled.[5]

Finally at the production helm, Brian immediately demonstrated his preternatural recording intuition. Working with rather primitive four-track equipment, one would literally have to splice recording tape together in the exact spot to edit and overdub sections accurately, or run the risk of ruining the track. Additionally, with the music being recorded live, split-second decisions were constantly required. It was here in this pressure-packed, do-or-die environment that Brian finally found a place where he was truly comfortable; he was home.

When the Capitol executives heard the winning results of Brian's demo productions for "Surfer Girl" and "Little Deuce Coupe," they were flabbergasted, and they granted him permission to continue to work at Western. Wilson's triumph of creative independence was not only a personal victory, it was an achievement that would wield a tremendous affect on a whole new crop of young, up-and-coming producers. Within five years, an entirely new breed of California producers would come to the forefront, an explosion that would not have been possible without Wilson's fiercely determined independence. With the arrival of these young, independent-minded producers, Los Angeles would supplant New York as the true center for recording.

Released in September 1963, *Surfer Girl* was the first Beach Boys album produced entirely by Brian. He threw everything he had into the marathon recording sessions that would stretch out over nine or ten hours, often obsessing over a single note or one instrumental part for hours on end. One of Wilson's innovative techniques was to record the same vocals twice, without using any echo. It was this pioneering use of "double-tracking" that provided the Beach Boys with their exceptionally bright, hallmark sound.

With the meticulously arranged, close harmonies of such ballads as the Four Freshman–influenced "Surfer Girl" and the Usher collaboration, "In My Room," the intense work had paid off. Nearly overnight, the Beach Boys had become the top rock 'n' roll group in America, and suddenly the California Sound was *the* sound. But all was not well with Wilson. Outside of the comfortable environs of Western, his demons began to manifest themselves in threatening ways. With the commercial and personal pressures mounting, Wilson was often unable to sleep, and when he did drift off, he was frequently jolted awake by ugly nightmares.

His inner turmoil growing, Wilson became hell-bent on outdoing himself on each subsequent recording session. Driving around town in his aquamarine Grand Prix one day in 1964, he heard a brand-new song on the radio and experienced an instant epiphany. The song was Phil Spector's Wall-of-Sound-defining production of the Ronettes' "Be My Baby." Completely stunned, Wilson immediately pulled over and concluded that it was the greatest song he had ever heard. Awed and inspired by Spector's latest creation, he bought ten copies of "Be My Baby" and played them incessantly, meticulously analyzing every note and nuance of the song.

Brian was particularly fascinated by Spector's method of forging new sounds by combining certain instruments together. "Rather than just say 'that's a piano, that's a bass,' now, we have what you call a piano-guitar. It sounds like something else. Although it may be two or three instruments combined playing the same notes, it now sounds different,"[6] Wilson explained. After he had thoroughly digested Spector's hit, he set out to top his idol with a new song he called "Don't Worry Baby."

Written with frequent Usher collaborator Roger Christian, "Don't Worry Baby" was a giant step forward in Wilson's production and songwriting progression. The song's yearning, angelic harmonies and deep, bassy groove intertwined majestically, and the metaphorical lyrics about drag racing and love were deceptively complex and ambitious. The song was nothing short of sublime. Wilson was clearly beginning to move away from simple teenaged anthems towards something far more mature and emotionally complex.

"Don't Worry Baby" was released as the flipside to "I Get Around," during the zenith of Beatlemania in the summer of 1964. On July 4th, the potent double-sided single became the Beach Boys' first Number 1 hit, while also serving as a subtle harbinger for the growing dichotomy within the California Sound. While "I Get Around" symbolized the sunshine ideal in all its carefree splendor, "Don't Worry Baby" suggested something entirely more pensive and even slightly dark underneath its pristine facade.

The demons were mounting for Brian Wilson, and, after suffering a nervous breakdown on a flight in December 1964, he permanently quit touring with the Beach Boys. Opting to stay home to compose and produce while the band spread the sunny California Myth to packed venues around the world, Wilson's songwriting and production conceptions continued to dramatically progress. In the spring of 1965, with "Help Me, Rhonda" at Number 1 and the successful release of the ambitious *The Beach Boys Today!*, the group was riding high on the charts, and Brian Wilson himself was doing the same at home.

Wilson had recently been introduced to marijuana, and the herb had an immediate effect on his songwriting and production style. Wilson wrote the entire second side of *The Beach Boys Today!* under the influence of pot. As a result, song tempos became more deliberate, arrangements grew more expansive, and the lyrics inwardly turned towards the ruminative. His thinking in regard to the recording process had changed radically, and his productions became denser and richer.

Wilson was now able to deconstruct songs into tiny increments and deal with each instrument individually, stacking sounds one at a time. This newfound insight was specifically demonstrated on "Please Let Me Wonder," a gorgeously lush, slow motion ballad that points the way towards Wilson's later masterwork, *Pet Sounds*. Further evidence was found on the pensive "In the Back of My Mind," whose stony lead vocal and warped string arrangement was Wilson's most ambitious arrangement to date.

Building on the momentum of *The Beach Boys Today!*, Wilson's songwriting and production skills continued to accelerate at the rapid pace necessary to keep up with friendly rivals the Beatles and the slightly more adversarial Spector. Now traveling in the bohemian Hollywood fast lane, Wilson began to experiment with LSD more than a year before the drug reached the mainstream. Unquestionably, acid wielded a great effect on Wilson's musical conceptions, as evidenced by the glorious keyboard and horns opening to the ultimate California sunshine anthem, "California Girls."

Opting to record "California Girls" at Gold Star Studios rather than Western, Wilson was not only using Spector's studio of choice, he was using his personal team of studio-aces, dubbed "The Wrecking Crew," as well. One of the musicians who played on the session was Carol Kaye, who supplied the song's famous loping bass-line. A frequent collaborator with the Beach Boys, Kaye recalled Wilson as a "fine guy to work for, who was intensive in his work. We had to create parts for all the other groups we cut for, but not Brian. We were in awe of Brian."[7]

Wilson's development continued to grow by leaps and bounds through the latter days of 1965. His production of "Guess I'm Dumb" (a song he also wrote) for Wrecking Crew guitarist and onetime Beach Boy touring member Glen Campbell was his most inspired yet.

With its surging, elegant Burt Bacharach–inspired string and horn arrangement and Campbell's forlorn Roy Orbison–like vocal, the song was equal parts artistic triumph and a commercial failure. Undaunted, Wilson's ambitions continued on the Beach Boys' daring single "The Little Girl I Once Knew," a song that featured several unpredictable tempo changes and a number of dead-stop "false endings." Needless to say, radio programmers were perplexed, especially by the dead air of the false endings. Brian Wilson had written his first Beach Boys flop.

• • • • •

Blonde, handsome, and wealthy, and the son of world-famous actress/singer Doris Day, Terry Melcher was the archetypal southern California golden boy. Melcher developed a passion for singing early in his youth, and, in 1961, at the age of nineteen (with help from Phil Spector compatriot Jack Nitzsche) he managed to scrape up $300 to cut a demo at the home of Spector's Wall of Sound, Gold Star Studios. The demo made such an impression at Columbia Records that Melcher was given an invitation to participate in its producer-trainee program in New York. After completing the program, Melcher returned home and struck up a fruitful partnership with singer/song-writer, and future Beach Boy, Bruce Johnston.

Thanks to the tremendously successful efforts of Wilson and Usher, a major market had been created around the fun-in-the-sun California Sound. Seeking to further capitalize on its success, Melcher and Johnston turned their attention to songwriters Ernie Bringas and

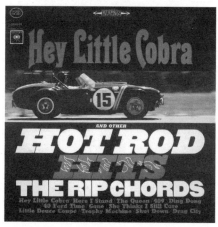

The Rip Chords
Hey Little Cobra and
Other Hot Rod Hits
(1964)

Phil Stewart and, dubbing them the Rip Chords, signed them up at Columbia. Hot rod music was currently the rage, and, after a couple of modestly charting singles, the Rip Chords struck it big with "Hey Little Cobra." The song, co-written by Melcher and songwriter Carol Conners, managed to race all the way to Number 4 in February 1964. Utilizing tireless Wrecking Crew session pros like drummer Hal Blaine and guitarist Glen Campbell, "Cobra"'s driving beat and sparkling production touches helped insure the song's success.

Rip Chords member Ernie Bringas named Melcher's production technique "cross-dubbing." Rather than over-dubbing the same voices on top of each other, Melcher would regularly layer the vocals with different voices. For example, Bruce Johnston would exactly duplicate Brian Wilson's falsetto, and this technique would be utilized for the other harmony parts and occasionally some leads as well. This innovative approach gave the whole sound a distinctive richness and vibrancy above and beyond what over-dubbing afforded at the time.

After a brief stint as a recording duo with Johnston, under the moniker Bruce and Terry that included the 1964 pseudo-surf hit "Summer Means Fun," the fledgling producer turned his sights on an exciting new L.A. band called the Jet Set. After cutting their teeth on the New York Greenwich Village folk scene, the band members relocated to Hollywood and began to merge the songwriting sophistication of folk with the exciting new Beatle beat.

When the band received a deal with Columbia upon the strength of a demo of an unreleased Bob Dylan song, "Mr. Tambourine Man," in the fall of 1964, Melcher was paired with the group. Accompanying their contract was a considerably more anglophilic new name, the Byrds. (They had previously recorded one failed single for Elektra Records as the Beefeaters.) Melcher heard great promise in "Mr. Tambourine Man" but realized that changes would need to be made in its arrangement and in its level of musicianship. Melcher concluded that guitarist Jim McGuinn was the only Byrd technically proficient enough to be involved in the recording and steadfastly insisted that the other members—David Crosby, Gene Clark, Chris Hillman, and Michael Clarke—sit out the session. Predictably, the other members, whose collective backgrounds were all in acoustic music, took the news hard; ultimately, though, they went along with Melcher's strategy.

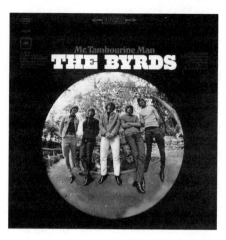

The Byrds
Mr. Tambourine Man
(1965)

Using his "normal guys" for the session—Hal Blaine (drummer), Leon Russell (keyboards), Larry Knechtel (bass), and Jerry Cole (rhythm guitar)—Melcher essentially copped the bass-drum groove from the Beach Boys' "Don't Worry Baby" and put the "Mr. Tambourine Man" melody over it. Then he had McGuinn weave his ringing Rickenbacker twelve-string through the song, which was overdubbed four times to create a rich jangly resonance.

With the newfound formula of twelve-string jangly guitar, punchy drumbeat, lopping bottom-heavy bass, and breathtaking group harmonies, "Mr. Tambourine Man" meteorically rocketed to a two-week stay at Number 1 in late June 1965. With the runaway success of the single, the Byrds promptly became the leading purveyors of the newly christened "folk-rock" genre. Melcher would go on to helm the first two Byrds LPs *Mr. Tambourine Man* and *Turn! Turn! Turn!*, and the title track from the latter became the band's second Number 1 single, in December 1965.

Catalyzed by their mixture of electrified Bob Dylan covers, traditional folk ballads and joyously jangly originals, both Byrds albums became instant cornerstones of folk-rock and introduced a new level of sophistication into the pop lexicon. Through Melcher's stewardship of the Byrds, folk-rock had become wildly popular, and the commercially golden formula was quickly co-opted by a myriad of L.A.–based artists including the Turtles, the Leaves, Sonny & Cher, and Barry McGuire. The teenaged record-buying audience was growing up fast, and the California Sound was becoming less about surfing and cars and more about social consciousness and personal awareness.

Emboldened by his groundbreaking work with the Byrds, everything was clicking for Melcher. He had been instrumental in the creation of a brand-new musical genre, garnered critical and popular success, and he was only 23 years old. His good fortune continued when he took up the production reigns for Columbia's newly signed band, Paul Revere & The Raiders. Hailing from the wild and wooly Pacific Northwest, the Raiders were an energetic, rag-tag party band that fused R&B and raw rock in such covers as "Fever," "Oo Po Pah Do," and "Louie, Louie." With Melcher now on board, he sought to tone down their roots rock tendencies in favor of a tougher, more contemporary alienated-teen approach. Replacing piano with Vox organ and virtually phasing out the earlier honking saxophone presence, Melcher attempted to recast the band as the American version of the Rolling Stones.

Ignited by their 1965 half-live/half-studio debut, *Here They Come* (Melcher produced the studio side), the Raiders were on their way to becoming one of the most popular rock acts of the decade. Continuing his practice of using top studio musicians for the recording sessions, Melcher crafted several highly successful, leanly rocking hits, including "Kicks," "Hungry," "Just Like Me," "Steppin' Out," "The Great Airplane Strike," and "Good Thing." In fact, the latter two hits were co-written by Melcher and charismatic lead singer Mark Lindsay. Often the band would be on tour and Melcher would have Lindsay fly in to record his lead vocals and then fly right back out to rejoin the band on the road, which became an obvious point of contention for the other Raiders. However, that was the reality of Melcher's exacting methods, and, with a long string of hit singles, it was difficult for the band to argue with success.

By the late 1960s, the band's Colonial uniforms and garage rock sound were wearing thin. Following the band's transitional 1968 album, *Goin' to Memphis* (which was essentially a Lindsay solo album in everything but name), Melcher ceased his involvement with the Raiders. Lindsay continued on with the band and as a solo act, enjoying chart success through the early 1970s. Today, one can go hardly ten minutes before one of the Raiders' snarling hits crops up on oldies radio.

On the flip side of Melcher's triumphs with the Byrds and Paul Revere & the Raiders was the star-crossed failure of the Rising Sons. One of most talented bands of the era, the L.A.–based Rising Sons are best remembered for featuring legendary musicians Taj Mahal and Ry Cooder. After making a splash around town with their prodigious amalgamation of country-blues, folk, and rock (legend has it that David Crosby once leapt up on a table after one of their performances, and led the crowd in a chant of "Long live the Rising Sons"), Melcher was assigned the unenviable task of shaping the eclectic band into a commercially successful outfit.

Despite musically conflicting ideas between the band members and simmering tensions with Melcher, several sessions were attempted between 1965 and 1966, although a completed album never saw the light of day. Much of the problem can be attributed to the dual character of the band, as the Rising Sons were really two different bands in one. With Mahal and Cooder they possessed an uncommon grasp of country-blues, while member Jesse Lee Kincaid's originals, such as "The Girl With Green Eyes," were decidedly more Beatlesesque and poppy.

If it wasn't for the ensuing fame of Mahal and Cooder, the band would most likely be remembered only as a curious footnote, but, instead, the Rising Sons' legend has continued to ascend throughout the years. Finally, in 1992, the Melcher sessions were officially released, and one has to wonder why they never came out in the first place. Containing several extraordinary performances of country-blues standards from immortals like Blind Willie McTell, Charley Patton, Sleepy John Estes, and Reverend Gary Davis, along with a handful of strong originals written by Kincaid, one can only wonder what might have been. Punctuated by Cooder's mind-boggling slide work and the band's assured arrangements, Melcher's recordings possess a dynamic energy and an authenticity uncommon to rock acts of the time. Had the album been released in 1966, the Rising Sons quite possibly would have become one of the more influential and important bands of the day.

• • • • •

The Beach Boys
Pet Sounds
(1966)

With the late-1965 release of the Beatles' near-perfect *Rubber Soul*, pop's stakes had been raised into the stratosphere. Suddenly, it was more about making a great album without filler than a great single, and, like many listeners, Brian Wilson's mind was blown. In an effort to record an album that would top *Rubber Soul*, Wilson realized he would need a new songwriting partner to help him achieve his mushrooming ambitions.

The collaborator he chose was Tony Asher, an ad-man who Wilson barely knew. With Asher on board, the 23-year-old Wilson began creating *Pet Sounds*, his loftiest and most personal artistic statement. *Pet Sounds* was the first album recorded without any musical contributions from any of the Beach Boys; instead, they were used solely for the vocals and harmonies. Expectedly, the band initially felt shut out from the process. However, once they heard what Brian was doing, they came around to support his decision.

From the winsome opening of "Wouldn't It Be Nice" through the plaintively auto-biographical "I Just Wasn't Made for These Times," to the heartbreaking closer "Caroline, No," *Pet Sounds* was pop's first true song-cycle, an album where all the songs were conceptually linked to a theme—in this case, the turbulent journey from adolescence to adulthood. The accompanying music was equally daring: nearly avant-garde string and horn arrangements enhanced by unorthodox instruments like theremin, bicycle bells, and makeshift percussion (from an overturned water bottle). Soaring above it all were the most majestic harmonies the Beach Boys had ever created.

The album even featured two emotional instrumentals, "Let's Go Away for Awhile," and "Pet Sounds," both of which bordered on a new form of modern symphonic music.

Perhaps the most enduring song on *Pet Sounds* is the almost impossibly beautiful single "God Only Knows." For its recording session, Wilson assembled 23 musicians in one studio, a quantity only matched at the time by rival Phil Spector. Constricted by the technical limitations of the studio, Wilson kept each distinct part in his head as he simultaneously conducted the ensemble and supervised the recording. Coupling an uncanny ability to make snap decisions with pitch-perfect hearing ensured the ballad's glorious immortality.

Fatefully, without one surfing or car song on it, Brian had tampered with the well-worn Beach Boys' formula and *Pet Sounds* became a commercial disappointment. Though both "Wouldn't It Be Nice" and "Sloop John B." performed modestly well as singles, it was the release of "God Only Knows" that became noteworthy as the first pop single to contain the word "God" in the title. Solely credited to Brian Wilson, the highly personal "Caroline, No" was also released as a single, but it only peaked at Number 32 on the singles chart.

Despite its commercial shortcomings, the album was enormously influential on Wilson's peers; in much the same way *Rubber Soul* blew Brian's mind, *Pet Sounds* had a galvanizing affect on Paul McCartney, who has often cited it as his all-time favorite album. Undeniably, the song-cycle construction of *Pet Sounds* was the catalyst for the Beatles' watershed *Sgt. Pepper* album released the following year. With folk-rock on the rise along with Wilson's artistic gauntlet, the California sunshine sound was expanding at the speed of light.

As the pressure of having to top himself with each new song mounted, Wilson embarked on the recording of a song originally slated for *Pet Sounds* entitled "Good Vibrations." According to Wilson, "'Good Vibrations' was going to be the summation of my musical vision, a harmonic convergence of imagination and talent, production values and craft, songwriting and spirituality."[8] The ambitious "teen-aged symphony to God," conceived while Wilson was tripping on LSD, was envisioned to be a production in the grandiose Spector mold.

Written in three separate parts, the electrically charged sessions sprawled out over several months and ended up costing Capitol over

The Beach Boys
Good Vibrations
(1966)

$50,000, an outrageous amount for a single in 1966. Fortunately, the lavishness paid off for Wilson, whose kitchen-sink instrumental approach included clarinet, harp, cello, and fuzz bass. Helping the song to stand out even further was the high-pitched wail of an electronic instrument called the theremin. Best known for its use in low-budget horror films, Wilson's use of the box-like theremin (which is manipulated by waving one's hand in different directions over the instrument to coax the sound waves) provided the song with a unique hook.

Everything coalesced when "Good Vibrations" hit Number 1 on December 3, 1966. Wilson had managed to merge the experimental with the commercial, and the song's thematically sunny lyrics and multi-sectioned construction boldly furthered the parameters of pop. "Good Vibrations" was a clarion call to music producers everywhere. Producing a pop record was now more about shattering musical boundaries then about exploiting existing trends. For a brief, shining moment, pop and art came together as unlikely commercial bedfellows.

• • • • •

In early 1966, Brian fired Murry Wilson as the Beach Boys' manager. The coast was now clear for Usher, and he and Wilson began to associate again. One fateful night at Studio Three West in Hollywood, during an Usher session for The Byrds' *Younger Than Yesterday*, the two-workaholic producers were stopped dead in their tracks by music coming from outside of their studio.

"All of a sudden, I heard a sound, and the instant I heard it, I froze, as if someone had thrown a bowling ball at me. My ears just perked right up. And Brian looked at me, I looked at Brian, and we both said simultaneously, 'What is that?'" Usher recalled.[9] The two began walking down the studio hallway following the trail of the music. As the sound grew louder and more exciting with each step, Usher and Wilson literally began to run towards the room from where the sounds came. They flung the door open to find what Usher described as a "little kid with an earring."[10]

That "kid" was Curt Boettcher, a short, curly-haired, upstart producer. The song he was recording was Lee Mallory's exuberant "That's the Way it's Gonna Be." Wilson was so flabbergasted by Mallory's harmonic sunshine pop song that his face turned white. Wilson became obsessed with the song and Boettcher's production, repeatedly bringing it up to Usher for a week straight. That was the first time Usher had met Boettcher, but it would certainly not be the last.

Boettcher had begun his career as member of the Minneapolis-based folk group, the Goldebriars, a unit that also featured two sisters, Dotti and Sherri Holmberg. With their unusual all black-clad attire, Boettcher's band released two albums of "progressive folk" for Epic Records. While still steeped in the folk music tradition, the Goldebriars arrangements and harmonies were breathtakingly fresh and unusually arranged. A late incarnation of the group featured future Music Machine drummer Ron Edgar, someone who would figure prominently in many of Boettcher's later projects.

Relocating to L.A., Boettcher assembled a coterie of like-minded musicians and formed the Ballroom. The band gigged around town from late 1966 through early 1967 with modest success, garnering minor notoriety from their frenzied version of Them's "Baby, Please Don't Go." Synthesizing delicate fairy-tale psychedelia and Mamas & Papas–style harmonic pop, the Ballroom had written several celestial originals, including "Would You Like to Go" and "Musty Dusty," that would be recycled for later Boettcher projects. After recording an unreleased album, the Ballroom disbanded and Boettcher focused on freelance productions that often utilized his ex-Ballroom band mates.

After submitting a demo recorded with cohort Victoria Wilson to ex–Vee Jay records executive Steve Clark back in 1965, the three banded together to form Our Productions. Clark then quickly dispatched Boettcher to work with the prolific pop star Tommy Roe. A fortuitous pairing, Roe and Boettcher's collaborations netted commercial gold.

With its woozy drums and swirling arrangements, Boettcher's reverb-heavy stamp on such Roe pop smashes such as "Sweet Pea" (arguably the first bubblegum song) and "Hooray for Hazel" is immediately apparent. Although Steve Clark retained production credit on these songs, Boettcher was the real studio producer. The infectiousness of the songs helped sustain Roe's sound and enabled him to maintain his popularity throughout the rapidly changing musical climate of the mid-sixties. The culmination of Boettcher's work with Roe can be heard on Roe's *It's Now a Winter's Day* album, which featured much of Boettcher's stable in supporting roles. Featuring a plethora otherworldly sound effects (courtesy of Boettcher's embryonic use of mellotron), beatific harmony arrangements, Eastern-derived rhythms, and luxuriant stereo panning, the album challenged Roe's primarily teenybopper fan-base towards something more daring, not to mention strange. *It's Now a Winter's Day* stands as one of the great, unsung 1960s pop releases.

As Boettcher took up residence in a gothic Spanish-style mansion in the old Hollywood neighborhood of Bronson Canyon (located in close proximity to Columbia recording studios, where he often worked), he began to dabble in mysticism. Future band mate Sandy Salisbury recalled driving up to Boettcher's home one night and finding him in the driveway with (ex-Ballroom member) Michelle O'Malley grinning strangely at him. When Salisbury inquired what the two were up to, Boettcher said, "We just got back. We've been flying over L.A." "I'm a witch, I took Curt with me" O'Malley added seriously. "Those two scared the shit out of me that night," Salisbury recalled.[11]

When not flying around L.A., Boettcher became involved with a new vocal group called the Association. One of its members, Ted Bluechel, admired Boettcher's cutting-edge vocal arrangements for Roe and suggested he produce the fledgling group. Boettcher agreed, and their initial collaboration was the Association's dynamic debut single, "Along Comes Mary." Bringing together a kicking drum groove, quasi-subversive lyrics, glorious harmonies, and crystalline production, Boettcher crafted a monstrous hit for the new band.

Boettcher scored an even bigger hit with the second Association single, the lovely, light-as-a-feather "Cherish," which occupied the Number 1 position for three weeks in the early fall of 1966. The runaway success of the singles introduced the Association as one of the main purveyors the harmonic, slightly psychedelic vocal music genre dubbed "soft pop" and, later, the retrospectively termed "sunshine pop." Updating traditional pop vocals with hip lyrics, breezy harmonies and an effervescent production style, soft pop quickly became a staple of AM radio and a decided antidote to the hard and heavy direction rock was taking on FM. Inspired by the overnight success of the Association as well as the Mamas & the Papas, soft pop bands like the Cyrkle, Harpers Bizarre, Spanky & Our Gang, and the Fifth Dimension quickly proliferated and prospered through the end of the decade.

Continuing to work with the Association, Boettcher helmed their debut 1966 album *And Then...Along Comes the Association*, a release that abundantly demonstrated his inspired production vision. Boettcher delighted in taking full advantage of the new possibilities that stereo offered, such as panning sounds from speaker to speaker and multi-layering vocals wherever possible. Drawing on his advanced techniques, Boettcher's productions possessed a magnificent three-dimensionality that set them apart from other contemporaries. Mysteriously, the band did not retain Boettcher for its follow-up album, and his association with the Association came to an abrupt halt. However, the California Sound was quickly moving in the sunshine-pop direction, due in large part to Boettcher. With several hit singles under his belt, the producer was left to plot his next move, a slated collaboration with admirer and fellow California sound visionary, Gary Usher.

• • • • •

By 1966, Usher's surf and hot rod sound was losing steam. Fortunately, his production skill and versatility enabled him to keep pace with the rapidly changing rock landscape. Working with the Byrds, Simon and Garfunkel, the Peanut Butter Conspiracy, and

British duo Chad & Jeremy, among others, his clean sound and ability to coax top-shelf performances from his artists kept him in high demand. Yet Usher, who was accustomed to having complete control during his surf and hot rod days, found working with many of these artists commercially fruitful yet artistically frustrating. "I had very little creative input. I was strictly a producer, and it was hard for me because of all I had done beforehand. It started eating away at me," Usher recollected.[12]

Creative frustrations aside, Usher's work, especially with the Byrds, represented the quintessence of the increasingly sophisticated and diverse California Sound. Outgrowing their early Terry Melcher–produced sound, the maturing Byrds enlisted Usher to helm their transitional 1967 release, *Younger Than Yesterday*. While the album's hodgepodge of styles and genres could have easily been a confused mess, Usher's studio command provided the album an impressively uniform consistency.

On *Younger Than Yesterday*'s hit opening track "So You Want to Be a Rock & Roll Star," Usher deftly layers samba-like percussion, mariachi-style horns, and sounds of screaming girls over one of the great sardonic rock anthems. The rest of the album glides effortlessly through shining folk-rock, jazz-influenced pop, novelty space rock, and colorful psychedelia. Significantly, the album also strongly flirted with country and bluegrass, elements that would soon come to dominate future Byrd releases.

Inching the California Sound even closer to towards country-rock was former Byrd Gene Clark's stunning debut, *Gene Clark with the Gosdin Brothers*. Produced in large part by Usher, the album was unfairly obscured by the bright commercial glare of *Younger Than Yesterday*, which was coincidentally released on the same day in February 1967. Using the workaholic Wrecking Crew, esoteric session man (and Brian Wilson collaborator) Van Dyke Parks, along with Byrds Chris Hillman and Michael Clarke, Clark's song's bridged the gap between *Rubber Soul*–influenced pop and nascent country-rock. With Clark's woebegone vocals taking center-stage, tracks such as "Tried So Hard" and "Set You Free This Time" sparkle with verve and vitality. With the country-rock explosion just around the corner, Clark and Usher managed to quietly turn in an album more than a year ahead of its time.

The Byrds
The Notorious Byrd Brothers
(1968)

With David Crosby out of the Byrds picture, Usher and the band went to work on yet another landmark, *The Notorious Byrd Brothers*. By no means a huge commercial success, the album's synthesis of rural psychedelia, space rock, and organic country was nothing short of astonishing. While sessions were by all accounts a tumultuous time for the band members, Usher helped the Byrds triumph over the tension as he crafted one of his most inventive productions. Clearly his mastery of layering, the availability of improved recording equipment, and the band's willingness to experiment all combined to make it a truly unique and subtle album.

The *Notorious Byrd Brothers* opens with its hardest rocking cut, "Artificial Energy," an amphetamine-fueled *tour de force* that is punctuated by staccato horns and heavy-phased guitar. The poignant antiwar song, "Draft Morning," is another standout that begins with the band's trademark chiming guitar and lush vocal combination before taking an expected turn into a cacophonous middle section of blaring horns, warped strings, fighter jet sound effects, and automatic gunfire. As a credit to Usher's skill, the sound collage somehow resolves seamlessly back into the delicate chiming and harmony that began the song. For the experimental, mantra-like track "Space Odyssey," Usher employed one of the first uses of Moog synthesizer in a rock context, and the spacey keyboard lends the composition a haunting, alien quality. Further defining *Notorious*'s diversity are the beautiful, fingerpicked country tunes "Old John Robertson," "Get to You," and "Tribal Gathering."

The third and final album of Usher's Byrds trilogy was the full-blown country-rock masterpiece, *Sweetheart of the Rodeo*. Bolstered by the addition of Gram Parsons (the former leader of the proto-country-rock group International Submarine Band), Usher and the Byrds recorded an album that redrew the boundaries of rock. Although it was not the first country-rock album, *Sweetheart of the Rodeo* was the release that truly cemented the genre.

With self-professed "cosmic cowboy" Parsons riding shotgun, Byrds leader Roger McGuinn had a new and formidable songwriting foil. Parsons and McGuinn were competitive and often adversarial, but the contentious environment helped elevate the project into the country-rock touchstone it has become. Tackling covers of such pure bluegrass, country, and Southern soul sources as the Louvin Brothers, Merle Haggard, and William Bell, as well as the customary Dylan reworking ("You Ain't Goin' Nowhere"), Parsons's energizing influence is omnipresent. Staying away from the dense sound-collages and multi-layered experimentation of *The Notorious Byrd Brothers*, Usher recorded the album in a crisply clean immediate style, designed to place full emphasis on the strength of the material. While this back-to-basics approach would soon become *de rigueur*, *Sweetheart of the Rodeo*'s sound lay in stark contrast to the prevailing heaviness of other defining 1968 releases as the Beatles' "White Album," Jimi Hendrix's *Electric Ladyland*, Cream's *Wheels of Fire*, Iron Butterfly's *In-A-Gadda-Da-Vida*, and the Jefferson Airplane's *Crown of Creation*.

As the usual acrimony swirled over the Byrds like a pestilence, and just before *Sweetheart*'s August release, McGuinn erased Parsons' lead vocals and replaced them with his own on a majority of the songs. (Years later, Parsons original vocals were restored as bonus tracks on the CD reissue.) Soon after, Parsons bolted from the Byrds for the greener pastures of his own seminal country-rock band, the Flying Burrito Brothers. Band in-fighting and duplicitous actions aside, the Usher-produced *Sweetheart of the Rodeo* was an undeniable catalyst for the burgeoning L.A. country-rock sound that would come to dominate much of the rock world throughout the 1970s.

Usher's triumphs with the Byrds notwithstanding, the producer was still unsatisfied with his lack of creative freedom. Without the luxury of the type of creative control that Brian Wilson enjoyed,

Usher was relegated to "doing money music" for Columbia Records.[13] "I was a hired gun. I worked 80 hours a week and I cranked 'em out. I put out a lot of product, and I didn't have time to sit back like Brian Wilson could do and take three, four, five months on a record. I was expected to turn one out in *days*," he said.

Ironically for Usher, the more production successes he enjoyed, and the more money he made for the record label, the less creative freedom he was granted from the record company executives. Usher yearned to arrange and produce his own music as he had done early in his career when he was "living in Brian (Wilson's) shadow as the 'King of Surf.'"[14] A natural seeker, Usher's thirst for knowledge led to an interest in the prevailing mysticism of the time, and he yearned to make more personal music. "The problem I had at CBS was that I could not do an inspirational album. There was no New Age stuff then," he said.

Usher was working extensively with the British duo Chad & Jeremy, helming their pastoral psychedelic-pop offerings *Of Cabbages and Kings* and *The Arc*. With their lightly trippy, harmonic sound, the band seemed like a natural fit for "My World Fell Down," an unusual new song that had been brought to Usher's attention. Somewhat surprisingly, Chad & Jeremy hated the song and refused to record it. The stubborn duo's resistance only strengthened Usher's resolve. More determined than ever to find an outlet for self-expression, he took matters into his own hands. Working with whatever free time he could muster—off-hours, late night sessions, weekends—Usher began to experiment with his own recordings.

Enlisting his trusty compatriots, the Wrecking Crew, Usher embarked on recording the song Chad & Jeremy had deemed "a piece of crap." Featuring vocal turns from (future Beach Boy) Bruce Johnston, colleague Terry Melcher and top studio-guitarist Glen Campbell, the song's vocals—"Call it wintertime, and the leaves are brown, since you went away, my world fell down"—were so somnolent that they bordered on the sinister. Featuring an eerie baroque opening, a sweeping, string-adorned chorus, and complex multi-part harmonies, the vanguard song contained enough commercial potential to impress legendary Columbia records honcho Clive Davis, who flipped over its originality. Davis was so impressed that he implored

Gary Usher/Curt Boettcher publicity shots for Sagittarius' *Present Tense*

Usher to sign the group that cut it. The only problem was that there was no real group to sign.

Ever since Usher's early surf and hot rod days, he had been creating fictitious studio groups such as the Super-Stocks and the Kickstands, imaginary bands to sate the hungry surf and hot rod record-buying audience. But this new project excited Usher in a different way; it represented the freedom of creative expression he had craved. With Usher afraid to admit that it was really just himself on "My World Fell Down," for fear of Davis thinking his top producer *actually* had free time, he said the band was called Sagittarius (Usher's astrological sign). Much to Usher's relief, Davis loved the name.

The single for "My World Fell Down" managed to not only delight Davis but confound him as well. In the song's middle section, the music drops out and gives way to a ringing alarm clock, a crying baby, and crowd noise from a bullfight! This type of avant-garde sound-collage was totally unexpected and unprecedented, especially for a single. While envelope-pushers such as the Beatles and the Beach Boys were moving in a similar direction, the song pre-dates both bands' multi-layered experiments. Davis was perplexed by the bizarre overdubs and sound-effect breaks and looked at Usher like he had lost his mind. After hassling with Davis, Usher finally agreed to remove the song's middle sound-collage section for the forthcoming album version.

Not a national smash by any stretch of the imagination, the single did manage to reside in the lower regions of the Hot 100 for five weeks during the mythical summer of 1967. In some of the more sophisticated markets such as San Francisco and Chicago, it actually became a Top 5 single. The regional success led to live appearance requests for the fictitious band that they obviously was unable to accept. Years later, the song would appear on the legendary Nuggets compilation that became instrumental in introducing a new generation of musicians and fans to the thrilling psychedelic songs of the mid-1960s. The song would also take on additional significance, as lead vocalist Glen Campbell soon became an MOR radio staple by pursuing a sound that was a far cry from the daring lysergic experimentalism of "My World Fell Down."

Turning his attention to recording Sagittarius's album *Present Tense*, Usher tapped the kid who had stunned him and Brian Wilson earlier that year, Curt Boettcher. Boettcher's influence was pronounced on the sessions as many of the psychedelic fairy-tale songs (such as "Musty Dusty" and "Would You Like to Go") came from his short-lived group the Ballroom. Furthering the album's unusual sound was the intriguing combination of Usher's oft-used session-pros and Boettcher's relatively unknown cabal of musicians. *Present Tense* is a special album, delicate but challenging, pillowy soft and decidedly hallucinatory. Not surprisingly, acid played an inspirational role in the album's creation as Boettcher explained:

> I was into LSD, but I did it way before everyone else was doing it. When everyone else was taking it, I had already done it. I did it for real reasons, not as a hedonistic self-stroke. I did it because I really wanted to find out more about myself. The music reflects it; it's not a period where you're landing, it's a period where you're stretching, and all that music was a stretch.[15]

• • • • •

Meanwhile, LSD was beginning to take its toll on the increasingly paranoid Brian Wilson. For Wilson the sunshine was dissipating and the darkness was creeping in. As usual, his desperate drive to top himself and the Beatles was in high-gear. Attempting to answer the Beatles' latest artistic gauntlet, *Revolver*, Wilson labored on a lavish concept album he was calling *Dumb Angel*. However, the Beach Boys' grip on reality was quickly loosening, exacerbated by drugs, unrelenting personal demons, professional pressures, and the influence of a new collaborator, the enigmatic and eccentric session man and songwriter Van Dyke Parks. Together, the two crafted a number of songs that were unorthodox and perplexing, especially to straight-arrow Beach Boy Mike Love, who considered the new material commercial suicide. Indeed there was something to Love's argument, as lofty new songs such as "Surf's Up," "Cabin Essence," and "Wind Chimes" possessed a darkly demented aura that would undoubtedly alienate nearly all of the Beach Boys' audience.

For the planned follow-up single to "Good Vibrations," Wilson and Parks tackled the mythical old American West in a song called "Heroes and Villains." Running more than seven minutes long, the sprawling, multiple-sectioned composition's radio potential seemed doomed from the start. Yet the indulgent Wilson was unconcerned about such matters, as reflected in the bizarre recording techniques utilized on the album he now titled *Smile*. These methods included recording at the bottom of an echoey, empty swimming pool, instructing vocalists to sing flat on their backs (stoned on copious amounts of hash), and infamously forcing a string section to don firemen's helmets as he burned buckets of wood in the studio for his intended "Fire" suite.

Directly following the recording of "Fire," a rash of real fires sprouted up around L.A. Wilson felt karmically responsible for the outbreaks, and in a fit of panic he burned the master tapes. Things were clearly racing out of control. Now totally paranoid, Wilson was unable to pull it all together. Finally, Capitol cut its loses and permanently shelved *Smile* in the summer of 1967. In its place, the band scurried to cobble together *Smiley Smile*. A pale interpretation of the doomed original, the un-cohesive album recycled several *Smile* snippets and ideas into new loose and stripped-down remakes.

The Beach Boys
Smile
(1967)

Three and a half decades later, *Smile*'s legend has only grown, and it now stands as the most famous unreleased album in rock history. Countless bootlegs abound with the uncompleted sessions, and indeed much of the music is as haunting as it is awe-inspiring. Had Wilson been able to connect all the dots, *Smile* would most certainly be regarded as one of the pop's major artistic statements, rather than an infamous, unfortunate footnote. The Beach Boys' fate was completely sealed when Wilson's paranoia forced them to pull out of the top spot of the Monterey Pop Festival in June 1967. Concurrently the Beatles released their *Sgt. Pepper*, which was similar to *Smile*'s structured song-cycle. Rock had opened a door to a new colorful world, but it slammed shut before the Beach Boys had squeezed through. Obsolete virtually overnight, the band is ironically pushed aside by a festival that it was to headline and an album that it inspired.

• • • • •

Conversely, Curt Boettcher's career was gathering momentum. After helming the fantastic 1968 debut LP from Eternity's Children with recording partner Keith Olsen, an album that featured the majestic, fuzz-toned sunshine-pop single "Mrs. Bluebird," Boettcher continued to further his boundary-stretching experiments with the formation of a new project. Utilizing the same coterie of homegrown musicians that contributed to the Ballroom and Sagittarius, Boettcher's new group was christened the Millennium.

Although Boettcher was unquestionably instrumental in the Sagittarius project, the album was clearly the brainchild of Gary Usher. With the Millennium, the original vision was finally all Boettcher's. For the studio group, Boettcher expanded his stable of local L.A. musicians to include Ron Edgar (a former member of Boettcher's Minneapolis-based folk-rock band The Goldebriars) and Doug Rhodes from garage-rock icons the Music Machine. Keith Olsen, Boettcher's studio engineer and co-producer, was also a former member of the Music Machine, a band best known for the snarling '60s punk anthem "Talk Talk." Boettcher's connection to the group stretched back to his Goldebriars days, when future Music Machine vocalist Sean Bonniwell served as the group's tour manager and subsequently adopted its black-clad, one leather glove look in the Music Machine. Rounding out the group were Boettcher studio veterans Sandy Salisbury and Lee Mallory and new songwriter acquaintances Joey Stec and Michael Fennelly.

Surprisingly, the seven-member group worked without the hindrance of egos that usually marred such a large gathering of creative talent. Different partners paired off and collaborated on different songs, and instrumental ideas were openly received by all of the members. "We were fairly engrossed in a group/cult mentality. The late-1960s "peace, love and understanding" mantra ran strongly within the band. "We were very enthusiastic about the creativity that was indeed at a high level for the initial writing, demo and master recording. It really was fun for everyone involved to be in the middle of such electricity," band member Mike Fennelly recalled.[16]

However this easy-flowing team spirit would seem to run contrary to Boettcher's growing reputation as an insecure, Napoleonic studio dictator. Millennium member Sandy Salisbury characterized Boettcher as "controlling," someone who always "had to be in the driver's seat."[17] Nonetheless, Salisbury had great respect for Boettcher and accepted his need to be always in the foreground, calling him a man who "knew where the sun came up."[18]

Ron Edgar respectfully characterized Boettcher as "a visionary, back in the day when you could sit around and talk about concepts, dreams, visions and perception."[19] By all accounts, Boettcher was a complex personality, a born leader, but he was also extremely insecure and impulsive. Boettcher sought constant approval of his work, and, when he did not receive it, he could become difficult. "He could give direction easily, sometimes good, sometimes bad. So you had to think for yourself and be on your toes at all times. It was hard to relax around him,"[20] Edgar said.

In early 1968, the Millennium embarked on the recording of its debut album, *Begin*. Produced by Boettcher and Olsen, the album, along with Simon & Garfunkel's *Bookends*, was the first to utilize sixteen-track recording technology. This was a quantum leap forward from the standard four-track and eight-track recorders currently in use. The clever ingenuity of this makeshift technology sheds light on the dynamic between curly-haired, pixie-ish look-alikes Olsen and Boettcher (both men were about 5'5"). As Mike Fennelly revealed: "Keith Olsen was extraordinary. We were in some otherworldly zone with the Millennium's music to begin with. Curt had a way of conveying that world to Keith, and Keith had a way of achieving the sound technically. Linking two eight-track machines together to record sixteen-track, or wrapping masking tape around the machine's capstan to vary speed, or flipping reels to record reverse echo. Nothing was taboo. If it had never been done before, so much the better."

Capitalizing on this cutting-edge technology and the seven-piece band's uncommon creative cohesion, *Begin* is one of those rare albums that exists on its own plane, a major statement from an unknown band. By the time *Begin* was completed in July 1968, Columbia Records had invested an astounding $100,000 in the recording of the album, making it far and away the most expensive album it had ever released up to that point. Much of the expense was a result of Boettcher's costly method of preparing to record while the studio's meter was already running. "We'd gather around the mic in the studio, then Keith (Olsen) would play the instrumental tracks with the lead vocal already complete. *Now* Curt began to think about arranging the harmonies. We'd stand there and he'd dictate our lines, always beautiful, always unique, and we'd memorize them on the spot. *Then* we'd start recording," Salisbury explained.[21] Cost aside, the sessions were an artistic achievement.

Begin's triumph is in its perfect cohesion and its uncanny ability to transport the listener completely into its own unique universe. Using incredibly lush, harmony-laden soft pop and a subtly dark and mystical strain of psychedelia as its jumping-off points, the album resonates with a delicate yet unshakably subversive vibe. With *Begin*, Boettcher was pushing the boundaries of pop with a seemingly inexhaustible well of ideas. "It was incredible, because Curt would have these out-there ideas, like fifteen layers of harmonies with reverse echoes on them, and Keith (Olsen) would make the stuff work," Joey Stec recalled.[22]

From the opening combination of harpsichord and looped drumbeats of "Prelude" (yes, looped drum beats in 1968!), which gives way to a playful, classically derived string arrangement, one is immediately lured into *Begin*'s paradoxical, futuristic-yet-baroque world. As "Prelude" seamlessly segues into the bossa-nova flavored (failed single) "To Claudia On Thursday," the syrupy vocals slowly drip into the mix and gently welcome: "Take off your shoes and fell the grass. Lie back and let the hours pass. Don't give a thought to anything in the world, except you and me." The album's strength lies in its ability to float seamlessly on emotions ranging from the psychologically chilling ("I Just Want to Be Your Friend") to the triumphant declaration of love ("It's You") to the magically transporting daytrip ("The Island"). A rare and dichotomous gem, *Begin* is as much sweet and sunny pop as it is furtively dark psychedelia. Intriguingly, its darkness is drawn from its tantalizing sweetness, and, as every kid knows, too much candy can rot your teeth—or, in *Begin*'s case, rot your brain.

Perhaps from lack of live tour support, or simply a matter of being too idiosyncratic for its time, *Begin* was a commercial disaster, magnified by the enormous expense Columbia incurred during its recording. Certainly, much of the problem can be traced to the fact that the album was perceived as too strange for conservative am pop radio and erroneously presumed too lightweight for the prevailing heaviness of late-sixties freeform FM radio. Whatever the case, the Millennium ended up scrapping a proposed follow-up record despite the fact that *Saturday Review* named *Begin* one of the top three albums of the 1960s. Following the commercial disappointment of *Begin*, Boettcher soon formed Together Records with Olsen and previous collaborator Gary Usher in the hope of securing greater artistic freedom.

Together managed to release a few albums during its short stint; among the highlights was a second Sagittarius album, *The Blue*

Marble. While the country-tinged soft pop effort prominently featured Boettcher, Usher was once again the guiding force. An underrated affair, the standout track is a sunshine pop reworking of the Beach Boys' "In My Room," the landmark ballad Usher had co-written with Brian Wilson back in 1963. Predictably, the album was almost totally ignored by the record-buying public.

• • • • •

Influenced by the hallucinatory soft pop being mined by Boettcher and Usher, Terry Melcher produced the obscure duo Gentle Soul's dreamy 1968 eponymous album. The group featured singer/songwriters Rich Stanley and Pamela Polland (who was best known for her song "Tulsa County," which was covered by both the Byrds and the Rising Sons) and for a time included a young Jackson Browne (although he was not featured on the album). *The Gentle Soul* was notable for Melcher's gorgeous orchestral pop arrangements for harp, tabla, cello, organ, and slide guitar—a marked departure from the sneering garage rock of Paul Revere & the Raiders. The presence of standout musical contributions from guitarists Mike Deasy and Ry Cooder (who turned in some of his most impressive slide guitar to date) and Van Dyke Parks on harpsichord has helped escalate the posthumous cult status that *The Gentle Soul* now enjoys. Today the album stands as a prime example of the psychedelic folky side of the California Sound.

After a four-year hiatus, Melcher reunited with the Byrds in mid-1969. After undergoing several lineup shifts, the band was now a full-fledged country-rock group. His work on *Ballad of Easy Rider* and the half-live/half-studio double-album *Untitled* saw an abandonment of the group's trademark harmonies (which he helped originally foster) in favor of a series of singular vocal leads from various band members. Utilizing the astounding talent of new lead guitarist Clarence White as their instrumental focus, Melcher and the Byrds fashioned an unpretentious, stripped-down sound that managed to be also muscular and full. Classic songs such as "Jesus Is Just Alright" (later a hit for the Doobie Brothers), "Ballad of Easy Rider," "Gunga Din," "Lover of the Bayou," and the ambitious suite "Chestnut Mare" all paved the way for the dusty, laid-back country-rock successfully mined by the Eagles, Poco, Linda Ronstadt, Emmylou Harris, and countless others throughout the 1970s.

Additionally, the direct, no-nonsense production style of Melcher's latter Byrds albums has served as a direct antecedent to modern alternative-country stalwarts such as Wilco, the Jayhawks, Whiskeytown, and the Mavericks, as well as platinum artists like Tom Petty and R.E.M. Unfortunately, Melcher's final outing with the Byrds, 1971's *Byrdsmaniax*, proved to be a low-point for both the band and producer. With its incongruous strings and weak material, the album is easily the most unsatisfying of the band's career.

By the time of his Byrds finale Melcher was something of a changed man. Four years earlier, in 1967, he had the good fortune of becoming the sub-publisher for the Beatles catalog for the U.S., Canadian, and Japanese markets. Seizing his high-profile connection to the Beatles along with his close friendship with Brian Wilson, an obscure songwriter came looking for Melcher in hopes of securing a record deal. The songwriter was a rather strange, quietly intense man named Charlie Manson.

Seeking a conduit to Melcher, Manson calculatingly infiltrated Melcher's inner circle (which included Beach Boy Dennis Wilson) via the promiscuous female members of his "family." Both Melcher and Wilson were notorious womanizers, and the appeal of orgies with Manson's female minions was too enticing for the two men to resist. Once Manson wormed his way into Melcher's world, he played him his oddly philosophical tunes such as "Look at Your Game Girl" and "Cease to Exist" on a beat-up acoustic guitar. Initially, Melcher was intrigued by Manson's musings, so much so that one of his songs managed to find its way to Dennis Wilson. Amazingly, the Beach Boys actually recorded Manson's "Cease to Exist" (re-titled "Never Learn Not to Love") for inclusion on their *20/20* album, but Melcher was not inclined to help the increasingly demanding Manson further.

Convinced that Melcher had somehow reneged on a recording deal, an enraged Manson and his "family" came looking to exact revenge on the producer at his home on Cielo Drive above Beverly Hills. Unbeknownst to the crazed cult leader, Melcher had recently moved, a fact that did not prevent Manson's followers from brutally murdering actress Sharon Tate, along with four other innocent victims who happened to be in the house on August 9, 1969. The savage slayings shocked the world and immediately transformed L.A. from the fun-in-the-sun capitol of good vibrations into a nightmarish netherworld paralyzed by paranoia and fear. The sixties were over: now *everyone* locked their doors.

The end of the sunshine myth, and the ascendancy of its sinister antithesis, was brilliantly captured by Joan Didion in her classic essay, "The White Album":

> I imagined that my own life was simple and sweet, and sometimes it was, but there were odd things going around town. There were rumors. There were stories. Everything was unmentionable but nothing was unimaginable.... A demented and seductive vertical tension was building in the community.... Many people I know in Los Angeles believe that the sixties ended abruptly on August 9, 1969.... The tension broke that day. The paranoia was fulfilled.[23]

• • • • •

One can view the evolution of the California Sunshine Sound as a mirror of the evolution of the 1960s. Commencing with its post-Eisenhower naïveté and insulated complacency, the early California Sound was predicated on Wilson, Usher, and Melcher's simple fun-in-the-sun ideals. With political assassinations and civil-rights upheaval, the climate had soured significantly by mid-decade and, as the Melcher-incubated folk-rock movement took flight, along with Wilson's daring interjection of art into pop, the California Sound assumed a more musically ambitious and mature world-view.

As a consequence of the escalation of the war in Vietnam the latter part of the decade became increasingly tumultuous, and the nation's shell-shocked youth responded by escaping inward, with the assistance of a myriad of hallucinogenic enhancers. This inward journey inspired the soft sunshine psychedelia of Usher and Boettcher's dreamy Sagittarius and Millennium recordings, as well as the city-escapism of the back-to-roots country-rock mined by Usher and Melcher's Byrds productions. The California Sound had once again traveled with the times.

By the end of the decade, an inevitable over-indulgence on the sunshine and sweetness advocated by the California Myth had led to chilling darkness and unsightly rot. With the multitude of hedonistic pursuits available to the California cognoscenti, decadence and decay became unsavory and dangerous realities. Wilson sunk deeply into a crippling miasma of substance abuse, and, without his leadership, producers, musicians, and fans abandoned his trailblazing brand of visionary pop. A direct result of this abandonment was the costly commercial irrelevance of Usher and Boettcher's ambitious late-1960s soft-pop undertakings. Compounded by Melcher's unfortunate and infamous connection to the horrifying Manson murders, southern California had completed its slide from sunshine paradise to infernal netherworld; it was the sunset of the original California Sunshine Sound.

• • • • •

Badly shaken by the Manson nightmare, Terry Melcher kept a low profile throughout the 1970s. With the exception of two unremarkable country-rock solo albums, his output was slim through the decade. He suffered a huge disappointment when he unsuccessfully tried to secure a mid-1970s deal for Brian Wilson through his Equinox production company, which he ran with former recording partner, Bruce Johnston. Melcher desperately wanted to help his old friend Wilson, whose mental and physical health were at their nadir. However, when Melcher brought the bloated, coke-addicted Beach Boy into the studio, Wilson was completely out of it. Sadly, all Wilson could do was quizzically stare at the mixing board, helplessly afraid to touch it. Wilson was so far gone he was unable to even recognize his former Wrecking Crew associates who Melcher had hired for the sessions. Melcher, who idolized Brian, was crushed.

Melcher's activity picked up through a slew of mid-1980s Brianless Beach Boy collaborations, including co-writing the 1985 Top 30 hit "Getcha Back" with Mike Love and producing a successful cover version of "California Dreaming." His greatest 1980s triumph with the Beach Boys was with "Kokomo," a "Margaritaville"-style song he co-wrote and produced for the soundtrack of the blockbuster film *Cocktail*. The tropically shimmering song featured former *Smile* collaborator Van Dyke Parks on a distinctively out-of-tune accordion and became the Beach Boys' biggest hit in decades. Something of a phenomenon, the song climbed all the way to Number 1 in 1988, ironically just as Brian Wilson released his critically acclaimed but commercially rebuffed debut solo album. Melcher now manages his mother's career, and the two are neighbors in the idyllic town of Carmel, California, where they manage a pet-friendly hotel, a world away from L.A.'s decadent fast lane.

• • • • •

Curt Boettcher continued to work sporadically throughout the 1970s. Inspired by his work with one-man pop band Emitt Rhodes, he released a stripped-down solo album, *There's an Innocent Face*, in early 1973. Prior to its release, on advisement from a numerologist, he changed the spelling of last name, first to Beotcher and then finally to the more phonetically correct Becher. An involvement with California Music, a group originally conceived by old partners Terry Melcher and on-and-off Beach Boy Bruce Johnston, led Boettcher to finally collaborate with the Beach Boys themselves. The result of the pairing was a bizarre, yet oddly gratifying eleven-minute disco version of the Beach Boys' 1967 blue-eyed soul ditty "Here Comes the Night," which was included on their uneven 1979 album L.A. (*Light Album*).

Following that curious undertaking, Boettcher drifted further into obscurity. He died at the age of 43 in 1987. Meanwhile, Olsen parlayed his studio skills into a successful engineering and producing career, working with such top artists as Fleetwood Mac, the Grateful Dead, and Foreigner, among many others. However, throughout the 1990s the legend of *Begin* began to grow as a new crop of pop-obsessed bands such as St. Etienne, the High Llamas, Olivia Tremor Control, and the Wondermints, along with vigilant record collectors and enamored critics, began to re-assess soft pop and the new belatedly dubbed genre, sunshine pop. Along with Sagittarius's *Present Tense*, the Millennium's *Begin* stands as perhaps the clearest distillation of California sunshine-pop.

In 2000, Boettcher's unreleased 1969 solo album *Misty Mirage* was finally released (bolstered by a slew of demo recordings, including a number of compelling jingles Boettcher recorded for Levis Jeans radio spots). The songs on *Misty Mirage* were sweetened by Boettcher's cherubic, man-child vocals and featured a pioneering early use of synthesizers inventively coupled with such unexpected instruments as pedal steel. The album also features a charged version of "That's the Way It's Gonna Be," the song he originally recorded with Lee Mallory that floored Wilson and Usher, and an inspired harmony and marimba-flavored take on the windswept Country nugget, "Tumbling Tumbleweed."

Furthering Boettcher's posthumous rediscovery was the release of *Magic Time*, a mammoth three-CD reissue consisting of all of the Ballroom and Millennium material that once and for all, put any argument about the historical importance of these recordings to rest. The unlikely attention generated led to an unexpected partial Millennium reunion, with members Lee Mallory and Joey Stec performing live shows everywhere from Tokyo to Los Angeles. Today, retrospectively, *Begin* is routinely cited by various sources as one of pop's most sumptuous delights.

· · · · ·

After a long period of inactivity throughout most of the 1970s and 1980s, things came full circle for Gary Usher when he was enlisted to contribute to Brian Wilson's 1988 self-titled solo album. Writing in Usher's garage, which doubled as a simple eight-track recording studio, the two men rekindled their relationship. Sadly, squabbles over production credit and money quickly ensued, and the two abruptly ended their collaboration in acrimony. Two years later, Usher died of a heart attack. With the recent rediscovery of sunshine pop building on a perennial interest in surf and hot rod music, Usher's California Sound legacy continues to grow.

· · · · ·

Trumped by the Beatles and haunted by the failure of the aborted *Smile*, Brian Wilson's mental health continued its downward spiral as his weight simultaneously ballooned. While he did manage to write some low-key gems for such solid offerings as *Wild Honey*, *Friends*, *20/20*, *Sunflower*, *Surf's Up*, and *Holland*, his participation with the Beach Boys had markedly dwindled. For Wilson, the sunshine had completely set into darkness, and it would take him nearly 20 years to rediscover the light.

With the deaths of brothers and bandmates Dennis (who drowned in 1983) and Carl (who died of lung and brain cancer in 1998), Brian is the unlikely Wilson brother survivor. He now enjoys an unexpected solo career and tours frequently. Revisiting his most creatively fertile material, he released a live version *Pet Sounds* played in its entirety in 2002. Even more astonishingly, in the spring of 2004 Wilson performed a full-fledged *Smile* concert in London backed by an 11-piece band. Miraculously, after nearly forty years, Wilson finally managed to pull all the loose ends together into a cohesive suite of music. By the time of the concert's triumphant conclusion, many of the enraptured attendees were reduced to a blubbering mess of tears; lending further proof that Wilson's divine innovations grow more influential and moving with each passing day.

KEY RECORDINGS
Brian Wilson

The Beach Boys –	*Surfin' Safari* (Capitol 1962)
	Surfin' U.S.A. (Capitol 1963)
	Surfer Girl (Capitol 1963)
	Shut Down Vol. 2 (Capitol 1964)
	All Summer Long (Capitol 1964)
	The Beach Boys Today! (Capitol 1965)
	Summer Days (and Summer Nights!!) (Capitol 1965)
	Pet Sounds (Capitol 1966)
	Smile (Unreleased) (1967)
	Smiley Smile (Capitol 1967)
	"Country Air," "Let The Wind Blow" (*Wild Honey* LP) (Capitol 1967)
	Friends (Capitol 1968)
	"Do It Again," "I Went to Sleep," "Our Prayer," "Cabin Essence," (*20/20* LP) (Capitol 1969)
	'This Whole World," "Add Some Music to Your Day," "At My Window," "Cool, Cool Water," (*Sunflower*) (Brother 1970)
	"A Day in the Life of a Tree," "'Till I Die," "Surf's Up," (*Surf's Up*) (Brother 1971)
	"Marcella" (Carl and the Passions/So Tough) (Brother 1972)
	"Sail on Sailor," "Funky Pretty," (Holland) (Brother 1973)
	The Beach Boys Love You (Warner 1977)
Glen Campbell –	"Guess I'm Dumb" (Capitol 1965)
Spring –	*Spring* (UA 1972)
Brian Wilson –	*Brian Wilson* (Warner 1988)
	I Just Wasn't Made for These Times (MCA 1995)
	Imagination (Giant 1998)
	Live at the Roxy Theatre (BriMel 2000)
	Pet Sounds Live (Sanctuary 2002)

Gary Usher

The Byrds –	*Younger Than Yesterday* (Columbia 1967)
	Notorious Byrd Brothers (Columbia 1968)
	Sweetheart of the Rodeo (Columbia 1968)
Gene Clark –	*Gene Clark with the Gosdin Brothers* (Columbia 1967)

Chad & Jeremy – *Of Cabbages and Kings* (Columbia 1967)
The Arc (Columbia 1968)

Firesign Theatre – *Waiting for the Electrician Or Someone Like Him* (Columbia 1968)

The Hondells – *The Hondells Greatest Hits* (Curb 1996)

Peanut Butter – *Is Spreading* (Columbia 1967)
Conspiracy *Great Conspiracy* (Columbia 1968)
For Children of All Ages (Columbia 1968)

Sagittarius – "My World Fell Down" (Columbia 1967)
Present Tense (Columbia 1968)
The Blue Marble (Together 1969)

The Spiral Staircase – *The Very Best of the Spiral Staircase* (Taragon 1995)

The Surfaris – *The Surfaris Hit City '65* (Decca 1965)

The Super Stocks – *The Super Stocks Complete Recordings* (One Way 1996)

Various Artists – *Gary Usher Greats Volume 1 – The Kickstands vs. The Knights* (AVI 1996)

Terry Melcher

Bruce and Terry – *Best of Bruce and Terry* (Sundazed 1996)

The Byrds – *Mr. Tambourine Man* (Columbia 1965)
Turn! Turn! Turn! (Columbia 1965)
Ballad of Easy Rider (Columbia 1969)
Untitled (Columbia 1970)

The Gentle Soul – *The Gentle Soul* (Columbia 1968)

Paul Revere and – *Here They Come* (Columbia 1965)
the Raiders *Just Like Us* (Columbia 1966)
Midnight Ride (Columbia 1966)
Spirit of '67 (Columbia 1967)
Revolution! (Columbia 1967)

The Rip Chords – *Hey Little Cobra and Other Hot Rod Hits* (Columbia 1964)
Three Window Coupe (Columbia 1964)

The Rising Sons – *The Rising Sons Featuring Taj Mahal and Ry Cooder* (Columbia 1992)

Curt Boettcher

The Association –	"Along Comes Mary" (Valiant 1966)
	"Cherish" (Valiant 1966)
	And Then…Along Comes the Association (Valiant 1966)
The Beach Boys –	"Here Comes the Night" (L.A. Light Album) (Caribou 1979)
Curt Boettcher –	*Misty Mirage* (Poptones 2000)
	There's an Innocent Face (Elektra 1973)
	California Music (Poptones 2001)
Eternity's Children –	*Eternity's Children* (Tower 1968)
The Goldebriars –	*The Goldebriars* (Epic 1963)
	Straight Ahead (Epic 1964)
Dotti Holmberg –	*Sometimes Happy Times* (Sundazed 2002)
Lee Mallory –	*That's the Way It's Gonna Be* (Rev-Ola 2002)
The Millennium –	*Begin* (Columbia 1968)
	The Millennium/Ballroom Recordings (Sundazed 2001)
Michelle O'Malley –	*Saturn Rings* (ABC 1969)
Tommy Roe –	"Sweet Pea," "Hooray for Hazel" (ABC 1966)
	It's Now Winter's Day (ABC 1967)
Emitt Rhodes –	*Emitt Rhodes* (mixed) (ABC/Dunhill 1970)
Sandy Salisbury –	*Sandy* (Poptones 2000)
	Falling to Pieces (Archive 2000)

THE MAVERICKS:
DAVID AXELROD AND
SHEL TALMY

In Hollywood in 1967 producer/arranger/composer David Axelrod had just completed recording the Electric Prunes' psychedelic God-rock opus, Mass in F Minor. *With its hallucinatory strings, Latin-chanted choral arrangements, and searing acid-rock underpinning, the concept album was totally off-the-wall—even by "Summer of Love" standards. As Axelrod sat in his Capitol Records A&R office, he received a concerned phone call from his boss, A&R honcho Voyle Gilmore.*

"Kid, I think I'm in some trouble here, do you have a copy of that damn thing? I have to take one in to Al [Livingston, Capitol president], he wants to hear it." Axelrod hung up nervously, called his secretary over, and handed her a freshly minted acetate of Mass in F Minor. *"They want to hear this upstairs," he said flatly.*

As she disappeared into the sea of executive offices, Axelrod was left alone to sweat out Livingston's likely confounded reaction. A half hour later, the phone rang—Gilmore again. Axelrod held his breath and gripped for the worst. "You gotta write an album for us," Gilmore said. As always, Axelrod played it cool—he quietly exhaled, agreed like he was expecting the unlikely offer all along, and then informed him of an idea he had already been gestating: "I want to do an album of tone poems based on a cycle of William Blake's poetry," Axelrod said deadpan. Amazingly, without hesitation, Gilmore agreed.

· · · · ·

David Axelrod

Among breakbeat worshippers the name **David Axelrod** invokes the image of the Holy Grail. A thoroughly enigmatic figure, he has served as a dependable A&R man, hit-making producer, and iconoclastic orchestral composer. Through his singular productions he established Los Angeles as a credible center for hard-bop jazz, boldly infused social-commentary into modern R&B, and drafted the commercially successful blueprint for soul-jazz. He was also responsible for perhaps the strangest acid-rock album of the '60s.

Meanwhile, his own compositions have juggled lofty liturgical concepts, William Blake–inspired imagery, avant-garde symphonic arrangements, and drumbeats so fat and funky they have become touchstones for eager hip-hop samplers and electronica purveyors around the world. The sum of these unique elements has made David Axelrod one of the quintessential studio visionaries.

Axelrod grew up in a rough section of Los Angeles, and, by his teens, he was fighting semi-pro boxing matches in various venues around town. After sustaining a severe eye injury in an overmatched bout, he began to gravitate towards the less physically violent world of music. Although L.A. was a mecca for soft and mellow West Coast jazz, Axelrod carted a burning passion for the town's under-appreciated, though talent-laden hard-bop jazz scene. Magnetically drawn to edgy and soulful rhythms, Axelrod began to spend his teenaged nights at primarily black Central Avenue nightclubs such as Jack's Basket Room and the Chicken Shack. Both of these clubs featured a mixture of jazz and rhythm and blues talent, and the impressionable teen was becoming equally enthralled with both styles of music.

After a spending a brief stint in New York soaking up the excitement of its bustling jazz scene, Axelrod returned home in 1951. Determined to infuse New York's earthy jazz style into L.A.'s decidedly more laid-back recording scene, Axelrod embarked on a nascent career in record production. Helming a string of hard-bop productions for several small local labels, Axelrod began to garner a reputation for decidedly tough and fiery recordings. Word spread all the way to the East Coast, where he was featured in the "jazz bible," *Down Beat* magazine. When interviewed by famed jazz critic John Tynan for the *Down Beat* article, Axelrod entertainingly showed his contempt for somnambulant West Coast jazz by likening it to a wet dream: "You knew something happened when you woke up, but there was no satisfaction," he disparagingly said of "cool jazz."

Axelrod's amusingly inflammatory comments in *Down Beat* rippled back to the West Coast, catching the eye of L.A.–based trombonist Frank Rosalino. Sharing Axelrod's sentiments, Rosalino called on the precocious producer to record his 1958 Specialty Records release, *Free for All*. Juggling well-worn standards and fresh originals, the exciting date was elevated by the presence of the gifted saxophonist Harold Land. The soft-spoken Land had made a name nationally playing with the high-profile Clifford Brown/Max Roach Quintet before returning to Los Angeles in the mid-1950s. Axelrod was astonished by his tough-yet-nimble tone, and quickly the like-minded men discussed cutting their own album together.

Recorded in August 1959, Land's Axelrod-produced, *The Fox*, was hard driving, visceral and soulful—everything West Coast jazz was reputed not to be. An influential landmark that irrefutably proved L.A. jazz had *cajones*, it served as a direct catalyst towards establishing the city as a credible jazz center. Suddenly, even the most biased East Coast jazz enthusiasts could not deny Land's innovative, edgy hard-bop. *The Fox* "changed music out here because Contemporary and World Pacific [Records] started signing guys like Carmel Jones and Ornette Coleman," Axelrod said proudly.

The same year Axelrod helmed Jimmy Witherspoon's *Singin'
the Blues*, a groundbreaking mélange of expressive R&B shouting
and sophisticated hard-bop backing. Never before had a fusion of the
two genres been forged so seamlessly or successfully on a recording.
Singin' the Blues helped reinforce Axelrod's rep as a versatile and
boundless innovator who was equally comfortable with complex jazz
and down-and-dirty R&B.

Like many in the jazz world, by the late '50s Axelrod had fallen
under the bewitching spell of arranger Gil Evans. Through his seductive and cerebral scores, Evans had transformed Miles Davis into a
virtual immortal, and his own visionary recordings contained an
intoxicating blend of swinging hard-bop and fearlessly avant-garde
arrangements. Heavily inspired by Evans's arrangements, Axelrod
began diligently teaching himself classical music theory around the
clock. Meticulously analyzing the intricacies of Stravinsky,
Beethoven, Schoenberg, Ellington, and Evans, Axelrod sought ways
to incorporate his newly acquired arranging acumen into his own
recordings. Soon he would get his chance.

• • • • •

After a successful producing stint at Hi-Fi Records, Axelrod parlayed his growing recognition into an A&R/staff producer position at
Capitol Records in early 1964. Duly impressed by his work on
Witherspoon's *Singin' the Blues*, Capitol's head of A&R, Voyle Gilmore,
immediately paired Axelrod with the label's smooth-as-silk, four-octave
voiced singer, Lou Rawls. A veteran of the gospel music circuit, Rawls
was now anonymously mining super-club material around L.A.

With Rawls as his first assignment at Capitol, Axelrod began to
scheme a new direction for the talented but struggling singer. Rawls's
initial Capitol albums featured a blues, jazz, and pop standards sundry
that failed to connect with the record-buying public. Enlightened by a
film class taught by gritty *cinema verité* auteur John Cassavetes,
Axelrod sought to infuse a similarly cinematic approach into Rawls's
productions.

"The song is your story, then you get an arranger. The arrangement then becomes the screenplay. The players and the vocalists are

your actors. The engineer is your director of photography. That's how I've always looked upon making records," Axelrod revealed.

Ready to apply his newly honed theory, Axelrod moved the singer towards a refined, yet funky brand of R&B. After continuously polishing their formula through a string of mildly received releases, success streamed in with Rawls's emotive 1966 single, "Love Is a Hurtin' Thing." Ignited by their breakthrough single, Rawls quickly caught fire with an impressive string of sublime Axelrod-produced hits that helped redefine rhythm and blues. The team enjoyed unprecedented R&B chart success over the next four years, culminating in the fortuitously titled single, "Your Good Thing (Is About to Come to an End)."

A particular Axelrod/Rawls standout was the devastatingly poignant "Dead End Street." Written by Axelrod, the tale of Chicago ghetto street-life was directly inspired by Claude Brown's powerful autobiography, *Manchild in the Promised Land*. Axelrod got the idea while laid up at home with the mumps one slow-moving afternoon. Unable to do anything but watch television, the housebound Axelrod was riveted by a Brown TV interview in which the writer detailed his tragic life as a juvenile junkie, hustler, and murderer.

"I'll never forget this—he found himself on a dead-end street. I went 'Oh! There is a song,'" Axelrod said, remembering the day inspiration struck. Bolstered by lyrical assistance from songwriter Ben Raleigh, Rawls's "Dead End Street" shot to Number 1 on the R&B charts and fetched a Grammy for Best R&B Vocal Performance of 1967. The impeccably arranged song solidified Rawls's career, and its pioneering socially conscious themes served as a clarion call to Motown's Norman Whitfield and Philly Sound masterminds Gamble and Huff.

• • • • •

Early into his Capitol stint, Axelrod began a long and fruitful partnership with the irrepressibly joyous alto saxophonist Cannonball Adderley. The two had first met in 1962 after being introduced by jazz singer Ernie Andrews in a Sunset Boulevard bar. "Cannonball stuck his hand out and went 'Ah-ha, *The Fox*, I knew our paths would cross someday!'" Axelrod recounted.

Along with leading his own crowd-pleasing band, Adderley had raised his profile through memorable turns on the landmark Miles Davis albums *Milestones* and *Kind of Blue*. When Capitol signed Adderley in 1964, the exuberant altoist immediately chose Axelrod as his producer, and the two became fast friends. Both shared a mutual appreciation for jazz and R&B, and, through a succession of phenomenally popular releases, Axelrod and Adderley fused the two styles together into the newly dubbed "soul-jazz" genre.

Featuring Adderley's brother Nat on cornet, a dynamic rhythm section, and Joe Zawinul (later of Weather Report) on Rhodes electric piano, Cannonball's remarkable quintet was equally at home with supple in-the-pocket soul grooves and brainy post-bop. Key among the Axelrod/Adderley sound was Zawinul's distinctively warm and fluid Rhodes piano. Emphasized in Axelrod's crisp mixes, the Rhodes piano would soon became a jazz and funk mainstay. Cannonball's band was "using it so much they really popularized the instrument," Axelrod said.

The Axelrod and Adderley team reached its zenith with the wildly successful *Live at the Club* album. Conceived to help promote a Chicago nightclub of the same name, in reality the sessions were actually held at a Capitol recording studio in October 1966. To enhance the mood of the recording, Axelrod furnished the studio as a faux nightclub, complete with tables and free drinks for an invitation-only gaggle of supporters. The highlight of the zestful session was Zawinul's laid-back, gospel-influenced "Mercy, Mercy, Mercy."

Cannonball Adderly
Mercy, Mercy, Mercy!
Live at the Club
(1966)

Bolstered by the studio audience's well-lubricated gregarious vibe, the infectious instrumental benefited from an impossibly catchy hook and Axelrod's uncluttered, relaxed production. The instrumental single rocketed up to Number 2 on the R&B chart (just behind Rawls's "Dead End Street") and became one of the biggest-selling jazz singles of all time. "My God, you couldn't turn on the radio without hearing it, it was getting embarrassing!" Axelrod said seriously.

Propelled by his soulful touch, assured production style, and uncanny ear for hit material, Axelrod had become one of the hottest producer/A&R men in the business by 1967. He had transformed Lou Rawls from an obscure crooner into a socially provocative, perennial chart-topper, and had laid the foundation for soul-jazz with his irresistible Cannonball Adderley recordings. His golden touch had even managed to make television's *Man From U.N.C.L.E.*, David McCallum, into an unlikely recording star with two surprisingly well-performing solo albums of pop and rock covers. Soon stretching his versatility and vision further than anyone could have predicted, Axelrod's next move was into the bizarre.

• • • • •

Best known for the 1967 fuzzbox-driven smash "I Had Too Much (to Dream)," the Electric Prunes were the perfect distillation of garage-punk posturing and acid-derived excess. Their in-your-face attitude, unsubtle hints at the joys of chemically induced mind expansion, and knack for sticky pop hooks made the Prunes one of the ripest bands in all of garage-psychdom. When the Prunes began to disintegrate into a morass of drugs and mysticism after their second album, *Underground*, their fate appeared sealed.

Axelrod was already hard at work on his own solo material when he got a strange offer form Lenny Poncher, his newly acquired manager. Poncher, who co-owned the Electric Prunes name (with producer Dave Hassinger), had just concocted an elaborate gimmick to rescue the band from its one-way ticket to obscurity: He wanted the Electric Prunes to record a rock mass! After the pop-oriented Hassinger balked at the idea, Poncher phoned the one man he knew could pull it off.

The Electric Prunes
Mass in F Minor
(1968)

"Sure, I can write anything," Axelrod said to his manager, half asleep one hazy Saturday morning. Axelrod had been up late at a session the night before, and, before Poncher could elaborate on the details, the exhausted producer hung up the phone and promptly fell back asleep. When Poncher called back a few hours later Axelrod was now fully awake, but there was a catch: "If it's not in Latin, get somebody else," Axelrod insisted. Poncher thought it over and, sensing the potential publicity a rock mass performed in Latin could trigger, agreed. A scant week later, Axelrod had completed the entire score.

Utilizing a combination of original Prunes and several session players that included members of the group the Collectors (later to become Chilliwack), Axelrod conducted the quasi-religious psychedelic opus himself. Titled *Mass in F Minor*, the album was a confounding, yet strangely satisfying, cauldron of Latin chants, cavernous cathedral organ drones, fuzz-faced guitar solos, and Axelrod's psychedelic string and horn arrangements. To achieve the Mass's swelling choral effect, Axelrod cleverly double-tracked Prunes singer James Lowe's voice to skirt the expense of hiring a real choir.

Predating the Who's rock-opera *Tommy* by two years, and eons ahead of *Jesus Christ Superstar*, *Mass in F Minor* was the original "God-rock" album. Reviews were savage; one critic characterized the sound "as if deaf monks were reciting Gregorian chants!" Almost inexplicably, the album actually sold copies and, when its opening cut, "Kyrie Elesion," was used in *Easy Rider*'s infamous graveyard scene, *Mass in F Minor* had ensured a permanent place in pop-culture history.

• • • • •

Since his late teens, Axelrod had been enamored of the painting and poetry of William Blake. "He had a terrible life. Until his last two years when people started to realize 'my God, this guy is a genius,'" he said. Axelrod had been toying with the idea of a Blake concept album for some time, and he already had a title: *Songs of Innocence*. Because of Capitol's surprising satisfaction with *Mass in F Minor*, Axelrod received his chance to move forward on the album. Finally, he was going to have an opportunity to fully showcase his imaginatively menacing yet funky, avant-garde vision.

Conceived as a seven-part suite, recording for *Songs of Innocence* began in the middle of the long hot summer of '68. For the sessions Axelrod tapped his trusty cabal of studio vets including bassist Carol Kaye, guitarist Howard Roberts, keyboardist (and session conductor) Don Randi, and incomparable drummer Earl Palmer. Although Axelrod had originally envisioned some of the compositions to feature a full-blown choir, he harbored doubts about finding the right ensemble. As a result, he opted to cut the album entirely instrumentally and include one Blake poem for each section of the score.

Unlike anything ever released before it, *Songs of Innocence*'s dramatically sparse arrangements played like an imaginary soundtrack to a Technicolor-soaked Italian gothic horror flick. Despite its occasionally harrowing moments, Axelrod kept most of the album rooted in a euphorically propulsive form of psychedelic R&B. By no means a commercial success, the uncompromising album, along with its similarly constructed 1969 follow-up, *Songs of Experience*, established Axelrod as nothing less than a wholly unpredictable and challenging conceptual artist.

In between solo albums, Axelrod also wrote and arranged *Release of an Oath*, the Electric Prunes like-themed follow-up to *Mass in F Minor*. Based on the ancient prayer Kol Nidre, Axelrod integrated a heavier, proto-progressive rock sound this time around, best exemplified on the mesmerizing and percussive "Holy are You." Fatefully, the cryptic album was a sales disaster. Without Axelrod, the Prunes cut one final album of tepid back-to-basics rock before making its final fade into obscurity.

In 1970 Axelrod continued to mine ambitious conceptual territory with his third solo album, *Earth Rot*. Subtitled "A Musical Comment on the State of the Environment," the ecological disaster–themed album featured two suites, ominously titled "The Warning" and "The Sign." Featuring Axelrod's masterful melding of sinister classical and sparse funk, for the first time his suites were augmented by a full choir. Originally planned for sale exclusively at college bookstores in celebration of the first Earth Day, *Earth Rot*'s timing could not have been worse. Released days before the Kent State killings, the record was immediately lost in the shuffle of the tragedy's aftermath.

In light of today's corporate-dominated music business, the notion that a major label would release such unwaveringly non-commercial albums remains astonishing. "The sixties were incredible, maybe the greatest decade ever for creative people, because you could do anything. What would happen today if somebody came in and said 'I want to do an album of tone poems on a cycle of William Blake's poetry?'—they'd throw you out the door," Axelrod quipped.

• • • • •

Throughout the '70s Axelrod drifted towards a more conventional funk-fusion direction through productions for keyboardist Merl Saunders and booty-shakers Funk Inc. He remained close friends with Cannonball Adderley, producing concept albums on the Bible, Africa, and the zodiac, among others, for the alto giant. In 1974 Adderley switched chairs with his producer to helm Axelrod's soul-fest *Heavy Axe*. The album was distinguished by the slow-building orchestral funk masterpiece, "Everything Counts." "That's the track! Jesus, it was terrific," Axelrod said of the composition that perhaps best crystallizes his singular avant-funk vision. Sadly, less than a year after *Heavy Axe*, Adderley suffered a fatal stroke.

Due to a string of faulty record deals, Axelrod's release output slowed to a trickle in the '80s. Fortunately, in the early '90s, a new breed of beat-diggers discovered the intoxicatingly spacious, ultra-fat drum sound that distinguishes nearly all of his recordings. Seemingly overnight, his long-out-of-print albums became highly coveted commodities, and in turn were routinely sampled by countless DJs and hip-hop artists the world over. Since his rediscovery, Axelrod's break-beats have formed the bedrock of recordings for artists, including Lauryn Hill ("Every Ghetto, Every City"), Dr. Dre ("Next Episode"), and DJ Shadow. Axelrod himself remained oblivious to his resurgence until large royalty checks began unexpectedly to appear in the mail. By the late '90s, his influence had spread to the rock world via trailblazers the Verve and Radiohead, who both used his albums to open their concerts.

With his profile percolating, Axelrod returned to action in 1998, re-mixing "Rabbit in the Headlights" for U.N.K.L.E., an experimental super-group featuring DJ Shadow and Radiohead architect Thom Yorke, among other notables. The U.K. chart success of the remix pre-cipitated the recording of *David Axelrod* for the Brit label Mo' Wax. For the album Axelrod recycled rhythm tracks originally recorded in 1969 for an abandoned third Electric Prunes collaboration (based on Faust). Novelly sampling himself, Axelrod mixed the old tracks with a newly penned orchestral score. Featuring contributions from old friends Lou Rawls and arranger H.B. Barnum, and new admirers such as rapper Ras Kas, the album touches on all of Axelrod's sonic hall-marks: ominous classical motifs, pitch black noir-jazz, mournful vocals, scorching acid-guitar, crystalline electric bass, and pregnant beats so rotund they threaten to burst at any moment.

Reinvigorated by his rediscovery, Axelrod is hard at work on a new album. Although he remains guarded when pressed for details: "I'm not going to talk about it, if I talk about it then I wouldn't have to write it. I'll just tell you it's going to be a motherfucker!"

• • • • •

In London in 1962, a brash, 21-year-old American named Shel Talmy had been kicking around Europe on an extended vacation. With his finances dwindling, he headed in the direction of Decca Records with an idea of how to prolong his stay abroad. Cockily strolling into the venerable label's office like he owned the place, Talmy took out a small stack of shiny new American 45 singles. "I produced these," he said poker-faced. Unbeknownst to Decca, Talmy had done no such thing.

• • • • •

Shel Talmy

Back in Los Angeles, Shel Talmy had begun to carve out a career as a recording engineer at Hollywood's bustling Conway Studios. Before jetting to Europe, he paid a visit to Capitol Records' head producer Nick Venet. Talmy had engineered a few sessions for Venet, and the two had become friendly. Before parting ways, Venet offered the fledgling engineer an armful of brand-new lacquers to take with him to Europe. Now, Venet's gifts were about to come in handy: Sitting face to face with Decca head Dick Rowe, Talmy passed off the singles as his own productions.

As Rowe listened attentively to Talmy's stack of singles, including the Beach Boys' "Surfin' Safari," a wide smile began to form on his lips. He was understandably flabbergasted by what he thought were Talmy's productions. England had yet to establish a viable rock scene, and the chance of landing a hot American producer was far too tantalizing for Rowe to pass up. "You start today," he said, hurrying the words out. Talmy had just calmly bluffed his way into a producing job for one of the most esteemed record companies in Europe. "I had a gig back in L.A., so it was no big thing. If Rowe discovered it was all bullshit, well then so be it," Talmy recalled matter-of-factly.

With nothing to loose, Talmy shot for the moon and demanded an agreement that would make him England's first independent producer.

"I knew enough that everybody in England at the time was on a salary and were not getting royalties. So I said 'I am an independent producer, I get royalties plus a retainer,'" Talmy said. Rowe had a decided fondness for Talmy's Yankee brashness, and he agreed to the unknown's unheard-of demands. The contract stipulated that Talmy would work exclusively for Decca, but it contained a loophole that permitted him to function as a free agent rather than as a label employee.

With the British Invasion more than a year away, Talmy began working with Decca's pop-oriented MOR artists. Following an unsuccessful debut production for Doug Sheldon on a cover version of "Lollipops and Roses," Talmy was paired with the Irish trio, the Bachelors. Talmy rehearsed the affable vocal group for six weeks in his tiny apartment before he felt they were ready. Finally, he brought them into the studio to cut the faux country song, "Charmaine." Talmy considered the song "crap" and spent a mere fifteen minutes disinterestedly cutting the session. Much to his surprise, the Decca brass loved it. Even more shocking to him, the song became a huge hit. Barely out of his teens, the fish out of water had become a bonafide hit producer an ocean away from home.

Settling into life in London, Talmy began to take notice of the thrilling new rock-oriented "Beat Boom" that was beginning to spark around the country. In autumn 1963, he briefly returned home to L.A. like a modern-day Paul Revere trumpeting a new British Invasion to all who would listen. Talmy visited nearly every label in town insisting that he could lock up every one of the new British bands from the Beatles to the Rolling Stones for a combined pittance of about $5,000. Unfortunately, his sensational claims fell on deaf ears. Deflated, he returned to England determined to discover his own new-breed British band.

• • • • •

One London afternoon Talmy was "standing around looking cute" in a Denmark Street publishing office when fate assumed the guise of a band manager named Robert Wace. Clutching a demo tape, Wace walked in the door and casually inquired if anybody would be willing to listen to his young group from the Muswell Hill area of

London called the Ravens. "Yeah, sure I'll listen to one," Talmy said effusively. Attentively listening to the crude demo tape, Talmy was summarily impressed by the group's unbridled exuberance and odd-sounding lead singer. Always one to make the most of an opportunity, he quickly agreed to help secure the band a record deal. Because Talmy's relationship with Decca had become recently strained (due to a royalty dispute over "Charmaine"), he instead brought the Ravens over to competitor Pye Records.

Pye was the runt of the major British labels. However, because it owned its own studios, recording sessions were cheap. As a result, taking a chance on an unproven band was not as risky a proposition as it was for Pye's competitors. Although there was a considerable amount of friction between Talmy and Pye's stingy label head, Louie Benjamin, a deal was struck for the Ravens. In January 1964 Talmy went into the studio to record the band's debut, a spirited version of Little Richard's "Long Tall Sally." Shortly before the single was released, the band changed its name. Now no longer the Ravens, it adopted the befittingly clever moniker, the Kinks. However, the hip name switch did not help its fortunes, as the single promptly flopped.

Led by frequently squabbling brothers Ray and Dave Davies, along with bassist Pete Quaife and drummer Mick Avory, the Kinks were Edwardian-clad, art-school smarties, hell-bent to make an imprint on the burgeoning British rock scene. The ever-wry Ray was clearly the leader of the band, and his remarkable gift of incisive, satirical songwriting was undeniable to Talmy from the onset. Musically, the band was formidable as well. Dave was a dynamic guitarist with a fiery approach, and Talmy considered Quaife "an extremely good bass player." Only Avory was not up to snuff, a fact that forced Talmy to use session drummer Bobby Graham on nearly all of the band's early recordings.

Talmy prized the raw immediacy of the best American rock records, and he quickly sought to inject that unrefined spirit into the Kinks' polite British sound. After a couple of false starts, Talmy's fusion became fully realized on the Kinks' third single, "You Really Got Me." With the song's raucous combination of crunchy, overdriven power chords, recklessly propulsive drums, and Ray Davies's expressively fey lead vocal, Talmy tailored a sound far heavier and louder than anything ever heard on either sides of the Atlantic. The single promptly skyrocketed to a U.K. Number 1 and became a revolutionary call to arms for all future hard rockers everywhere.

Due to Pye's tightwad budget, Talmy was forced to cut the song with shoddy three-track mono recording equipment. To achieve the separation of sound he knew the song required he harkened back to his long days spent as an engineer at L.A.'s Conway Studios. Working on seminal sessions like the Marketts' reverberating "Surfer's Stomp," Talmy and his cohort Phil Yend would spend endless hours in pursuit of better acoustics by constantly adjusting recording levels, building homemade baffles, and covering platforms with carpet. "We were the first people in L.A. at the time to really go heavy into isolation of instruments and guitar sounds, and how best to do drums," Talmy said.

When Talmy arrived in England he was surprised to find that drums were still being recorded with only three or four microphones. Utilizing his L.A.–honed recording techniques, Talmy upped the ante (and the volume) considerably and began to utilize up to twelve microphones for the drums alone. Despite the supreme skepticism and occasional hostility he received from the English engineers, Talmy demonstrated that his multi-mic technique could succeed without distortion. His sound had a bite unlike anything heard before, and everyone began to take note. Within six months nearly every rock producer in London was using the technique in an attempt to replicate his speaker-rattling sound.

Although Ray Davies possessed a cocky confidence in his songwriting abilities, he was not so comfortable with his admittedly ragged rhythm guitar playing. As a result, he opted not to play on "You Really Got Me," and Talmy recruited the top British session guitarist Jimmy Page in his place. Through the years Page has periodically taken credit for playing the lead guitar and solo on "You Really Got Me," but Talmy insists that the Led Zeppelin mastermind was solely responsible for the song's rhythm. A true rock landmark, "You Really Got Me" introduced the almighty power chord into the rock lexicon.

During the early half of the British Invasion, the pool of London session men available to pull off a genuine rock sound was extremely shallow. Besides Graham and Page, Talmy primarily used organist (and future Deep Purple co-founder) Jon Lord, versatile guitarist "Big" Jim Sullivan, drummer Clem Catini, and legendary keyboardist Nicky Hopkins. "If you didn't use them, then you were really shit out of luck," Talmy recalled. As the British rock scene matured through the decade, a new larger crop of able session players would eventually become available. However, it was the small nucleus of original session players that supplanted the bulk of Talmy's sessions.

Riding the tidal-wave momentum of "You Really Got Me," the Kinks' next three Talmy-produced follow-up singles, "All Day and All of the Night," "Tired of Waiting for You," and "Dedicated Follower Fashion," burned up the British charts. Aided by the Kinks' unique songwriting perspective and contagious charm, Talmy was now firmly established as one of rock's major producers. As Ray Davies churned out his unique brand of pointed, often-amusing of social observation at an astoundingly prodigious rate, Talmy himself selected the strongest material to record. "Ray was one of the more prolific songwriters I've ever known. He used to come in with 20 songs he'd written overnight and we would sit and go through them," Talmy said.

By 1964 America's appetite for anything British was becoming insatiable, and the Kinks signed a U.S. deal with Reprise Records. Much to Talmy's dismay, Reprise promptly reprocessed the band's early mono material for stereo. The stereo reprocessing took the bite out of Talmy's ballsy mono productions and left many of the band's American-released records sounding muddy and neutered. However, ignorance was bliss to the Kinks' newly rabid American fans, and, despite Reprise's sonic undermining, the band established a fervent fan base in the United States. Enjoying a string of Top 10 U.S. hits from late 1964 through the first half of 1965, the Kinks were one of the most popular exports of the British Invasion.

• • • • •

With his hard-rock hit-making reputation rising, Talmy found his services in demand. Among the callers was a London-based mod band called the High Numbers. The hard-charging band liked what Talmy had done for the Kinks and convinced the producer to attend one of its rehearsals. Although the raucous quartet had been making a racket around town with its wild stage antics, so far the group had been unable to satisfactorily capture its dynamic sound on tape. By the time the band auditioned for Talmy, it had returned to one of its earlier names, the Who.

Talmy was literally blown away as he absorbed the Who's ear-splitting, self-proclaimed "Maximum R&B" up close. This was exactly the type of band he was looking for. "I loved them when I first saw them," he said. Coupling incredible musicianship with incendiary showmanship, the band's raw talent was nearly overwhelming. Powered by Roger Daltrey's nifty microphone twirling and charismatic R&B shouting, Pete Townshend's ferocious windmill guitar strumming, John Entwistle's effortlessly nimble bass playing, and Keith Moon's violently frenetic drumming, Talmy thought the band was almost too good to be true.

Charged by the band's electrical rehearsal, Talmy moved quickly to sow up the Who. First he signed the quartet to his production company, and shortly after he began financing its recordings himself. Sweeping aside his past issues with Decca, Talmy brought the band to the label, and the Who was promptly signed to a long-term contract. As the High Numbers, they had already released only one single "I'm the Face/Zoot Suit," a rather tamely produced record that belied the group's inherent pugnacity. With Talmy now confidently at the controls, he sought to shape a sound more akin to their wild and wooly live performances. His first Who production came with the proto-power pop debut single, "I Can't Explain." Initially written by Townshend in a deliberately power-chorded Kinks' style to pique Talmy's interest in the band, the sparse yet tuneful single was an auspicious beginning for the band.

Utilizing the similar multi-mic methods that had catalyzed the Kinks, Talmy startlingly added intentional feedback to the mix of the band's boisterous second single, "Anyway, Anyhow, Anywhere." Consciously using feedback on a recording was tantamount to audio anarchy in 1965. Many colleagues were shocked, while others were confused by Talmy's heretical decision. Of course, the most perplexed was the band's new label. After Talmy sent the tapes of the single to Decca America for its U.S. release, he promptly received a telegram that read: "We think you sent us the wrong pressing with these strange screechy sounds—we're sure that's not the way it was supposed to be." Rather brashly, Talmy assured them that it was exactly the way it was supposed to be. Predictably, baffled American marketing executives botched "Anyway, Anyhow, Anywhere," and the single did nothing in the States. Conversely, England embraced its sonic chaos, and the song crashed into the U.K. Top 10 in late 1965.

Although the Americans didn't seem to get it, Talmy knew he was onto something, and he tested the limits even further for the Who's next single, "My Generation." Working with his ace engineer, Glyn Johns, Talmy heaped even more feedback and dissonance onto the recording than its predecessor. Although "My Generation" began as a ponderous Jimmy Reed–like talking blues number, over the course of three sessions Talmy had whipped the song into a frenzy of lightening-fast drum fills, savage feedback, careening guitar noise, and spry key changes à la the Kinks. Corralling an eternal theme of youthful alien-ation, Daltrey's pill-popping vocal stutter, Entwistle's rumbling bass solo, and an Armageddon-like drum and guitar assault from Moon and Townshend, "My Generation" served as a letter-perfect distillation of the Who's defiant essence. The song rudely stormed to Number 2 on the U.K. charts and endures as one rock's most powerful anthems.

While Talmy is cautious to unfairly grasp the glory of his clas-sic productions, he does claim responsibility for the bulk of the arranging, including "My Generation." "Did the bands come in with prearranged stuff? No. They came in with stuff and I worked on it with them. I always did. I never took any credit for songwriting when I contributed to it. But that's the way it was," he said.

After producing the Who's 1965 debut album, *The Who Sings My Generation*, disagreements between Talmy and the band's wild-card co-manager Kit Lambert forced an abrupt ending to the pairing. Talmy surmises the friction was a result of Lambert's legendary paranoia and a perceived power play to wrestle control away from him. However, he contends that he just wanted to make hit records. Nonetheless, the Talmy-owned master tapes became a protracted point of contention between him and the band, preventing the album's proper re-release for years. Fortunately, in 2002, the dispute was finally settled, and the album was properly remixed by Talmy and reissued issued on CD.

• • • • •

Despite frequent physical and verbal rows between the Davies brothers, Talmy continued to net stunning results with the rapidly maturing Kinks. The band's sound had grown by leaps and bounds in the year Talmy had paired with the band. Seeking to stoke the band's creative growth even further, Talmy played Ray Davies an East Indian–influenced song he was producing for Jon Mark (later of Mark-Almond). Davies was wowed by the song's unusual structure and exotic tunings and quickly went to work on his own Indian-derived pop song. Demonstrating his amazingly swift songwriting skill, Davies arrived in the studio a day later with the haunting raga "See My Friends."

Released in the summer of 1965, the minimalistic, droning Eastern-scaled single became the first rock song to utilize a sitar sound, predating the Beatles' "Norwegian Wood" by several months. "Of course we didn't have a sitar, we had to tune down a guitar and double-track it," Talmy recalled. Cited as Talmy's proudest production, the groundbreaking "See My Friends" was slightly too far out on the cusp, and it became the Kinks' first bomb on the charts.

Undeterred by the failure of "See My Friends," the Kinks continued to take chances with their sound. With their growth process continuing at an astonishing rate, they released the loosely structured concept album *Face to Face* in 1966. Something of an equivalent to the Beatles' transitional *Revolver*, *Face to Face* was a fantastic collection of diverse

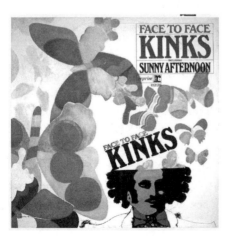

The Kinks
Face to Face
(1966)

art-pop that included the mesmerizing Eastern trance number, "Fancy," the mock Hawaiian rock tune, "Holiday in Waikiki," and the sublime English music hall hit "Sunny Afternoon." With its superb songcraft and stylistic diversity, *Face to Face* proved that the Kinks were no mere British Invasion flash-in-the-pan content to milk the same commercial formula until it ran dry. Rather, the Kinks were now among rock's most ambitious and elite innovators.

Following *Face to Face*, Talmy was back for the band's irrepressible 1967 offering, *Something Else By the Kinks*. Another pillar of brainy pop, the album was marked by the songwriting emergence of guitarist Dave Davies, illustrated on his wonderfully self-pitying "Death of a Clown" and his grungy garage nugget, "Love Me 'Till the Sun Shines." Meanwhile, Ray's marvelous knack for finely chiseled character portraits was amply evidenced with the bouncy and mocking, "David Watts," the fly-on-the-wall observation "Two Sisters," the droll "Situation Vacant," and the peerlessly refined "Waterloo Sunset," easily one of the most gorgeous pop songs ever penned.

In two short years together, Talmy and the Kinks had ascended from obscure art-school unknowns to untouchable rock royalty, but *Something Else* would be the Kinks' final chapter written with Talmy. Although the Kinks would continue to scale dizzying artistic heights with conceptual landmarks like *Village Green Preservation Society* and *Arthur*, the band missed Talmy's chart savvy, and its fan base began to erode. Ironically, it was only after the Kinks returned to the earlier Talmy-like formula for the hit 1970 single, "Lola," that it was able to regain a commercial foothold.

• • • • •

Along with his Kinks and Who landmarks, Talmy crafted several memorable freelance hits throughout the decade. Among the highlights was the Easybeats' transcendent pop-psych masterpiece "Friday on My Mind," Manfred Mann's U.K. chart-topping Dylan cover "The Mighty Quinn," and Chad & Jeremy's "A Summer Song." He also worked with young Anthony Newley–obsessed art student David Jones on several ignored singles released between 1964 and 1966. By the early 1970s, Jones would attain worldwide fame as rock's foremost chameleon, David Bowie. "It was completely evident to me that he was going to be a major star. I got him when he was seventeen. Unfortunately, I was about six or seven years ahead of the market," Talmy said.

Some of Talmy's finest work came with the tragically underrated cult band, the Creation. Led by the astonishing Eddie Phillips, the Creation was a thrilling amalgamation of tough mod posturing, flowery pop-art imagery, and flashy guitar-driven pyrotechnics. Talmy calls Phillips "the greatest unknown guitarist off all-time," a claim supported by the fact that he was asked by Pete Townshend to join the Who—a flattering offer that he inevitably turned down. A true trailblazer, Phillips invented a violin-bowed electric guitar style that would later be co-opted by Jimmy Page in Led Zeppelin. With Phillips harnessing his feedback-generating bowing technique on explosive singles like "Making Time" and "Biff, Bang, Pow," the Creation began to cultivate notoriety around several European countries, including Germany and Holland.

Mysteriously, the Creation never managed to truly break through in its native England. Even worse, the band remained virtually unknown in the United States. Dispirited by its commercial shortcomings, Phillips turned his back on rock for the steady paycheck of bus driving. His timing could not have been worse. Just as Phillips dissolved the Creation, Talmy was finalizing negotiations for an American record deal. "He should have been as well-known as Clapton," Talmy said, lamenting that he "could not hold them together." Posthumously, the Creation's cult has steadily expanded through the decades, and today it is are routinely recognized as one of the finest British bands of its era.

Talmy ended the decade by turning down the decibels. Proving his versatility, he helmed a trio of gentle acoustic-based albums for the magnificent British folk rock quintet Pentangle. Featuring the dazzling dueling acoustic guitar virtuosos Bert Jansch and John Renbourn, the gifted and jazzy rhythm section of Danny Thompson and Terry Cox, and the luminous-voiced Jacqui McShee, Pentangle was a staggeringly eclectic quintet. Stylistically restless, the group's oeuvre included medieval chants, pop standards, modern jazz, and sizzling acoustic folk. Talmy recalled his Pentangle work as "really good fun," and the pristinely recorded, marvelously performed albums have worn surprising well through the decades. "It worked because of the variety of what we did," Talmy said fondly.

Not as much fun for Talmy was his work on British folk-rock eccentric Roy Harper's *Folkjokeopus* album. "He wasn't one of my favorites, he had at least a couple of chips on each shoulder. I never understood him and actually never wanted to," Talmy said of the notoriously nutty songwriter. Negative memories aside, *Folkjokeopus* is often an intriguing collision of Harper's impenetrable musings and inventive folk-psych backing courtesy of Talmy's dependable cabal of session men. The uneven, though often oddly charming 1969 album would serve as a springboard for Harper's excellent early '70s albums, *Stormcock* and *Lifemask*.

As the '60s gave way to the '70s, Talmy grew bored of the increasingly corporate music climate, and his output slowed. Later in the decade, he briefly dabbled in punk (a genre whose ferocious sound was directly rooted in his spirited Kinks and Who productions), helming the Damned's 1977 release *Music for Pleasure*. The release proved to be a disappointment for all involved. Clearly, Talmy's heart was not in it from the start: "I didn't like punk, I just wanted to make sure that I wasn't going to enjoy it," he said. After a long layoff, Talmy returned to action in the mid-1990s with the debut album from Nancy Boy, a retro new wave band fronted by blue-blooded pretty-boy Donovan Leitch, Jr. Ultimately, *Nancy Boy* was a victim of style over substance, and despite sporadic moments of inspiration, the album failed to generate any significant heat.

Talmy, who suffers from a longtime degenerative vision condition, continues to receive frequent offers from bands but remains unenthused by the current crop of artists. "The art of songwriting seems to have died at least in the last ten or fifteen years or so," he observed. However, he stays up on modern recording techniques and remains open-minded about future possibilities. Whether he works again or not, Talmy's maverick coupling of raw power-chorded distortion and sticky harmonic hooks will eternally remain among rock's key building blocks.

KEY RECORDINGS
David Axelrod

David Axelrod –	*Songs of Innocence* (Capitol 1968)
	Songs of Experience (Capitol 1969)
	Earth Rot (Capitol 1970)
	Pride (Warner Bros. 1970)
	The Auction (Decca 1972)
	Heavy Axe (Fantasy 1974)
	Seriously Deep (Polydor 1975)
	Strange Ladies (MCA 1977)
	Marchin' (MCA 1980)
	David Axelrod (Mo' Wax 2001)
Cannonball Adderley –	*Mercy, Mercy, Mercy! Live at the Club* (Capitol 1966)
	Accent on Africa (Capitol 1968)
	Black Messiah (Capitol 1972)
	Inside Straight (Fantasy 1973)
	Pyramid (Fantasy 1974)
Nat Adderley –	*Soul of the Bible* (Capitol 1972)
	Soul Zodiac (Capitol 1972)
Gene Ammons –	*Brass Wind* (Prestige 1974)
Electric Prunes –	*Mass in F Minor* (Reprise 1968)
	Release of an Oath (Reprise 1968)
Funk Inc. –	*Superfunk* (Prestige 1973)
Hampton Hawes –	*Northern Windows* (Fantasy 1974)
Harold Land –	*The Fox* (Hi-Fi Jazz 1959)
David McCallum –	*Music: Another Side of Me* (Capitol 1966)
Letta Mubulu –	*Free Soul* (Capitol 1968)
Lou Rawls –	*Soulin'* (Capitol 1966)
	Carryin' on (Capitol 1966)
	Too Much (Capitol 1967)
	You're Good for Me (Capitol 1968)
	The Way It Was: The Way It Is (Capitol 1969)
Howard Roberts –	*Spinning Wheel* (Capitol 1970)
Frank Rosolino –	*Free for All* (Specialty 1958)
Merl Saunders –	*Merl Saunders* (Fantasy 1974)
U.N.K.L.E. –	"Rabbit in Your Headlights" (Remix) (Mo' Wax 1999)
Jimmy Witherspoon –	*Singin' the Blues* (1959 World Pacific)

Shel Talmy

Amen Corner –	*The Return of the Magnificent 7* (Immediate 1971)
Chad & Jeremy –	"A Summer Song" (World Artists 1964)
The Creation –	*We Are Paintermen* (Hit-Ton 1967) *How Does it Feel to Feel?* (Edsel 1982)
Dave Davies –	"Death of a Clown" (Pye 1967)
The Easybeats –	"Friday on My Mind" (United Artists 1967)
David (Bowie) Jones – and the Lower Third	"I Can't Help Thinking About Me" (Pye 1966)
Roy Harper –	*Folkjokeopus* (World Pacific 1969)
Bert Jansch –	*Birthday Blues* (Reprise 1969)
The Kinks –	*The Kinks* (Pye 1964) *You Really Got Me* (Reprise 1965) *Kinda Kinks* (Pye 1965) *Kinks-Size* (Reprise 1965) *The Kink Kontroversy* (Reprise 1966) *Face to Face* (Reprise 1966) *Something Else by the Kinks* (Reprise 1967)

Manfred Mann –	"Semi-Detached Suburban Mr. James/
	    Morning After the Party" (Fontana 1966)
	"Ha! Ha! Said the Clown/Feeling So Good"
	    (Fontana 1967)
	"The Mighty Quinn (Quinn the Eskimo)/
	    By Request – Edwin Garvey" (Mercury 1968)

Nancy Boy –	*Nancy Boy* (Sire 1996)
Pentangle –	*The Pentangle* (Reprise 1968) *Sweet Child* (Reprise 1968) *Basket of Light* (Reprise 1969)
Various Artists –	*The Best of Planet Records* (RPM 2000)

The Who –	"I Can't Explain/Bald Headed Woman"
	    (Decca 1965)
	"Anyway, Anyhow, Anywhere/
	    Daddy Rolling Stone" (Decca 1965)
	The Who Sings My Generation (Brunswick 1965)
	"Substitute" (Decca 1966)

4

THE CHEMISTRY
BEHIND THE BOARD:
JIMMY MILLER AND GLYN JOHNS

American producer Jimmy Miller sat in the control room of Olympic Studios in London in summer 1967, helming a session for an exciting new quartet called Traffic. The song the group was working on had the potential for greatness, but, as each member recorded in his own separate isolation booth, it clearly lacked the vitality it so desperately required. For Miller, the vibe was not right, and for the burgeoning producer nothing was more paramount than the right vibe.

Suddenly Miller had an idea, and he told the band to take a break. He ordered his assistants to set up the band's equipment together on a giant riser at one end of the studio—and then called them back in for another attempt. With the band playing live together on the mock stage (straight into a four-track recorder), the song began to magically transform. Miller openly grooved at the mixing board as the band jammed the song—but in mid-take, he abruptly got up and bolted from the control room. A moment later, he reappeared on the other side of the glass, grabbed a pair of maracas, and leaped onto the riser. The band glanced over at Miller quizzically as he began to furiously shake the maracas, exhorting them to speed up the tempo. The band got the message and followed his lead straight into a final frenzied rave-up. Miller just channeled the mercurial "perfect vibe" for an impending rock classic called "Dear Mr. Fantasy."

"That to me, was the most remarkable piece of production assistance I'd ever seen," legendary recording engineer Eddie Kramer recalled. "They were shocked to see him out there, exhorting them to double the tempo. Their eyes kind of lit up. It was amazing. That was Jimmy!"[1]

Jimmy Miller

Photo: Meredith Day/Clear Pond

• • • • •

t was 1966, and Jimmy Miller arrived in England just in time to help pop music flip the switch from black and white to Technicolor. Hailing from New York, the tall, mustachioed Miller began his musical career as a singer and drummer, and by the early '60s he had secured a recording contract with Columbia Records. Shortly after, he entered a studio and dipped his feet in the recording process for the first time. He was utterly fascinated, and it became self-evident that his true passion was not performing, but producing.

By mid-decade Miller had produced a slew of demos and obscure singles. One release, an R&B song called "Incense," caught the attention of fledgling Island Records mastermind Chris Blackwell, who released the song in England. Blackwell was also managing a soulful rock combo named the Spencer Davis Group, a Birmingham-based band that featured the prodigious musical talents of its wunderkind 15-year old singer/ keyboardist, Stevie Winwood. Although the band had garnered impressive U.K. recognition, it was unknown stateside. Red-hot American producer Shel Talmy had recently broken both the Who and the Kinks in the States, and Blackwell figured an American producer might just be what his band needed as well. So in September 1966, Miller flew out to work on the new Spencer Davis Group's single, "Gimme Some Lovin'."

Arriving in England, Miller found the song's core elements already recorded, including its incessantly deep bassline, ringing church organ, and Winwood's Ray Charles–like lead vocal. At its heart "Gimme Some Lovin'" was a dance song, but, like many British recordings of the day, the song lacked a punchy drum sound. With his background in drumming, Miller introduced his hallmark percussive sound by remixing the drums and overdubbing a crazed cowbell and adding new backing vocals. Miller's mix was soulfully sweaty, and the song's compact sound was a perfect match for the compressed dynamics of AM radio. "Gimme Some Lovin'" rose to Number 2 on the U.K. charts and, more significantly, stormed to Number 7 in America.

Miller and Winwood developed a strong rapport, that quickly led to a songwriting collaboration on the band's follow-up release, "I'm a Man." Darker in tone than its celebratory predecessor, the sexually charged single was propelled by Winwood's astonishingly mature lead vocal, gutbucket organ washes, and Miller's rattling voodoo percussion sound. Contributing to the song's exotically charging rhythms were outside musicians Dave Mason, Jim Capaldi, and Chris Wood, all fellow members of the Birmingham rock scene. The deviously danceable "I'm a Man" became a monster hit, cracking the U.S. Top 10 in May 1967. Meanwhile, as Winwood's talents rapidly blossomed, it became clear that he had gone as far as he could with the Spencer Davis Group. Just as the song became a hit, he split to form Traffic, taking "I'm a Man"'s ancillary percussionists with him.

• • • • •

Seeking to galvanize its wide-ranging musical ideas, Traffic holed up in a country cottage in the rural English area of Berkshire. Living communally, the four musicians began to carve out their eclectic identity through ongoing songwriting and jam sessions. Predicating its sound on diversity and experimentation, Traffic's explicit mantra was "to sound like the same group, but never to sound the same."

By the summer of 1967, Miller had produced two fantastical psychedelic singles for Traffic: Winwood and Capaldi's tabla and sitar-driven "Paper Sun" and Mason's whimsically surreal, backwards-tracked "Hole in My Shoe." After meticulously rehearsing the album's songs under

Miller's auspice, the band began to record its debut at Olympic Studios. Olympic was one of the few non-label affiliated recording studios in London at the time, and, with its enviable acoustics and relatively advanced equipment, it would become Miller's studio of choice for years to come.

Continuing with the lysergic sonics of their two singles, Miller and his gifted engineer, Eddie Kramer, dunked the album's songs in buckets of multi-colored mellotron tones, lavish tape phasing and echo effects, and heavily manipulated percussion. While Miller pushed the four-track recording equipment to the brink of experimentation, he was careful not to smother Traffic's extraordinary musicianship and top-notch songwriting. Miller was all about *feeling* the music, and he was determined to make sure the band felt it too.

Miller's good humor and unbridled enthusiasm catalyzed the band throughout the recording of its first album, *Mr. Fantasy*. From the flute and flamenco-flavored shuffle "Dealer," to the heavy organ-blues jamming of "Coloured Rain," to the pensive acoustic ballad "No Face, No Name, No Number," to the future classic rock staple "Dear Mr. Fantasy," Traffic's virgin foray was a richly tailored, auspicious debut. Following its release, squabbles ensued between Winwood and Mason over the band's direction. Soon after, Mason quit Traffic, but he was coaxed back to the fold for its eponymous second album.

Yearning to get back to basics, Traffic ditched the candy-colored surrealism of its debut in favor of an organic sound closer to its stunning live performances. Once again, Miller spread his positive vibes throughout the sessions, and his spontaneous approach imbued the songs with a marvelous improvisational elasticity. Miller's mix emphasized crisply layered percussion, evident in the propulsive "Pearly Queen," the calypso-influenced "Vagabond Virgin," and the soul-stirring "Feelin' Alright" (later a memorable hit for Joe Cocker). With its tonally diverse arrangements and spatial sound, *Traffic* was marvelous from beginning to end. Among those taking note was a downtrodden band called the Rolling Stones.

• • • • •

Traffic
Traffic
(1968)

By early 1968, the Rolling Stones were in trouble. Rapidly out-growing their teeny-bopping audience, the band tried to catch the magic bus with the messy post-*Pepper* psychedelic album, *Their Satanic Majesties Request*. While the album contained a few kaleido-scopic winners, it was a commercial disaster. Clearly the Stones were ill at ease with the paisley-patterned optimism of psychedelia, and the band's future was in legitimate jeopardy as it struggled with the shift-ing musical winds.

Miller and the Stones first met at Olympic Studios on a night when Traffic was recording at Studio B and the Stones were toiling on *Majesties* in Studio A. According to Miller, the Stones walked in on a "beautiful moment" during a Traffic session: "We were giving it a loud playback and the vibes were wonderful, but when I later dropped by the Stones' session it was rather bogged down and Mick (Jagger) was complaining to me that he couldn't be on both sides of the control room glass at once. So I just gave him some words of encouragement and told him to hang in there," Miller said.[2]

Two days later Miller was invited to Jagger's estate, where he was asked to produce the next Stones album. Like many, Miller had become a huge fan of the band after hearing their immortal "Satisfaction," and he quickly, if a little nervously, agreed to take the job. Jagger then played him a new acoustic demo of a song he proclaimed to be the band's new single. The original lyrics featured Jagger singing "I *feel* like Jumpin' Jack Flash." Miller loved the song, but he convinced Jagger that he wasn't *like* Jumpin' Jack Flash, rather he actually *was*

Jumpin' Jack Flash. "Just sing 'I'm Jumpin' Jack Flash,' Miller suggested. Jagger thought about it for a moment, then agreed.[3]

Entering Olympic with Britain's top rock engineer Glyn Johns in March '68, Miller and the Stones went to work on "Jumpin' Jack Flash," a scintillating cousin to "Satisfaction." The Stones had always worshipped American roots music, and working with Miller proved to inspire the band. Buoyed by his cheerleader-like enthusiasm and refreshed by his patient support for in-studio songwriting, the band began to recuperate from the confusion of *Their Satanic Majesties'* acid-hangover. Well aware that inspiration could not be rushed, Miller somehow managed to keep the Stones relaxed and focused at the same time. He realized they were onto something glorious with the new song.

Released in May 1968, the tumultuous "Jumpin' Jack Flash" (coupled with the cosmically pastoral B-side, "Child of the Moon") was a sneak preview for the looming long, hot summer. Ignited by a stuttering, barbed-wire sharp guitar riff and Jagger's malevolent vocals, the song rumbles into a crossfire hurricane of darting bass, rat-a-tat-tat drums, and esoteric East Indian instruments. With relentless maracas reverberating around the catchy "Jumpin' Jack Flash, it's a gas" chorus, the song builds towards a frenetic coda then releases into a frenzied half-minute of serpentine jamming, before slowly disappearing over a protracted fadeout. The structure was intoxicatingly captivating, and Miller and the Stones would utilize it often in the coming years. With the mercurial new producer at the helm, "Jumpin' Jack Flash" fought its way to the to the top of the U.K. charts and became the Stones' first Number 1 in two long years. There was no doubt: The Rolling Stones were back.

By early summer, the Stones began sessions for their new album, *Beggars Banquet*. Among the songs they tackled was the incendiary single "Street Fighting Man." The song's unorthodox construction resulted after Richards played Miller a demo he had recorded at home on a mono cassette player. As they listened, Richards outwardly longed to get the same savagely distorted sound in a proper studio. "Why not record your acoustic on a cassette here in the studio?" Miller asked, and then he quickly procured a cheap Philips tape recorder.[4]

The Rolling Stones
Beggars Banquet
(1968)

Recording on a cheap tape deck inside one of England's top studios was a bold, if not heretical, move by the freethinking Miller. Without a background in sound engineering, he was unencumbered by traditional recording methods, and his "anything goes" spirit was as inspired as it was defiant. Of course, it helped that Miller had brilliant engineers like Johns and Kramer to oversee the technical details while he focused on the bigger picture at hand.

Using the crude cassette machine, Miller recorded two viciously strummed acoustic guitars played by Richards, Brian Jones's sitar, and a directly miked miniature drum set played by Charlie Watts. He then transferred the cassette recordings onto one track of a standard four-track recorder. With three free tracks available, Miller added multiple overdubs, including a bass played by Richards (the only electric instrument on the recording), Nicky Hopkins's piano, and the droning Eastern instruments *tamboura* (played by Jones) and *shenai* (played by Traffic's Dave Mason). Lastly, Jagger's bellicose vocal was added. "You can't really tell that a cassette is being played in there when you listen to the finished record, but if you ever took that track out the whole sound would change and become very sterile," Miller said.[5]

If "Jumpin' Jack Flash" was the preview to the wicked, long hot summer of '68, then the chiming "Street Fighting Man" was its theme song. Unfortunately, the single's truculent, though slurred, themes made the song a political pariah. As a result, several radio stations boycotted the single, and it died quickly on the bottom end of the U.S.

charts. Nonetheless, the song's intentionally crude production aesthetic portended both the DIY movement of the late '70s/early '80s, as well as the more recent lo-fi genre purveyed by artists like Guided By Voices, Pavement, and Beck.

Never a political band, it was *Beggars Banquet*'s demonic opener, "Sympathy for the Devil," that would define the band's notorious image for years to come. "Sympathy" was recorded while French New Wave director Jean-Luc Godard filmed the band for "One Plus One," a short and ultimately disjointed documentary centered on revolt and revolution. With numerous film crew distractions exacerbating the usual in-studio mayhem, the band worked through the song on camera. Soon, the song began to mutate from its gothic acoustic blues origins into what Richards later called "a mad samba." Miller was thrilled by the direction it was taking, and he took to sashaying around the control room, cheering "whoo, whoo" along with the song. Quickly, his backing vocals infected the band and its entourage, and everybody began singing the rapturous "whoo, whoos." Inspiration struck Miller, and he ran to set up a microphone in the control room. Eventually, much of the impromptu reveling made it into the final mix. Thriving on spontaneity, Miller had wrung inspiration out of sheer chaos. With its crisp exotic rhythms and darkly seductive piano/guitar groove, "Sympathy for the Devil" was in many ways the perfect embodiment of Miller's loose-limbed vibe.

In keeping with the emerging rootsy Americana sound instigated by the Byrds, the Band, and Dylan, the Stones explored gothic territory throughout *Beggars Banquet*. Songs like the mandolin- and fiddle-sweetened Appalachian folk tale "Factory Girl," and the hillbilly harmonica cornpone "Dear Doctor" were appropriately dusty and damaged. The Hawaiian slide guitar-enhanced "No Expectations" laconically conjured an atmosphere soaked in lazy afternoon humidity, achieved by recording the band with open microphones as the band sat performing on the floor. Other rich banquet courses included the leering, Velvet Underground–mimicking "Stray Cat Blues," the lo-fi blues "Parachute Woman," and the gospel-tinged album closer "Salt of the Earth."

Beggars Banquet made it to Number 5 on the U.S. album charts in early 1969 and re-established the Rolling Stones as the world's preeminent rock band. Clearly, Miller's encouragement of experimentation and indomitable positivity had proven to be just what the Stones needed. On an unprecedented creative roll, the team quickly reconvened to begin work on a new album.

Re-assembling in Olympic, Richards began to open up the band's sound by experimenting with obscure, open country guitar tunings. The importance of Richards's growth was underscored by Brian Jones's glaring absence; Jones was well into his drug-addled long goodbye. Although Jones would occasionally show up to the studio, it was usually with an inappropriately exotic instrument for what the session dictated. Miller sympathized with the beleaguered Jones and would try to placate him, going as far as to record him in a separate booth and on a different reel than the rest of the band. Sadly, though, Jones had slipped so deep into twilight that he did not know the difference.

However, the band was out of patience with its fallen band member and dismissed him from the group during the sessions; shortly after, Jones drowned in his swimming pool. After the Stones mulled over several different options, the spectacular young guitarist Mick Taylor, who was fresh from a stint in John Mayall's Bluesbreakers, finally replaced Jones. Bolstered by Taylor and an expanded lineup of session players, the Stones' sound was suddenly injected with a newfound instrumental robustness.

Prior to the album's completion came the new single, "Honky Tonk Woman." Stoked by a hoedown drum kick (taught to Watts by Miller), countrified guitar lick, Miller's clanking cowbell, and soulful backup singers, the tune was a joyously bawdy barroom sing-along. Recorded in just five hours, the country rock classic was perhaps the epitome of Miller's party-in-the-studio tenet. When the magical session was completed just before dawn, Jagger accurately predicted a Number 1 single.

Meanwhile, the lengthy flipside, "You Can't Always Get What You Want," was as contemplative as it's A-side was raucous. Something of an answer to the Beatles similarly extended "Hey Jude," the song was as much a rumination on the band's consumptive lifestyle as a larger commentary on the death of sixties idealism. Not exempt from the lyrical concerns was the increasingly hedonistic

Miller, illustrated in Jagger's line: "I went down to the Chelsea drug-store to get your prescription filled, I was standing in line with Mr. Jimmy and man did he look pretty ill."

Supplying the sublime gospel-infused drums on the song was no less than Miller himself, who sat behind the kit after Watts was unable to nail the tricky drum accent:

> I heard what I thought would be a good drum part, but couldn't get Charlie to play it—you know he just couldn't feel it. When you don't feel something, you can have someone explain it to you all night long and you still won't get it. Finally, out of frustration, Charlie handed me the sticks and said, "Here, you play it." By then, feeling that our getting the track depended on getting that drum part, I was very willing to take the sticks and play it myself.[6]

"Honky Tonk Woman"/"You Can't Always Get What You Want" was a Number 1 smash and stayed on top for a full month in August 1969. Following in November was the album *Let it Bleed*, a cheeky swipe at the Beatles' recently released single "Let it Be." With its immaculate Glyn Johns–engineered sound, peerless performances, and often troubling material, *Let it Bleed* was the Stones at its most darkly inspired.

Nowhere was this dark inspiration more evident than on the eerie masterpiece "Gimme Shelter." One of Miller's finest produc-tions, "Gimme Shelter"'s chilling stage was set by a sinister slow fade-in of guitar, electric piano, scrapping gourd percussion, and

The Rolling Stones
Let It Bleed
(1969)

menacing backing vocals. To harness Richards's creeping sound, his guitar was split through two different amps, with one amp heard in the right speaker, the other in the left. "That intro happened pretty much by accident," Miller recalled. "Out of all the takes, it was the only one that built like that—everybody came in at exactly the right time."[7]

Another song to evolve accidentally was the parched country blues "You Got the Silver," which became Richards's first lead-vocal. The circumstances arose after Miller and Johns had decided to backward echo a bottleneck guitar track for the song. The inventive technique involved flipping the tape over and adding echo to an open track; then the tape was flipped right-side-up, resulting in a backwards echo effect. However, after all the tape-flipping, Johns got confused as to what part was on each track, and he inadvertently erased Jagger's vocal. With Mick nowhere to be found, Miller suggested Richards step in and sing it himself, and his hoarse vocal provided the song with the perfect outlaw grittiness.

Quiescent country blues "Love in Vain," brutish horn-charged riff-rockers like "Live with Me" and "Let It Bleed," the Boston Strangler narrative "Midnight Rambler," and the pernicious junkie tale "Monkey Man" rounded out the album. With its nefarious horn-section, soulful back-up singers, and expanded lineup of session players, *Let it Bleed* drew a new blueprint for the band's sound that would last well into the next decade.

• • • • •

Miller was also active away from the Stones throughout the late 1960s. He produced "Scene Through the Eye of a Lens," the fantastic, tempo-shifting first single for proto-progressive rock geniuses Family, in 1967. A year later he began to work on its trailblazing debut album, *Music in a Doll's House*, but commitments to *Beggars* allowed him to only produce two of its tracks. Miller also enjoyed a memorable turn with the innovative pop-art rockers the Move.

The Move was one of the most renowned bands on the British scene, due in part to destructive early live performances that featured onstage power-tool-wielding demolitions of television sets. Gimmickry aside, the band possessed a glorious pop sense, and, despite a long string of popular singles, it had been unable to reach the top spot on the U.K. singles charts. After the disappointing failure of the single "Wild Tiger Woman," the band vowed to the British press that it would break up if its next release did not reach Number 1. Recognizing that its previous release had suffered because of its murky mix, the Move recruited Miller for "Blackberry Way," its last shot. Sure enough, Miller coaxed a special performance out of the band, and the cello-colored lament "Blackberry Way" marched to a U.K. Number 1 in early 1969. By the early 1970s, the Move would morph into E.L.O. and eventually become one of the most popular rock acts of the decade.

Once again teaming with engineer Glyn Johns, Miller produced British blues rockers Spooky Tooth's 1968 debut, *It's All About*. The overlooked album mixed surprisingly effective covers of Janis Ian's "Society's Child" and the venerable "Tobacco Road," with a clutch of driving psychedelic originals (several of which were co-written by Miller). He also returned for Spooky Tooth's bluesy follow up, *Spooky Two*, which was marked by the muscular "Evil Woman" and the convincing country/blues hybrid "That Was Only Yesterday." With their echoed, crunchy guitar riffs and dense organ, both albums helped open the floodgates on 1970s jam-style hard rock.

Following the triumph of Traffic's glorious second album, Miller returned to produce its outstanding late 1968 single "Medicated Goo." Unfortunately, battles between Mason and Winwood raged on, and following its release Traffic disbanded. With the band broken-up, Miller was forced to cobble together the posthumous, part-live *Last Exit*. Soon after Traffic's demise, rumors circulated of a new project featuring Winwood and Eric Clapton, whose own mega-band Cream had recently called it quits.

Officially forming in the spring of 1969, the band dubbed Blind Faith featured Winwood and Clapton, along with flashy Cream drummer Ginger Baker and ex-Family bassist Rick Grech. The band attempted to self-produce the album, but there were serious problems with the recordings, and Miller was called in at the 11th hour for an independent opinion. Due in only four days (a deadline imposed to coincide with the band's upcoming tour), Miller was shocked to discover that the record was nowhere near finished. "I went down to Olympic to hear what they'd done, and they brought up something like 38 boxes of tape, most of which was jams!" Miller said.[8]

With no time to spare, Miller quickly had the band re-record three of the album's key songs, "Presence of the Lord," "Sea of Joy," and "Do What You Like," and scurried to extensively edit the remaining cuts. With only two days now remaining before the deadline, Miller was forced to mix each side of the album in a night apiece—just under the wire. "After that ordeal, I was really numb," he said.

Bowing in July 1969 with a great deal of fanfare and anticipation, *Blind Faith* introduced rock's first real supergroup. While several of the tracks fulfilled the promise of the grouping, the fifteen-minute plus jam "Do What You Like" clearly smacked of filler. Miller was unhappy with the severely rushed release and wondered what might have been with more time to cut the album his way. Nonetheless, the record quickly rose to the top spot in the United States, continuing his astounding slew of produced hits.

Clapton quickly grew disenchanted with Blind Faith's burdensome performing demands and promptly quit the band after its tour (Winwood would soon reform Traffic without Dave Mason). Almost immediately, he began to take musical refuge in one of Blind Faith's opening acts, Delaney and Bonnie. The American husband and wife team played an unpretentious, passionate country/blues hybrid, and Clapton joined them for a tour, thankfully serving as just another musician in a band. With Clapton relaxed and playing better than ever, Miller was rushed in to produce a document of the band's smoking live performances.

Recorded at the tail-end of 1969, the scorching *Delaney and Bonnie & Friends on Tour with Eric Clapton* featured roughhewn gems such as the stinging soul of "Things Get Better" and the expressively bluesy "Comin' Home." Following its release, Clapton would poach Delaney and Bonnie band members Jim Gordon, Bobby Whitlock, and Carl Radle for the short-lived, but legendary, Southern rock project, Derek and the Dominos. Once again, Miller had overseen another rock classic, but it was time to return to the Stones.

• • • • •

In the winter of 1970 Miller and the Stones began sessions for their new album, *Sticky Fingers*, at Jagger's stately country manor, Stargroves. With the band's recently constructed 34-foot mobile studio semi-truck parked out in front, recording commenced in the mansion's spacious parlor. Surrounded by plaster walls, hardwood floors, and a large bay window that stretched from the floor to the ceiling, Stargroves provided what Miller deemed "a very good acoustic environment."[9] As microphones sprouted from the chimney and a guitar amp oddly rested in a large fireplace, the Stones began to jam songs that would become "Sway," "Bitch," and "Moonlight Mile." The initial sessions were inspired, and, after getting the feel at Stargroves, recording moved to the familiar environs of Olympic.

While Glyn Johns was involved in some of the engineering duties, the bulk of the album's recording responsibilities fell to his younger brother, Andy. Generally, when it came to capturing the actual sound, Miller usually deferred to his far more technical engineers, but he was not afraid to push for a particular sound when the circumstance arose. Once the sound levels and microphones were properly set, Miller would have the band run through the song; then everyone would listen to the playback together. The band was usually amenable to Miller, except for Jagger, who would often nit-pick the recordings. "There was nothing that you could ever put over on him, and I liked that," Miller said of the singer.[10]

The only true source of friction between Miller and Jagger concerned their frequently differing ideas on the vocal levels. Miller constantly tried to mix Jagger prominently, but Mick would inevitably barge into the control room clamoring that the mix was too heavy on the voice. Miller would counter that "he could barely hear the vocals," but Jagger wanted to create a mystique akin to the often-indiscernible lyrics of early blues songs.[11]

Preceding the release of *Sticky Fingers* was the band's new single, "Brown Sugar," which was first cut in late 1969 at the hallowed Fame Studios in Muscle Shoals, Alabama. Powered by a marvelous staccato opening guitar riff, walloping drums, clicking castanets, roadhouse piano, and sleazy horns, the playfully scandalous song was an unmitigated masterpiece. Remarkably catchy, the song sailed straight to Number 1.

Sticky Fingers followed a month later and brilliantly continued the Miller/Stones wining streak. With the combination of Taylor's fluidly clean guitar and the horn section of Bobby Keys and Jim Price spurring the band to dizzying new heights, the album was loose, decadent, and dangerous. Propelled by the Latin rock jam "Can't You Hear Me Knocking," prickly powerhouses "Bitch," and "Sway," the orchestrated musical haiku "Moonlight Mile," and somnolent ballads "Sister Morphine" and "Wild Horses," *Sticky Fingers* grabbed the Number 1 spot in several countries around the world. With its sleek sound and heavily medicated undercurrent, the album instantly became one of the cornerstones of the emerging "party 'til you drop" '70s hard rock aesthetic.

The Rolling Stones were bigger than ever. But instead of cutting its next album in the tried-and-true surroundings of Olympic, the band would strangely find it recording in a dank basement in the French Riviera. This album would become the Stones' unlikely masterpiece...

• • • • •

With the Stones plagued by tax trouble in England and unwelcome in the United States (due to a recent Jagger drug bust), the band relocated to the south of France in the spring of 1971. Unable to locate an appropriate recording studio in the French Riviera, the band decided to record its new album, nicknamed "The Tropical Disease Sessions," in the basement of Richards's rented villa, Nellcote—an edifice that eerily served as the site of an SS headquarters during the Nazi WWII French occupation. Miller was back as what Richards often described as "the chemistry behind the board," but, in trying to keep pace with the band's debilitating party habits, he began to fall victim to its perils.

Utilizing the mobile recording studio, the sessions immediately hit a snag when it was discovered that the ancient villa could not support the equipment's heavy-duty electrical currents. To solve the problem, members of the sound crew snaked thick cables up from the basement through the kitchen and illegally tapped into a nearby railway power line. Further complicating matters was the segmented layout of the basement. Rather than one large room, the basement actually consisted of several rooms, which prevented the band from playing entirely together as a single unit. The guitar and drums would be in the main room, Nicky Hopkins would be in the "Piano Room," Price and Keys in the "Horn Room," and bassist Bill Wyman was often relegated to playing in the hall.

"The sound was really harsh, and no matter how hard we tried, no matter how many microphones we tried, and no matter how many different positions we tried, we could never get it right," Miller remembered.[12] Despite the adversity, the band continued to plug away, and through the early summer both the concrete basement and the band began to heat up dramatically.

The material itself was the rootsiest and raunchiest of the Stones' career, and the bulk of the album was recorded live with very few guitar overdubs. Miller ended up playing a lot of the drums himself during the sessions, including "I Just Want to See His Face," "All Down the Line," and Richards's dazzling "Happy." The latter had transpired after Richards showed up early for a session and found only Miller and saxophonist Keys on hand. Playing as a trio, the three quickly fell into a blazing jam. By the time the rest of the Stones straggled in, the song had essentially been completed.

That off-the-cuff casualness was indicative of most of the basement sessions—but somehow, miraculous results were being pulled from the decidedly wasted chaos. Eventually, Miller, Jagger, and Richards flew to L.A. and pieced together the final mix at Sunset Sound Studios. Fleshing it out with several overdubs from keyboardists Billy Preston and Dr. John, acoustic bass from Bill Plummer, and a group of female gospel singers, the album was finally ready to go.

Released in May 1972, the murky *Exile on Main Street* was a densely sprawling double-album full of sepia-toned delta blues, outlaw acoustic country, divine gospel, and pure rock 'n' roll. Each side was consciously sequenced to form its own distinct character and contained enough power and emotion on its own to sate even the most voracious musical appetite. Explosive rock 'n' roll declarations "Rocks Off," "Rip This Joint," and the hit single "Tumblin' Dice" paced the first side. The second side was devoted to moonshine country like "Sweet Virginia," "Sweet Black Angel," and "Loving Cup."

Side three housed the swampy and cryptic "Ventilator Blues," "Let It Loose," and "I Just Want to See His Face." The final side brought the album triumphantly home through the soulful closing numbers "Shine a Light" and "Soul Survivor." *Exile on Main Street* grabbed the top spot in the States, and, for many, it is simply the greatest rock album ever recorded.

Miller completed his run with the Stones on 1973's slick but uneven *Goats Head Soup*. Primarily recorded in Jamaica, the album sounded great, but with its spotty material it was an inevitable come-down after *Exile*. With Jagger and Richards often at odds, their collaborative songwriting style had been largely abandoned, and the album suffered for it. To compound matters, Miller was becoming increasingly addled and his once commanding presence had been severely compromised by drug abuse.

"Jimmy went in a lion and came out a lamb. We wore him out completely. Jimmy was great, but the more successful he became, the more he became like Brian (Jones)," Richards recalled in 1975.[13] By the time Miller began to burn out, one of his old colleagues had become his prime successor.

· · · · ·

As a teenaged tape operator at London's IBC Studios in the late 1950s, Glyn Johns's youth was his greatest asset. With the onset of rock 'n' roll, old guard engineers versed in tamer musical styles were quickly out of their element with the new music. Because of their reluctance to embrace the upstart genre, the young Johns became the *de facto* engineer for all of the rock recorded at IBC. Johns spent four highly educational years as a tape operator at IBC Studios, working with a variety of producers and bands, most significantly with the American ex-pat producer Shel Talmy.

Working with Talmy on watershed sessions like the Kinks' "All Day and All of the Night" and the Who's "My Generation," Johns was afforded the opportunity to participate in some of rock's most defining sessions. "Glyn was one of the great engineers of all-time, no doubt at that," Talmy said.[14] As the first independent producer in England, Talmy enjoyed unprecedented control over his sessions, and his autonomy was an inspiration to Johns. Following Talmy's lead, Johns seized the opportunity to become England's first freelance engineer.

Johns soon discovered his bold move towards free-agency had consequences, and as a result he was initially unable to find work at nearly all of England's studios. Each facility had its own in-house engineers and hierarchies, and Johns's independence was viewed as a thumb-nosing threat to the existing old-guard system. After sticking around IBC longer than he had hoped, he finally secured some work, first at Pye Studios and then at the mighty Olympic Studios.

Johns was remarkably efficient as an engineer, and his clear-eyed approach was a perfect complement to the bigger picture methodology of many of the producers he worked with. With an amazing ear for acoustics and an expert understanding of microphone and amp placements, Johns demonstrated deft skill at coaxing clean, natural sounding recordings. Furthermore, his clear-eyed work ethic and accommodating attitude towards experimentation helped further his reputation. For all of his skills, Johns quickly became the engineer of choice for most of England's top rock bands. Although he preferred live-sounding recordings, he also was flexible enough to take of advantage of emerging studio effects and technologies—exemplified on his engineering of the Small Faces' landmark single, "Itchycoo Park."

By 1967 the Small Faces had grown from mod stalwarts to psychedelic-pop experimentalists. Musically accomplished and restlessly innovative, the Small Faces were constantly seeking to charter new sonic territory, and "Itchycoo Park" was its most ambitious song yet. As the band prepared to cut the day-dreamlike single, Johns was introduced to "phasing," a new recording effect perfect for the song. Invented by George Chikiantz, one of Johns's assistant's at Olympic, the effect utilized three separate tape machines and, when applied to a recording track, resulted in a rising, shimmering envelope of sound. Tailor-made for the playful vividness of psychedelia, Johns chose to phase sections of singer Steve Marriott's vocal and parts of Kenny Jones's tumbling drum fills, which were also panned one from one speaker to the other.

"All I had to decide was where to use it, it was that simple, yet it was so revolutionary, I'd never heard anything like it before," Johns said.[15] Soon the phasing technique became a recording studio staple, but, having made his statement with it, Johns never used it again on any recording.

Johns also endured a long and sometimes contemptuous relationship with the Rolling Stones. After working with the band on some of the earliest sessions, he found himself quickly at odds with its manager/producer, Andrew Oldham. More of a promoter than a producer, Oldham's brashness coupled with his lack of studio skill constantly rankled Johns. "Andrew Oldham couldn't produce an apple and bleedin' orange at the time," he remarked.[16]

Johns engineered often for the Stones during its mid-1960s Oldham period and frequently during the band's more sophisticated Miller years. With Miller generally deferential to his more technically savvy engineers, Johns's contributions to *Beggars Banquet, Let it Bleed, Sticky Fingers,* and *Exile on Main Street* were weighty, so much so in fact that he has often claimed more responsibility for their success than Miller himself. For the latter two albums, Johns's younger brother Andy was also involved in the sound engineering responsibilities. Although the two brothers rarely worked together during the sessions, Andy would also become a top engineer and would go on to produce Television's untouchable rock cornerstone *Marquee Moon* in 1977.

By the late 1960s Johns had become one of the most accomplished and well-regarded engineers in England, but he became a frustrated victim of his own success. He had harbored the intention to become a producer since he first went independent, but most bands simply thought of him as an engineer, and the label became nearly impossible to alter. Frequently, he would request production credit, especially from the Stones, only to find his queries quickly quashed by the band. (Johns was given a production credit for the Stones' 1970 live album *Get Yer Ya-Ya's Out.*) Finally in late 1967, he received his first break to produce with a promising, but unproven American group called the Steve Miller Band.

After amassing songs while working as a janitor in a Texas recording studio, Miller headed out to San Francisco to form the Steve Miller Band along with fellow songwriter/guitarist Boz Scaggs. After several well-received gigs around town and a spot at the Monterey Pop Festival, heavy label interest found the group. Soon after, it signed to Capitol Records for $50,000—the most lucrative deal ever offered to an unknown band at the time. With its fondness for British rock, the band opted to record in London at Olympic Studios, with Steve Miller slated as producer. After much persuasion, Miller's manager convinced the highly skeptical Johns to take the engineering job.

Miller's producing inexperience was glaring, and the sessions were a mess, "just total, absolute nonsense," Johns recalled.[17] After three weeks of getting nowhere, Johns was exasperated and announced that he was quitting the sessions. The band was already in over its head and, realizing Johns's absence would spell disaster, pleaded for him to stay on the project. Johns told Miller he would only remain if he were allowed to produce the album himself. He got his wish—finally, he was officially producing an album.

Johns promptly asserted control over the Steve Miller sessions, demonstrating a methodology of focused discipline that what would define his career. Where maverick producers from Phil Spector to Jimmy Miller had been able to leisurely pull inspiration from studio chaos, Johns's engineering background left him exacting in the studio with little time for bullshit or indecision. In this respect, his approach resembled the approach championed by illustrious Atlantic Records engineer/producer Tom Dowd, who was turning out naturalistic productions for everyone from Aretha Franklin to the Allman Brothers.

Released in 1968, the Steve Miller Band's *Children of the Future* was a highly inventive merging of American blues and British-styled psychedelia. Trippy songs like "In My Mind First" and "The Beauty of Time is That It's Snowing" segued into each other, forming surprising suites. To help foster a surreal atmosphere, Johns poured numerous sound effects into the album's adventurous mix. "I did all kinds of things on that record that I'd always wanted to do. For example, I cross-faded two tracks and one pushed the other off the record, using the stereo. There were lots of little things I'd always wanted to try and I never wanted to give to anyone else, so I did them on that album," Johns said.[18]

Johns continued with the Miller Band on *Sailor*, this time recorded stateside in L.A. The original idea for the album was to stitch several songs around the concept of a sailor returning home to

Steve Miller Band
Sailor
(1969)

the States after an extended absence, only to find that the country had completely changed since he left it. Although Miller's material was not entirely successful in maintaining the intended concept, several of the album's songs centered on the original idea. *Sailor* was distinguished by its spacey instrumental opener, "Song for Our Ancestors," a painstakingly constructed song that became one the most creative mixes of John's career.

Seeking to get an authentic foghorn sound, he went down to Los Angeles harbor in San Pedro with a portable tape recorder. After eventually capturing the perfect foghorn, he returned to the studio and began to mix it together with a bounty of nautical sound effects. He then recorded eight seconds of an organ and several voices all tuned to the same note; then he doubled then halved the speed of the tapes that created three separate octaves. Next, Johns combined the tapes into a two-minute tape loop and wrapped it around the opening chord of the song for a mesmerizing affect. "All the people at Wally Heider's studio thought I was mad. They'd never seen anything like it—I kept wheeling more machines in," Johns recalled.[19]

With a large debt to Johns'ss ingenuity, the sparkling *Sailor* became a Top 25 hit and a high point in Miller's career. Johns continued to work with Miller following Scaggs's departure from the band (Johns would produce Scaggs's '71 solo album, *Moments*) helming the two solid, although less adventurous follow-ups, *Brave New World* and *Your Saving Grace*. Unfortunately, both albums were devoid of any hits, which was reflective of Johns's clear preference for albums over singles, "I'm not terribly interested in singles. If I'm making an album with somebody, I see it more as a complete statement of where the artist is at, and that, to me, is what I'm good at," Johns said reflecting on his Miller albums.[20]

Undoubtedly, Johns's predilection for albums over singles facilitated the oncoming rise of the AOR (album-oriented rock) format rock, which would soon dominate FM radio for decades to come. With improving studio technology encouraging producers' adventurousness, and listeners' tastes growing more sophisticated, the single was rapidly becoming supplanted by the album. Fittingly, Johns's next project would be with a band that would personify AOR radio more than any other: Led Zeppelin.

• • • • •

With the intriguing combination of well-known session vets Jimmy Page and John Paul Jones, and two relative unknowns, Robert Plant and John Bonham, Led Zeppelin began its heavy flight in early fall 1968. Page and Johns had known each other, dating back to their shared youth in the English town of Epsom. More recently, the two had crossed paths on numerous sessions ranging from the Kinks, to the Who, to Joe Cocker. Now, with Page's newly formed band preparing to record, he called on his old mate to co-produce his band's debut album.

Through rigorous rehearsals, Zeppelin quickly rounded into marvelous shape. With its astonishing balancing act of hard rock

Led Zeppelin
Led Zeppelin
(1969)

ferocity and acoustic folk finesse, the band's sound was clearly special from the onset. Installed at Olympic Studios, recording for *Led Zeppelin* began in October 1968. Johns was instantly awestruck by the band's astounding musicianship: "I'd never heard arrangements of that ilk before, nor had I ever heard a band play in that way before—it was just unbelievable, and when you're in a studio with something as creative as that, you can't help but feed off it," he said.[21]

With Zeppelin and Johns focusing with laser-like intensity, the stunning sessions were completed in a mere nine days. From volcanic eruptions like "Good Times, Bad Times" and "Communication Breakdown," to epic bluesy workouts "You Shook Me" and "Dazed and Confused," to the acoustically textured "Baby, I'm Gonna Leave You" and "Black Mountain Side," the performances were incredible and the sound was utterly titanic. "I think it is one of the best sounding records I've ever done," Johns has said of the landmark.[22]

Subsequent to *Led Zeppelin*'s completion, disagreements over producing credit surfaced. Johns was only awarded a "director of engineering credit," while Page was credited as the sole producer. Unfortunately, Johns still remained only an engineer in the eyes of most English bands. Johns contends that, in an avaricious move, Zeppelin went back on a verbal agreement and refused to pay him his fair share for co-producing. "There's no question at all that I co-produced the record with them. Listen to it; it's got me all over it, and if anybody's got half an earhole they can tell what I did. Just compare the album I made with them to the next one (*Led Zeppelin II*) and my contribution is obvious," he said.[23] Johns's point is well taken. As mighty as *Led Zeppelin II*'s material is, its sound is as muddy as its brown album cover. Strangely, Page had initially invited Johns to work on *Led Zeppelin II*, but he quickly declined and never worked with the band again.

While Johns was beginning to establish a name as a producer, he continued to take prestigious engineering assignments, including one for the Beatles' ill-fated *Get Back* album. With the band unhappy with the recordings, and its release in serious jeopardy, Johns was asked to piece together a temporary version of the album from the countless boxes of recordings. True to his production aesthetics, Johns's mix emphasized the ragged aspects of the performances, as he chose to include in-studio banter and false starts. Ostensibly crafting a Beatles bootleg in the process, Johns's album mix is as ironic as it is raw, considering that the band perhaps best exemplified the "produced record." Initially, the irony was lost on the Beatles themselves. They hated Johns's mix, and the album was indefinitely shelved.

Surprisingly, while the Beatles were well into cutting *Abbey Road*, the band's final studio album, if returned to Johns. "I got a call from John and Paul asking me to meet them at EMI, which I duly did. They pointed to a big pile of tapes in the corner, and said 'Remember that idea you had about putting together an album?' and I said yes. They said, 'Well there are the tapes—go and do it,'" he said.[24]

Johns was "absolutely petrified," but obviously flattered.[25] He had just been asked to produce the Beatles! The assignment was as arduous as it was daunting, as Johns sifted through the mountains of recording tape like a junk scavenger with a metal detector. After countless hours, he finally crafted a finished version of *Get Back*. Sticking to his bold bootleg idea, Johns eschewed any overdubs and included several false starts along with jokey banter from the band. Despite the acrimonious tension of the sessions, Johns made sure to preserve the unique camaraderie that still existed within the band. McCartney was enthused over Johns's rough mix, but Lennon and Harrison were not so enamored, and it was rejected. Shortly after, the tapes were handed to Phil Spector, who controversially lavished string and choral overdubs onto the album, newly renamed *Let It Be*. In his typically blunt fashion, Johns has since characterized Spector's final mix as everything from "embarrassing"[26] to "utter puke."[27]

As the 1970s dawned, Johns quickly rebounded from the *Get Back* disappointment. Album rock was on the rise, and his career was about to kick into overdrive.

• • • • •

By 1970, the Who had clawed its way to the top of the rock heap with its rare pairing of brawn and brains. After the rock opera triumph *Tommy* and the pedal-to-the-metal *Live at Leeds*, the band went to work on Pete Townshend's lofty concept album, *Lifehouse*. Drawing on elements of science fiction and Meher Baba-influenced mysticism, the project was originally envisioned as an elaborate mixed media coupling of film and music. Unfortunately, Townshend was over-reaching, and by the spring of 1971 the project stalled. The Who had already recorded over 20 songs for the project with producer Kit Lambert, but Townshend was unhappy with the production's lack of cohesion. To salvage the situation, he turned to Johns, the band's old engineer from its Talmy days, to remix the songs.

After scrutinizing the existing tapes, Johns suggested the band scrap any traces of *Lifehouse* and re-record the best songs from scratch. Townshend trusted Johns's musically savvy instincts and the decision was made to take the strongest existing material and craft it into a traditional collection of stand-alone songs. Looking to instill fresh atmosphere into the material, Townshend wanted to try some of the re-recording at Mick Jagger's country manor, Stargroves. Having previously engineered a number of *Sticky Fingers* sessions there, Johns agreed that it was a good idea, and arrangements were made.

Although the concept of *Lifehouse* was convoluted, the songs on their own were proving to be as accessible as they were radical. Townshend frequently incorporated new synthesizer technology into the songs, and his prompt mastery of both the ARP and the Moog lent a fresh dimensionality to the compositions. With the Rolling Stones' sixteen-track mobile studio parked out in front of Stargroves, the band set up in the mansion's long hallway and tackled new versions of *Lifehouse*'s defiant centerpiece, "Won't Get Fooled Again," and the rollicking, gypsy-themed "Going Mobile." The new versions succeeded in liberating the songs from their doomed concept album trappings, and the remainder of the sessions moved to Olympic Studios.

The sessions progressed spectacularly through May and June for the album newly titled *Who's Next*. Townshend was thrilled with John's expertise: "We were just astounded at the sounds Glyn was producing. For the first time, the Who were recorded by someone who was more interested in the sound than in the image of the group. Glyn's not particularly interested in the Who image, whereas when Kit Lambert was producing us, that was all he cared he about."[28]

The Who
Who's Next
(1971)

Released in August 1971, *Who's Next* became the gold standard of '70s rock. From impassioned hard-rocking anthems "Baba O'Riley" and "Won't Get Fooled Again," to tough-but-tender ballads like "Behind Blue Eyes" and "Bargain," the album featured exuberant but nuanced performances by the band and magnificent sonic clarity from Johns. With its remarkable power and honesty, the album has endured as one of the most influential rock albums ever cut—and one of the few as revered by the rock underground as by the mainstream. Although his contributions were enormous, Johns was only awarded an "associate producer" credit on the album. Nonetheless, they had proven to be a fantastic team and, while they would never quite scale *Who's Next*'s heights again, Johns would continue to work with Townshend and the Who throughout the decade.

• • • • •

By the early '70s, rock had ditched most of its acid-tinged baroque hippie vibes in favor of an amphetamine-stoked, amps-to-eleven hard-rock style. Having already worked with nearly all of the British rock royalty, Johns had carved a reputation as perhaps the premiere hard rock producer, a perception that was furthered through two albums helmed for British bloozers, Humble Pie. Led by the diminutive but throaty ex–Small Faces shouter Steve Marriott and boyishly flashy guitarist Peter Frampton, the band had begun life as a pastoral late-1960s band in the eclectic mode of Traffic. However, by the time

Johns got to it for its self-titled 1970 release, Pie had begun to transition to a savage, take-no-prisoners hard rock style. The path was furthered the following year with the Johns-produced *Rock On*, which featured a white-hot, live-in-the-studio sound. With the inclusion of scorching boogie classics "Stone Cold Fever" and "Sour Grain," the album established Humble Pie as one of hard rock's mightiest bands, and its sound would influence contemporary acts ranging from the Black Crowes to Queens of the Stoneage.

Soon after, Johns turned his attention to a commercially unsuccessful band called the Faces. Rising out of the ashes of the Small Faces in 1969, the charismatic lineup featured bassist Ronnie Lane, organist Ian McLagan, and drummer Kenny Jones from the original band, along with guitarist Ronnie Wood and a singer named Rod Stewart. With a boozy sound that fell somewhere in between the Who and the Stones and a reputation for boisterous onstage carousing, the band could be alternately sloppy or masterful on any given night. When Johns signed on in 1971 to produce its third album, *A Nod's as Good as a Wink... to a Blind Horse*, Stewart was already becoming a worldwide solo star, and his personal wattage had begun to outshine his part-time band. Johns had longstanding friendships with Lane, McLagan, and Jones stretching back to the Small Faces days, but he was disdainful of Stewart's supremely cocky, bigger-than-the band attitude and his annoying predilection for constantly re-singing vocal tracks. "They were a fantastically exciting live band, but it became abundantly clear very early on that his solo success was where his real interests lay," Johns said of Stewart.[29]

Luckily, the issues between the two did not blemish the album, and *A Nod's As Good as Wink* became the band's best-selling release. Stoked by the thrilling single "Stay With Me," the release reached Number 6 and became the band's highest charting album. Johns returned two years later for the Faces' *Ooh La La*. Although the material was a tad spotty, the record still contained the tightly rocking songs "Cindy Incidentally" and "Borstal Boy," along with the wistful mandolin-strummed title track. But by then, Stewart's jet-set persona had far eclipsed the band's humble identity, and *Ooh La La* would become its swansong. With their zestfully unpretentious sound and devil-may-care attitude, the Faces albums have aged far more gracefully than many of their contemporaries. As a result, the Faces would become one of the few dinosaur bands championed by late '70s blank generation punk bands such as the Sex Pistols and the Damned, as well as later alternative acts from the Replacements, to REM, to Wilco.

• • • • •

As Johns's sterling credits piled up, the latest to come courting was an obscure American country-rock band called the Eagles. Recently signed to fledgling Asylum Records, the Eagles had a diamond-in-the-rough quality but lacked a cohesive sound. The band had long admired Johns's work, and the producer agreed to fly out to Colorado to see the Eagles perform in person. After watching the band sprint through a bland mishmash of Chuck Berry–style rock and lukewarm country-rock, Johns concluded that the band was "blatantly, bloody awful"[30] and flatly rejected its production offer.

Not taking no for an answer, Eagles manager David Geffen relentlessly pestered Johns to give the band one more chance. Geffen insisted that if he came out to one of its rehearsals, he would not be disappointed. Johns finally relented, but his low opinion remained unchanged as the band limply rocked out in front of him. Johns, after all, had worked with the greatest rock bands in the world, and in his mind the Eagles were not even on the same planet as the Stones, the Who, and the Faces. Never one to beat around the bush, Johns clearly let on that the band had again failed to impress him.

With Johns wholly unconvinced and the audition essentially blown, the Eagles took a break from its performance. After failing the second tryout, the pressure was off. Now relaxed, someone instinctually grabbed an acoustic guitar and the band broke out into a staggering four-part harmony. Like a bright lightening flash, Johns was struck with a glimpse of the band's capability. In that moment it became clear to him that the Eagles was a harmonic country-rock act, not a bash-it-out rock 'n' roll band. Suddenly intrigued by its country-rock possibilities, Johns made a dramatic about-face and agreed to produce its debut album.

Sessions for the Eagles debut began at Olympic in February 1972. Johns was unusually tough with the green band, and he rode the Eagles hard through grueling and long late-night rehearsal sessions. Displeased with the way the band was playing, Johns instituted a policy of no drugs in the studio, with the hope of sharpening up their questionable performances. Throughout the recording, band members Glenn Frey and Don Henley continuously harangued Johns into moving the album in a more rocking direction, but the producer was defiantly unyielding and insisted on keeping it on its acoustic course. By emphasizing Bernie Leadon's country banjo and delicate guitar picking, along with the band's crystalline harmonies, Johns was determined to do things his way.

As was his usual methodology, Johns set the group up in the studio as if it was playing live and rehearsed the band until the sound was just right. In typical fashion, once the arrangements were solidified, he worked quickly, and *Eagles* was completed in just two weeks. Expectedly, Frey and Henley were unhappy with the mellow country-rock sound taking precedence over their charging, Chuck Berry–like material, and they openly professed a dislike of the album. However, the release performed respectably and spawned Top 10 hits with the Jackson Browne–penned "Take It Easy" and the quasi-mystical "Witchy Women." With its laid-back country-rock sound, *Eagles* helped set the template for "California rock" and its subsequent decade-long chart domination.

Although the Eagles detested Johns's tyrannical methods, the band could not argue with its debut's success, and he was retained for their follow-up album, *Desperado*. Intended as something of a concept-album revolving around the old West's outlaw Dalton gang, Johns was pleased to see the band embracing the cowboy themes. Although its concept was promising, the actual material was generally weak and unfocused. As a result, the album was a commercial bomb, failing to break into the Top 40. The Eagles blamed Johns for making a record that was too country for rock audiences and too rock for country fans. Although Johns admittedly had poor instincts for hit singles, he always made sure he worked with artists who had a strong songwriting vision, but with *Desperado*'s tepid material, he found himself on unfamiliar terrain.

Despite the failure of *Desperado*, the Eagles retained Johns for *On the Border*, its decidedly harder rocking third album. Predictably, old issues quickly appeared between the band and the producer, and after six weeks in the studio only "The Best of My Love" and "You

Never Cry Like a Lover" had been deemed acceptable. Johns was fed up with the Eagles' lack of productivity. Feeling that the band had not accumulated enough quality material, he left the project and never worked with the Eagles again.

· · · · ·

Johns continued with notable projects throughout the decade, including the homespun Pete Townshend/Ronnie Lane album *Rough Mix*. Featuring contributions from Charlie Watts and Eric Clapton, the album featured a thoroughly enjoyable mix of lean rock and cozy folk, alternately sung by Lane and Townshend. He also mixed the Who's *Quadrophenia*, produced its underrated *Who By Numbers*, and co-produced its rock-solid 1978 follow-up, *Who Are You*—which hit Number 2 in the United States.

One of Johns's biggest commercial hits was scored on Eric Clapton's subdued 1977 album *Slowhand*. One of Clapton's most consistent and successful efforts, and an FM radio staple, the album was marked by the country-steeped smash single "Lay Down Sally," the laconic J.J. Cale-penned shuffle "Cocaine," and the moving pop "Wonderful Tonight." A year later Johns returned for Clapton's similarly low-key although less inspired *Backless*.

Johns also worked extensively with Joan Armatrading, helping her to become one of the more heralded female singer/songwriters of her generation. The West Indian–born Armatrading had kicked around since the early '70s, but her eclectic mixture of jazz and folk, soul and reggae, left her initial albums unfocused. In 1976, Johns stepped in for her eponymous third album, and his sympathetic, crystal-clear production finally garnered Armatrading the notice she deserved. He continued with Armatrading, producing several further releases for her through the end of the decade.

While his productions tailed off considerably through the '80s, Johns continued to work with quality artists. His endeavors included mixing the Clash's *Combat Rock*, a release that saw the former punk icons successfully move to mainstream rock mega-success. More recently, Johns has taken turns with alternative rock act Belly (*King*) and singer/songwriters Linda Ronstadt (*We Ran*), Nanci Griffith (*Storms*), and John Hiatt (*Slow Turning and Stolen Moments*). As his work has slowed down, Johns's son Ethan has followed the bloodline, engineering and producing albums for a number of alternative country and rock acts.

• • • • •

After *Goats Head Soup* in 1973, Jimmy Miller worked only sporadically through the rest of the 1970s. One of his finest efforts came with his production of ex-Millennium member Joey Stec's eponymous 1976 release, a latter-day sunshine pop/California rock mini-masterpiece. At the end of the decade he had a brief but concentrated flurry of activity. In 1979 he produced two influential albums for metal god Motörhead (*Bomber* and *Overkill*) and in 1980 the outrageous novelty punk debut from the Plasmatics (*New Hope for the Wretched*). He also presided over several sessions for ex–New York Doll/Keith Richards doppelgänger, Johnny Thunders.

After a long hiatus, Miller returned to action in the early 1990s, producing a single for beloved Scottish indie-rockers the Wedding Present. He also had a turn with Stones-worshipping Brits, Primal Scream; producing a couple of tracks on its '90s rock pillar, *Screamadelica*. Included on the influential album was the exciting "Movin' on Up," a cut that featured Miller's trademark, distinctly layered percussion sound.

Fatefully, Miller's substance-abusive lifestyle got the best him. In the early 1990s he had stopped using the drugs that derailed his career for nearly two decades, but sadly he replaced them with heavy drinking. In October 1994 he succumbed to liver failure, at the age of 52. However, the repercussions of Miller's vibe-driven recording technique are felt stronger than ever. In many ways his lack of engineering knowledge and non-technical vision portended the spontaneity-courting style of modern producers ranging from Brian Eno to Rick Rubin.

These days, one cannot listen for more than a few minutes to any classic rock radio station, watch a block of television commercials, or browse in nearly any store without hearing the handiwork Johns and Miller. The best of their productions clearly distill the timeless essence and enduring passion of rock. And while they often worked with the same bands, clearly each one brought his own aesthetic to the table. Indeed much of Miller's greatest contributions could only stem from his saintly patience and anything-goes cheerleader-like approach, in much the same way that Johns's best work resulted through his exacting, engineer-pedigreed approach.

KEY RECORDINGS
Jimmy Miller

Blind Faith –	*Blind Faith* (Atco 1969)
Delaney and Bonnie –	*On Tour with Eric Clapton* (Atco 1970)
Family –	"Scene Through the Eye of a Lens/Gypsy Woman" (Liberty 1967) "The Breeze," "Peace of Mind" (tracks appear on *Music in a Doll's House*) (Reprise 1968)
Wynder K. Frog –	*Out of the Frying Pan* (United Artists 1968)
Ginger Baker's – Air Force	*Ginger Baker's Air Force* (Atco 1970)
Motörhead –	*Overkill* (Bronze 1979) *Bomber* (Bronze 1979)
The Move –	"Blackberry Way" (Regal Zonophone 1968)
The Plasmatics –	*New Hope for the Wretched* (Stiff 1980)
Jim Price –	*Kid's Today Ain't Got No Shame* (A&M 1971)
Primal Scream –	"Movin' on Up," "Damaged" (tracks appear on *Screamadelica*) (Sire/Warner Bros. 1991)
The Rolling Stones –	"Jumpin' Jack Flash" (London 1968) "Street Fightin' Man" (London 1968) *Beggars Banquet* (Decca/London 1968) "Honky Tonk Woman/You Can't Always Get What You Want" (London 1969) *Let it Bleed* (London 1969) "Brown Sugar" (Rolling Stones 1971) *Sticky Fingers* (Rolling Stones 1971) *Exile on Main Street* (Rolling Stones 1972) "Tumblin' Dice" (Rolling Stones 1972) *Goats Head Soup* (Rolling Stones 1973) "Angie" (Rolling Stones 1973)
Savage Rose –	*Refugee* (Gregar 1972)
Sky –	*Don't Hold Back* (RCA 1970) *Sailor's Delight* (RCA 1971)

Spencer Davis Group –	"Gimme Some Lovin'" (United Artists 1966)
	"I'm a Man" (United Artists 1967)
	I'm a Man (United Artists 1967)
Spooky Tooth –	*It's All About* (Island 1968)
	Spooky Too (Island 1969)
	Tobacco Road (A&M 1971)
Joey Stec –	*Joey Stec* (Playboy 1976)
Johhny Thunders –	*Too Much Junkie Business* (ROIR 1983)
	In Cold Blood (New Rose 1983)
Traffic –	"Paper Sun/Giving to You" (Island 1967)
	"Hole in My Shoe/Smiling Phases" (Island 1967)
	"Here We Go 'Round the Mulberry Bush/Coloured Rain" (Island 1967)
	Mr. Fantasy (Island 1967)
	Traffic (Island 1968)
	"Medicated Goo/Shanghai Noodle Factory" (Island 1968)
	Last Exit (Island 1969)
Various Artists –	*The Rolling Stones Rock and Roll Circus* (Abkco 1996)
The Wedding Present –	"Boing!" (First Warning 1992)
Bobby Whitlock –	*Raw Velvet* (Dunhill 1972)

Glyn Johns

Joan Armatrading –	*Joan Armatrading* (A&M 1976)
	Show Some Emotion (A&M 1977)
Belly –	*King* (Sire/Reprise 1995)
Eric Clapton –	*Eric Clapton's Rainbow Concert* (engineered) (RSO 1973)
	"Lay Down Sally" (RSO 1977)
	Slowhand (RSO 1977)
	Backless (RSO 1978)
The Clash –	*Combat Rock* (mixed) (Epic 1982)
Bob Dylan –	*Real Live* (Columbia 1984)
Eagles –	"Take it Easy" (Asylum 1972)
	The Eagles (Aslylum 1972)
	"Witchy Woman" (Asylum 1972)
	Desperado (Asylum 1973)
	On the Border (Asylum 1974)
The Faces –	*A Nod Is As Good as a Wink...to a Blind Horse* (Warner Bros. 1971)
	"Stay With Me" (Warner Bros. 1971)
	Ooh La La (Warner Bros. 1973)

Fairport Convention –   *Rising for the Moon* (Island 1975)

Family –   *Family Entertainment* (Reprise 1969)

Fanny –   *Mother's Pride* (Reprise 1973)

Green on Red –   *This Time Around* (Mercury 1989)

Nanci Griffith –   *Storms* (MCA 1989)

The Groundhogs –   *Live at Leeds '71* (engineered) (EMI 2002)

John Hiatt –   *Slow Turning* (A&M 1988)
Stolen Moments (A&M 1990)

Humble Pie –   *Humble Pie* (A&M 1970)
Rock On (A&M 1971)

Ronnie Lane –   *Anymore for Anymore* (GM 1974)

Led Zeppelin –   *Led Zeppelin* (Atlantic 1969)

McGuinness Flint –   *Happy Birthday, Ruthy Baby* (Capitol 1971)

Midnight Oil –   *Place Without a Postcard* (Columbia 1981)

Nine Below Zero –   *Don't Point Your Finger* (A&M 1981)

The Ozark Mountain –   "Jackie Blue" (A&M 1975)
Devils

The Rolling Stones –   *Get Your Ya-Ya's Out* (London 1970)
Jamming With Edward (Rolling Stones 1972)

Linda Ronstadt –   *We Ran* (Elektra 1998)

Linda Ronstadt/ –   *Western Wall: The Tucson Sessions* (Elektra 1999)
Emmylou Harris

Boz Scaggs –   *Boz Scaggs and Band* (Columbia 1971)
Moments (Columbia 1971)

Small Faces –   "Itchycoo Park" (engineered) (Immediate 1968)

Steve Miller Band –   *Children of the Future* (Capitol 1968)
Sailor (Capitol 1969)
Brave New World (Capitol 1969)
Your Saving Grace (Capitol 1969)

The Subdues –   *Annunciation* (High Street 1994)

Pete Townshend/ –   *Rough Mix* (Polydor 1977)
Ronnie Lane

The Who –   *Who's Next* (Decca 1971)
"Behind Blue Eyes" (Decca 1971)
"Won't Get Fooled Again" (Decca 1971)
Quadrophenia (mixed) (MCA 1973)
Who By Numbers (MCA 1975)
"Who Are You" (MCA 1978)
Who Are You (MCA 1978)
It's Hard (MCA 1982)

Ron Wood/   *Mahoney's Last Stand* (Atco 1976)
Ronnie Lane –

THE SKY'S THE LIMIT:
R&B GOES FUNKY:
WILLIE MITCHELL AND
NORMAN WHITFIELD

In Midland, Texas in 1968 Willie Mitchell's Memphis-based
R&B band rehearsed for a show at a sawdust-floored roadhouse. As
a trumpeter and bandleader, Mitchell's career was at its apex, thanks
to the recently released instrumental hit "Soul Serenade." Relaxing
before the show, the dapper, pencil-thin mustachioed bandleader sat
at a table drinking a beer when a scrappy looking young man
approached him. The man sheepishly arrived at Mitchell's table and
introduced himself as the opening singer for the night's performance;
his name was Albert Greene. Mitchell racked his brain momentarily,
then asked: "Didn't you have a song sometime back...somethin'
about a train?"[1]

"'Back Up Train.' Yes, sir I did," Greene answered.[2]

"Never liked that song. Like trying to make somethin' out of
nothin',"[3] Mitchell said bluntly, sizing up the man's nappy hair and
ragged appearance.

Mitchell called over to his band—which included his horn-playing
brother James, a young trio of brothers with the last name of Hodges
and the venerable skinsman Al Jackson, Jr.—to rehearse the night's
opening singer. Freshly wounded by Mitchell's pointed criticism,
Greene took the stage and began to run through "Back Up Train." As
the band ably launched into the opening chords of the song, Greene
stepped to the microphone and began singing in a way he never had
before. Instead of performing the tune in its customarily gruff style,
Greene delivered it slowly and quietly, delicately caressing drama from
every syllable. The band sympathetically followed his smoothed-over
lead and skillfully downshifted the groove.

With just a few words, Willie Mitchell had inspired the young Greene to mine a previously uncharted region deep within him: "In that moment, the music had become a sweet meditation on making more out of less, putting the feeling in spaces instead of the notes," the singer said.⁴ The meeting between Mitchell and Greene would be among the most propitious of their lives. Within two years, Albert Greene would become Al Green, and, with Mitchell as his producer, the team would create some of the most memorable and timeless recordings in pop history.

• • • • •

Growing up in Ashland, Mississippi, Willie Mitchell was fascinated by the expressive harmonics of jazz trumpeters like Harry James and Roy Eldridge. At the age of eight he began to study the instrument and quickly demonstrated a natural musical talent. During high school he moved to the Southern music hub of Memphis, and quickly he cultivated a reputation as a skillfully swinging trumpeter, which led to a featured player spot in the popular local big bands of Al Jackson, Sr. and Tuff Green. Still a teenager, Mitchell got his first taste of the recording studio when he contributed to several early sessions for up-and-coming electric bluesman B.B. King.

By the late '40s, Mitchell had enrolled at Rust College, where he studied for three years under the auspice of Duke Ellington disciple Onzie Horne. An ambitious, natural born leader, Mitchell assembled his own seventeen-piece dance band and began to play a wide variety of gigs, from sporting events, to society formals. Particularly notable among the musicians his band backed was the blues master Howlin' Wolf, a larger-than-life figure who would repeatedly ridicule Mitchell's brainy be-bop style in an effort to get the group to play more down and dirty.

After a stint in the Army, Mitchell was back home and fronting his own combo again by the mid-1950s. Post-war Memphis was brimming with remarkable musical talent, and several future jazz luminaries passed through Mitchell's urbane outfit, including inventive hard-bop saxophonists Booker Little, Charles Lloyd, George Coleman, and the prodigious pianist Phineas Newborn, Jr. Mitchell continued to hone his chops by playing residencies at every important club in town, and on several occasions his group performed at private parties for Memphis's favorite son, Elvis Presley.

Mitchell's well-established local presence led to a producing gig with the Home of the Blues record label, and he began to work with popular Memphis R&B artists such as Roy Brown and the 5 Royales. After minimal success, Mitchell left Home of the Blues for another local label called Hi Records. Founded by a former Memphis record retailer named Joe Cuoghi, Hi Records was known as the "home of the instrumental" through a run of popular honking rockabilly sides from the likes of the Bill Black Combo and the "Yakety-sax" man, Ace Cannon.

Signed to double duty at Hi as a recording artist and producer, Mitchell's classy, swinging instrumentals helped keep the label going past the rockabilly era and through the 1960s. Following a slew of modest instrumental successes such as "Sunrise Serenade," "20-75," "Percolatin," "Buster Browne," and "Bad Eye," he finally broke into the R&B Top 10 in 1968 with the greasy-smooth dance tune "Soul Serenade." Mitchell toured the "chitlin circuit" virtually non-stop throughout the next two years in support of the hit, which led him to the fateful gig at the Texas roadhouse. It was there that Mitchell met his future, and his name was Al Greene.

• • • • •

As a child living in rural Jacknash, Arkansas, Albert Greene found music's divine inspiration everywhere—from church sing-alongs to the chirping melodies of the birds he heard from his bedroom window. Nearly everyone in his family sang, and when Greene was nine he and his three siblings formed a family gospel quartet called the Green Brothers. The group began to perform at various churches around town and soon became a local attraction. However, Greene loved pop music as much as gospel, and, after he was caught listening to the secular soul sounds of his idol Jackie Wilson, his church-devoted father fired him from the quartet. After his family relocated north to Grand Rapids, Michigan, the teen-aged Greene assembled the Creations, a new vocal group formed with some high school friends.

In early 1968 the Creations had become Al Greene and the Soul Mates, and the group scored an out-of-nowhere hit with the tough R&B shouter "Back Up Train." The song chugged all the way to the Top 5 on the R&B charts and even managed to scrape the Top 50 on the pop charts. Suddenly hot, the hit song took Greene and his group all the way to the hallowed Apollo Theatre. Their performance that night was legendary, evidenced by an unprecedented nine encores from the adoring Apollo crowd. Things looked bright for Greene, but, by the time he met Willie Mitchell later that year, his fortunes had turned. Unable to replicate the success of "Back Up Train," the impetuous singer had broken with the Soul Mates and was almost at the end of the line.

As Mitchell watched Greene deliver his improvised, slow-burning version of "Back Up Train," he caught a glimmer of something special in the singer. Hi Records's reputation as the "home of the instrumental" had become an albatross, and Mitchell was keenly aware that the times were beginning to pass the label by. A promising vocalist like Greene was just what the flagging label needed, but Mitchell played it cool. As the roadhouse rehearsal came to a close, Greene chatted Mitchell up, essentially giving him his life story in the process. He was sure he had charmed him into a production offer, but Mitchell simply wished him luck with an air of finality. Nearly destitute, Greene was crestfallen; it looked like his music career was over.

After the gig, Greene gave it one last desperate shot and hitched a ride in Mitchell's van for the long drive back to Memphis. With Greene precariously squatting on the hump in the van's front seat, sandwiched between Mitchell and his brother, the men bonded on the dark highway through the long Southern night. Finally, Greene bluntly asked if Mitchell he could make him a star. Mitchell assured him that he could, but there was a catch: It would take a year and half of hard work to get there. To Greene, who had been beaten down by the endless grind of one-night shabby club stands, eighteen months seemed like an eternity. When they finally reached Memphis early the next morning, Greene politely informed Mitchell that he could not wait a year and half longer to make it.

As Greene slowly prepared to hop out of the van by the side of the highway on the outskirts of Memphis, he had one more question

for Mitchell: Could he lend him $2,000 to pay back some debts he
had accrued back in Grand Rapids? Mitchell paused for a moment,
surprised by the audacious request, then he shot a glance over to his
brother and told him to bring the van over in front of a pay phone.
Moments later Mitchell returned to the van and told James to head
down to the bank for a withdrawal. Unbeknownst to Greene, the
money he was about to receive was actually an advance on a recording contract for Hi Records.

. . . . .

From the fertile Beale Street blues clubs to the rock 'n' roll cradle of Sam Phillips's Sun Studios, Memphis was the beating heart of
Southern music throughout the 1950s. Early in the following decade,
Memphis-based Stax Records emerged as a decided rough and tough
alternative to Detroit's commercially calculated, smoothly polished
Motown sound. Propelled by its estimable house band, Booker T. &
the MGs, and augmented by the Memphis Horns, Stax churned out
one thrillingly tough horn-punctuated hit after another for artists like
Rufus Thomas, daughter Carla Thomas, Otis Redding, and the MGs
themselves. When Mitchell became house producer at Hi in the mid-
1960s, he borrowed members from the Stax brood to cultivate his
own house band, commonly known as the Hi Rhythm Section.

Beginning in 1966, Mitchell began to revamp the Hi Rhythm
Section with younger musicians, including three Hodges brothers:
bassist Leroy, nicknamed "Flick" after his unique plucking style; guitarist Mabon, dubbed "Teenie" because of his diminutive size; and
pianist Charles, a.k.a. "Do Funny," inspired by his unusual swooping
keyboard style. Mitchell had taken the Hodges brothers in to his
home, essentially becoming a second father to the young men as he
molded them into his emerging musical vision. Rounding out the
band was second keyboardist Archie Turner, Mitchell's brother James
on sax, and Memphis mainstay drummer Al Jackson, Jr. Mitchell
worked closely with his young 20-something band, scrupulously
refining his clear-eyed "less is more" philosophy. Although the
rhythm section featured Stax's Jackson, and quite frequently its
famed Memphis Horn section, Mitchell was developing a sound that

eschewed the go-for-the-throat grittiness of Stax for a more subtly grooving sound.

It was around this time that Mitchell was approached by Back Beat Records's Don Robey to produce tortured Southern soul vocalist O.V. Wright. Like many others, Wright had spent his formative years on the gospel circuit before crossing over to the pop world. In 1964 Wright had originally recorded the searing ballad "That's How Strong My Love Is," but it was quickly eclipsed by Otis Redding's hit version for Stax and soon after memorably covered by the Rolling Stones. Employing the new Hi Rhythm Section, Mitchell produced Wright's heartbreaking "Eight Men, Four Women," a deep soul gem that clawed its way to Number 4 on the R&B charts in 1967. Thrilled by Wright's success, the Houston-based Back Beat quickly dispatched regal bluesman Bobby "Blue" Bland down to Memphis, where Mitchell produced half of his *A Touch of the Blues*.

While Mitchell continued to work closely with Wright for Back Beat on emotionally possessed powerhouses like "Ace of Spades" and "A Nickel and a Nail," Hi primarily remained a novelty R&B instrumental label. With the public's tastes markedly changing by the late 1960s, only Mitchell's own recording success was keeping the flailing Hi afloat. It was obvious that he needed to find a vocalist with crossover commercial potential if Hi was going survive into the coming decade. Fortunately, Mitchell soon got the break he needed after watching sultry St. Louis–bred singer Ann Peebles unleash a dynamo performance at Memphis's Rosewood Club in 1969. Promptly taken by Peebles's commanding voice and seductive stage presence, Mitchell approached her after her set and asked her where she lived. When Peebles answered, "St. Louis," Mitchell countered, "Not anymore."[5]

With Peebles initially splitting time between St. Louis and Memphis, Mitchell went to work on her debut Hi single, "Walk Away." Although the song was not the massive hit Mitchell was after, it did begin to establish a new identity for Hi, reaching a respectable Number 22 on the R&B charts. After a decent showing for the follow-up release, "Give Me Some Credit," Peebles finally landed an R&B Top 10 with the 1970 single "Part Time Love." While the diminutive singer demonstrated encouraging promise, her releases remained tethered to the R&B charts. It now became imperative to Mitchell to recruit a strong male vocalist with both black and white appeal to truly turn around Hi's waning fortunes. Fatefully, he found what he was looking for in the Midland Texas roadhouse....

• • • • •

It wasn't until years later that Al Greene realized that the $2,000 loan Mitchell gave him after their all-night van ride was actually a signing advance to Hi Records. As Greene rode a bus back to Grand Rapids, he began to reconsider the proposed eighteen-months-to-stardom plan. Once home, it became obvious that he had no future in the rather bleak Michigan town. His mind was made up. He took what was left of the loan, bought a used Ford, and drove straight to Mitchell's Memphis home. Perpetually playing it cool, Mitchell seemed unsurprised to see the singer, and he immediately whisked him across town to Royal Studios.

Located on the former site of the Royal Theatre movie palace, Royal Studios was the official recording headquarters for Hi Records. It still had its large lobby and candy counter, but the screen had been torn down. The ratty chairs had also been removed from the large sloping floor, and Mitchell soon discovered that the further down the slope the band was placed, the more the sound would separate and swell in size. The actual recording booth was archaic, with two Ampex four-track recorders that, had been connected together to form one makeshift eight-track recorder. Rather than the prevailing "solid state" circuitry of most studios, Mitchell's recording set up utilized tube-technology, and the acoustical warmth it generated was a paramount component of the seductive Hi sound.

Greene looked skeptically at the simple set up and asked if eight tracks were enough to do the job. Mitchell assured him that, in fact, he generally only used four of the tracks for most of his recordings—one for the drums, one for the bass, one for the guitar and keyboard, and the last held open for a vocal. Mitchell's sound was predicated on a combination of simplicity and execution, and employing a minimal amount of tracks enabled him to get the immaculately spacious sound he desired. Indeed, the modest set-up perfectly complemented the economically lean sound that he squeezed from his personally trained house band.

After his studio tour and introductions to the Hi band, Greene appeared to scoff at Royal's funky accommodations. Unsure of the shoddy set up, he told Mitchell that he had to think it all over. Greene spent the next three days shuffling aimlessly around Memphis before finally deciding he was ready to give himself over to Mitchell and his eighteen-months-to-stardom plan. It was 1969, and a new decade was dawning.

· · · · ·

With the 1970s looming, R&B was at a crossroads. Out on the West Coast, Sly Stone and his interracial, mixed-gender backup band, the Family Stone, had jubilantly merged the hard-driving rhythms of James Brown with a loopy horn-accentuated, acid fuzz-toned psyche-delic rock sound. Stone first came to prominence as an influential and outrageous San Francisco radio DJ, shaking up his station's rigid R&B music format with tracks from the Beatles and Dylan. His local notoriety led to a deal as house producer for Autumn Records, where he worked with a number of Bay Area garage rock acts, including the Mojo Men, the Great Society, and Bobby Freeman. He scored his most notable production success at Autumn with a streak of British Invasion–style hits for the Beau Brummels, including the harmonica-laced smash "Laugh, Laugh" in 1965.

Craving the spotlight himself, Stone formed Sly and the Family Stone in late 1966 and began to forge a revolutionary mixture of rock and soul whose edict was reflected in the title of its debut album, *A Whole New Thing*. Through its effortless blend of irresistible bass-slapping dance rhythms, free-form doo wop harmonies, and tripped-out studio innovations, Sly and the Family Stone ran off an inspiring string of pragmatic hits (including "Dance to the Music," "Everyday People," "You Can Make it If You Try," and "Stand,") that functioned as a rainbow bridge between the ever-widening chasms between black and white audiences. After the group's electrifying performance at Woodstock, Stone was catapulted to superstardom, and his dynamic sound revolution sent shockwaves rippling throughout the world of R&B. Perhaps most acutely feeling the effects was Motown's ascending producer, Norman Whitfield.

· · · · ·

*Psychedelic-soul
integrationists,
Sly and the
Family Stone*

Born in Harlem in 1943, Norman Whitfield's musical interests grew exponentially after his family relocated to Detroit in the late 1950s. Whitfield quickly glommed onto Detroit's talent-rich local musical scene, and by the time he was a teenager he had already finagled a job at Thelma Records as a songwriter and producer. While at Thelma he got his feet wet by working with local R&B combos like the Synetics and the Distants, although his early outings met with only minimal success. Unusually driven, Whitfield soon outgrew Thelma and began to hang around the hallowed halls of Motown Records just as the label was beginning to hit its stride. Whitfield's pesky persistence eventually paid off, and in 1962 he was offered a job in the label's shadowy quality control department.

With its bureaucratically compartmentalized system, Motown had separate departments for songwriters, musicians, artists, a finishing school for its performers, and an in-house test-marketing team called "quality control." Working for $15 a week, Whitfield would scrutinize stacks of demo recordings, assess their commercial viability, and report his findings to the label's executives. Using the quality control gig as a stepping-stone, Whitfield soon joined estimable talents Mickey Stevenson, Harvey Fuqua, and the holy trinity of Holland-Dozier-Holland in Motown's venerable songwriting department.

Competition with the intimidating songwriting talent was expectedly stiff, and Whitfield initially struggled to write material that could stand up against his far more experienced colleagues. Barely out of his teens, the lanky and reserved Whitfield continued to plug away and refine his skills through a succession of rejected songs. His first real break came when the song he had co-written with Eddie Holland, "I Couldn't Cry if I Wanted to," was cut by the Temptations, one of the label's newest and most promising acts. Whitfield was already well acquainted with the Temptations, having previously worked with several of its members at Thelma Records when they were part an earlier group, the Distants. Disappointingly, the song failed to catch on and Whitfield continued to toil somewhat anonymously in the songwriting department. In 1964 he finally broke out, writing the Marvelettes' wonderfully catchy "Too Many Fish in the Sea" and the soulful hand-jiving number "Needle in the Haystack" for the Velvettes. A year later, he would also helm the latter Girl Group's saucy Northern soul classic "Really Saying Somethin'."

From the beginning, Whitfield's goal at Motown was to arrange and produce, and with his recent successes he was finally given the opportunity to cut the Temptations' single "Girl (Why You Wanna Make Me Blue)." With charmingly mellifluous Smokey Robinson-produced hits like "The Way You Do the Things You Do" and "My Girl," the Tempts had climbed the ladder to become one of the crown jewels in Motown's budding dynasty. Unfortunately, Whitfield's "Girl (Why You Wanna Make Me Blue)" met with only modest favor, and, failing to make the Top 20, it was deemed a flop by Motown's rather lofty expectations.

Spoiled by success, Motown head Berry Gordy Jr. had little patience for failure, and Whitfield was relegated to producing secondary sessions and B-sides while Robinson was kept as the group's primary "A material" producer. Whitfield worked tirelessly to sharpen his songwriting acumen, and most of his early Temptations productions drew from his own compositions (usually co-written with

Eddie Holland and Barrett Strong). Sweetly soulful winners like "The Girl's Alright With Me," "Everybody Needs a Love," and "I Gotta Go Now," which all appeared on the late 1965 release, *Temptin' Temptations*, proved that Whitfield was finally becoming a functioning cog in the humming Motown machine.

After the Tempts' Robinson-produced 1966 single "Get Ready" barely scraped the Top 30, it became readily apparent that the group's sweet but tame sound was being muscled aside by the brawny deep Memphis soul of rising stars like Otis Redding, Wilson Pickett, and Sam and Dave. Meanwhile, Whitfield was beginning to pick up steam, after scoring with his expansive production of the Supremes' hit *I Hear a Symphony* album. Demonstrating that he was in tune with the shifting musical winds, he was given another shot with the Tempts. This time around, Whitfield came out of the gate strong with the David Ruffin–sung "Ain't Too Proud to Beg," a muscular R&B pleader that introduced a tougher-sounding Temptations, more in step with the turbulent times. Utilizing Motown's extraordinary house band, the Funk Brothers, Whitfield began to coax a considerably looser and more aggressive sound than the musicians had previously been permitted to explore.

Gordy was clearly dismayed with "Ain't Too Proud to Beg" and its tampering of the smooth and pleasant Motown formula, but its ascension to the Top 15 quickly muzzled his displeasure. Whitfield had finally proven himself and was ceded primary production control of the group. Keeping charismatic and versatile singer David Ruffin out in front as ostensible lead-vocalist of the Tempts, Whitfield continued the group's identity makeover on its glockenspiel-chiming follow-up R&B chart topper, "Beauty Is Only Skin Deep," and the scintillating "(I Know) I'm Losing You." By instilling a gospel-infused grittiness into the Tempts' inherently honeyed-harmonies, Whitfield's visceral productions ably answered the challenge mounted by his Memphis soul competitors.

· · · · ·

With his infectious songwriting and adventurous productions successfully shaking up Gordy's easily digestible formula, Whitfield had become Motown's top producer. Along with his stewardship of the Tempts, Whitfield also continued to write and produce fresh, hook-laden material for a number of other Motown artists. After an arduous journey through the Motown pipeline, one particularly unusual Whitfield song would eventually become one of pop music's greatest triumphs.

The song first came together in the middle of 1966, after songwriter Barrett Strong approached Whitfield with a new melody he had been toying with. Strong (who's own 1960 hit, "Money," had helped Gordy originally build his Motown empire) had left the label more than a year earlier in a bid for independence. Finding little success outside of Motown's confines, Strong hoped to be allowed back into the family fold with his latest song. Whitfield listened attentively as Strong plunked out some Ray Charles–inspired gospel piano fragments and sang the only words he had thus far: "I heard it through the grapevine." Whitfield's eyes lit up immediately; he knew this could be the song that could make his career, and he and Strong quickly went to work on finishing the tune.

By August, the duo had completed "Grapevine," and Whitfield began deliberating over which Motown artist to entrust it to. Reputedly, it was originally intended for the recently signed Isley Brothers, but instead it was given over to label perennials Smokey Robinson and the Miracles. Unfortunately, Smokey's breezy rendition fell far short of conveying the inner turmoil that boiled beneath the song's surface. With his producer's mentality, Whitfield was a firm believer that song quality was a far greater factor than the artist who sang it, and in turn he blamed its subsequent failure on Robinson's mismatched lilting delivery.

Whitfield remained committed to exposing "Grapevine's" raw-nerved emotion and went back in the studio six months later; in a brilliant move he slowed the song's tempo to an ominous crawl. Seeking to bring out its anguished tension even further, he fashioned a starkly percussive arrangement replete with slinky high-hat, rattling gypsy tambourine, and reverberating electric piano, which was joined by loping bass, slithering strings, forlorn trumpet, and luscious female backing vocals. With the song completely reworked, Whitfield recruited Marvin Gaye to give the bold new version a shot.

With his irrepressible charm and astounding talent, Gaye was among Motown's most dynamic and popular performers. Having racked up numerous debonair hits such as "Hitch Hike," "Can I Get a Witness," "Pride and Joy," in addition to a string of stirring duets with Mary Wells, Kim Weston, and Tammi Terrell, Gaye had become one of R&B's top male vocalists. Like the title of one of his songs, Gaye truly was "a stubborn kind of fellow" and, with the headstrong Whitfield calling the shots, the two volatile personalities were often at odds during the recording. As a result, the session often became a test of will between Gaye and Whitfield that teetered on the brink of violence on more than one occasion.

Further fanning the contemptuous flames was Whitfield's unorthodox insistence that Gaye sing "Grapevine" in a key higher than his natural range—an artist-irking technique that the producer would continue to employ throughout his career. Although Gaye was one of the label's biggest stars, he still rated below the producer in Motown's hierarchy of power. Forced to defer to Whitfield's stringent demands, Gaye's throat veins literally bulged as he painfully strained to hit the song's high notes—but the producer was clearly on to something and succeeded in coaxing one of the most heartbroken and vulnerable vocals of all-time from Gaye.

With Gaye's "Grapevine" resting in the can, Whitfield had to engage in yet another struggle on the song's behalf. This time the battleground was the label's quality control department—ironically, the very place where he had begun his Motown career five years earlier. One of the department's many litmus tests involved pitting prospective Motown releases against the current Top 5 hits and analyzing if the songs fit any of the current molds. Clearly though, Whitfield's revolutionary "Grapevine" was out to break a mold, not to congeal to one. Ever the conservative, Gordy made the call not to release the song as a single and instead selected Gaye's rather tame romantic ballad "Your Unchanging Love." Whitfield exploded when the word trickled down to him of Gordy's decision. But vindication came quickly after "Your Unchanging Love" promptly bombed on the charts, and Whitfield renewed his campaign for the release of Gaye's "Grapevine."

Seething and indignant over Gordy's snub, Whitfield flagrantly usurped his authority by reworking the song into an up-tempo Aretha Franklin–like gospel number. Unbeknownst to Gordy, he then surreptitiously recorded the new version with Motown's Gladys Knight and the Pips. Less daring than Gaye's version, the song was green-lighted for release, and it lodged itself at the Number 2 spot on the pop charts for three weeks in December 1967. Whitfield would subsequently produce two additional Top 20 hits for Knight, "Nitty Gritty" and the thrilling "Friendship Train."

Reinvigorated by Knight's hit version, Whitfield continued to mercilessly hound Gordy into releasing Gaye's "Grapevine" to the point of obsession. Ultimately forcing a showdown, Gordy angrily warned Whitfield that he would be fired if he mentioned the song again. Despite the warnings, Whitfield's dogged determination persisted and finally, in a move of appeasement, Gordy agreed to tack the song on to Gaye's 1968 album, *In the Groove*. Seemingly buried on the album, it wasn't until three months later that a Chicago disc jockey named Phil Jones started playing the album cut on his popular evening show. From the first moment Jones dropped the needle on Gaye's "Grapevine," the phones lit up like a Christmas tree. A phenomenon was born.

Motown quickly took note, rushed the song out as a single, and hastily renamed the album *I Heard It Through the Grapevine*. The song hogged the top spot on the pop charts for an incredible seven weeks, eventually sold over four million copies, and became Motown's biggest selling record of all time. Trying to replicate their success, Whitfield helmed Gaye's 1969 follow-up *That's the Way Love Is*. Although the "Grapevine"-like title cut was a classic, Gaye was already working towards recording autonomy, which would soon be achieved on his self-produced 1971 watershed, *What's Goin' On*.

Coinciding with Motown's rush release of "Grapevine" was the Temptations' mind-blowing "Cloud Nine"—yet another revolutionary Whitfield production that reached stores in the same autumn week of 1968. With his drug-themed wide-screen production of "Cloud Nine," Whitfield's makeover of the Temptations, from old-school balladeers into Motown's resident funky bunch, was complete. To complement the changing sound came a change in image, as group members

Marvin Gaye
In the Groove
(1968)

ditched their clean-cut appearance and matching suits in favor of nappy afros, paisley shirts, striped bellbottoms, and assorted hippie accoutrements like Indian headbands and colorful knotted scarves.

Further hastening changes within the group was the regrettable departure of David Ruffin, who bolted after the group refused his demand to be billed as David Ruffin and the Temptations. Under Whitfield's auspice, Ruffin had magnificently sung most of the group's recent leads, including their glorious Top 5 hit "I Wish It Would Rain," but with his elevated visibility the singer now considered himself bigger than the group. Finding a suitable replacement for the gifted, though difficult, Ruffin was daunting. Finally, the less mannered but appropriately earthy-voiced Dennis Edwards was recruited from Motown's atypically raw act, the Contours.

Co-written by Whitfield and Strong, "Cloud Nine"'s charging conga rhythms, fluttering wah-wah guitar, counterpoint harmonies, alternating fire and brimstone lead vocalists, and overt drug references (a particular sticking point with Gordy) became the producer's boldest step yet toward updating the Tempts and Motown. Whitfield, who himself had recently grown out his own afro, had clearly fallen under the psychedelic-soul spell cast by freak-flag wavers Jimi Hendrix, Funkadelic, and especially Sly and the Family Stone. As one of the few at Motown in tune with the new world, Whitfield took it upon himself to uphold the famous company motto, "The Sound of Young America." In January 1969 "Cloud Nine" floated its way to a Number 6 spot on the pop charts just as Gaye's "Grapevine" was

The Temptations
Cloud Nine
(1969)

enjoying its reign at Number 1. Inarguably, Whitfield's Motown risks had netted remarkable rewards.

While the full-length album *Cloud Nine* still featured several straightforward R&B ballads, it was also home to "Run Away Child, Running Wild," a song that, along with "Cloud Nine," obliterated the compact Motown formula. A socially conscious slab of heavy funk rhythms, whiplash guitar, and fervent group vocals, the densely layered story-song stretched out for an amazing nine and a half minutes. In an edited form, it also became a hugely successful single. From now on, there was no looking back to the Motown sound of old.

Mightily assisting Whitfield's brazen Motown remodeling was a newer and younger crop of Funk Brothers. Making significant contributions was drummer Uriel Jones, who supplanted the legendary Benny Benjamin after his passing in 1968, and bassist Bob Babbitt, who admirably filled the enormous shoes of the increasingly flaky James Jamerson. Also making their presence felt were Dennis Coffey and Melvin "Wah-Wah" Ragin, versatile guitarists who were as at home with slashing funk as they were with acid rock.

Whitfield's preferred song construction method was having Jones ride a cymbal for several minutes, after which the producer would inevitably call out for a bass drum accent. Then he would order as many as a dozen Funk Brothers to join in and jam until settling into a satisfactory groove. In similar fashion to Phil Spector's unyielding taskmaster approach, Whitfield worked the musicians hard through elongated sessions—and, like Spector, he had become the star and focal point of the recordings himself. Although his demanding, unorthodox ways often rankled the Funk Brothers, the consistently golden results the sessions netted proved that there was a method to Whitfield's madness.

Taking full advantage of the talents of the revamped Funk Brothers, as well as improving studio technology, Whitfield crafted a succession of colorfully funky releases for the Tempts through the late '60s. Saturating the recordings in copious amounts of echo, over-the-top stereo panning, and a multitude of other stony sound effect gimmickry, Whitfield's own presence loomed larger with each release. Removing the last traces of the old Tempts' sound, 1969's *Puzzle People* became the first album to fully integrate Whitfield's lavishly psychedelic multi-tracked vision. From the wah-wah and enveloped harpsichord "Message From a Black Man," to the hard-bitten horns and playful party-in-the-studio ambience of "I Can't Get Next to You," to the fuzz guitar and bass freakout that overtakes the middle section of the epic chain-gang tale "Slave," Whitfield freely experimented on every track, deftly fading instruments in and out of the mix at will.

Puzzle People's most experimental mix was reserved for the Tempts' stab at the Isley Brothers recent hit "It's Your Thing." With its thumping bass, ultra-echoed mix, and continuously rising and falling recording levels, the song is a precursor to the forthcoming early '70s dub experiments of Jamaican producers Lee Perry and King Tubby. Additionally prescient was Whitfield's method of incorporating lyrics from previous hit songs into new ones, a technique that prefigured hip-hop sampling by two decades. The group's cover of "Hey Jude" weaves in a line from "Runaway Child, Running Wild" and from "Don't Let the Joneses Get You Down," borrows from "Cloud Nine" and "Message From a Black Man," and snatches a bit from James Brown's "Say It Loud (I'm Black and I'm Proud)."

By the time of 1970's *Psychedelic Shack*, Whitfield and Strong were writing virtually all of the group's material. With its curious embracing of oddly passé flower power themes, *Psychedelic Shack* is in many ways a time warp back to 1967 and the Summer of Love that originally passed Motown by. Nonetheless, Whitfield's production trickery was highly compelling, especially on the fuzz-drenched hit title track, which rushes in on a savage wave of wah-wah distortion and free jazz drums and again samples lyrics from an earlier song

("I Can't Get Next to You"). Fittingly, the song's incessant guitar line itself was sampled 20 years later on Public Enemy's menacing hip-hop touchstone "Welcome to the Terrordome." Other notable *Psychedelic Shack* cuts include the nearly avant-garde string arrangement on "You Make Your Own Heaven and Hell Right Here On Earth," the supremely spaced-out eight-and-a-half-minute "Take a Stroll Thru Your Mind," and the elongated "Friendship Train," which is enhanced by panning train sound effects and continuously shifting percussion.

Whitfield continued to triumph with the Tempts on the fantastic state-of-the-world smash single "Ball of Confusion (That's the World Is Today)" and on 1971's transitional *Sky's the Limit*. Downplaying the hippie themes in favor of a decidedly more urban sensibility, *Sky's the Limit* was distinguished by the dreamy Eddie Kendricks–sung ballad "Just My Imagination (Running Away With Me)," a Number 1 pop hit that ranks among the group's finest performances. Also included was the sinister "Smiling Faces Sometimes," twelve minutes of creeping urban paranoia that would soon become a Top 3 hit for Whitfield's newest group, the Undisputed Truth.

During the *Sky's the Limit* sessions Kendricks left to pursue a solo career and new recruit Damon Harris was enlisted to fill his falsetto spot. Troubled founding member Paul Williams exited shortly after Kendricks and was ably replaced by tenor Richard Street. Sadly, a year and half later the alcohol-plagued Williams (who had continued to oversee the group's onstage choreography) would die from a self-inflicted gunshot wound.

With the Tempts' new lineup in tow, Whitfield helmed 1972's *Solid Rock*, another winning effort that moved the band closer into outright funky soul territory. The album was marked by the rocking "Superstar (Remember How You Got Where You Are)," a pointed swipe at ex-members Ruffin and Kendricks, the delicately arranged social commentary "Take a Look Around," a stretched-out take on Bill Withers' "Ain't No Sunshine," and the killer funk "What It Is?" Only a cover of Edwin Starr's "Stop the War Now," the most tedious of all Whitfield's sprawling sound-collages, revisited the protest themes of previous releases. Notably, the producer's puppet-master image continued, evidenced by *Solid Rock*'s inside cover, which featured a photo of Whitfield and Strong that was as large as the accompanying photo of the Tempts themselves.

• • • • •

Compounded by Otis Redding's 1967 death in a plane crash and exacerbated by Whitfield's successfully updated Motown sound, Memphis soul was free-falling out of commercial favor by the end the 1960s. While Greene had largely patterned his earthy vocal approach on Redding's gruff style for his early hit "Back Up Train," Mitchell knew he needed to coax a more mellow and sophisticated sound to soothe the ears of the battle-wearied public. With his emerging new Mitchell-dictated style, the singer dropped the extra "e" on his last name and was now simply Al Green.

Summarily, Mitchell went to work on seasoning his new protégé. Sensing an almost unlimited reservoir of versatility and vocal expression, Mitchell began to experiment with a wide variety of material for Green to tackle—from jazz standards, to contemporary country, to British Invasion rock. With Hi's well-oiled rhythm machine setting a spare, laid-back groove, Mitchell exhorted Green to slow down his phrasing and soften up his timbre to a whisper. He wanted him not just to sing the lyrics but to *feel* them, explaining that it was the band's responsibility to be rough and gritty on the bottom and Green's job to be smooth and silky on the top.

Mitchell continued to rehearse Green for several months, fostering the singer's emerging style and bolstering his confidence in a relaxed and unhurried atmosphere. Finally, Mitchell was convinced that Green was ready to record, but the resulting 1970 album *Green Is Blues* was somewhat of a tentative affair. It featured much of the wide range of material that Green had been rehearsing the previous months, including covers of Gershwin's "Summertime," the Temptations' "My Girl," the Box Top's "The Letter," and the Beatles' "Get Back," but the arrangements and vocal performances lacked the subtly assured sound of impending releases. Further sealing its fate was the miscalculation to release the album's other Beatles cover, "I Want to Hold Your Hand," as a single. A glaring misstep, the inappropriately chosen song flopped miserably and almost doomed the Mitchell/Green partnership.

More determined than ever, the duo rebounded strongly on the rapidly recorded follow-up, *Al Green Gets Next to You*. Green's highly personal style began to emerge on several of its cuts, especially on the swaggering reworking of the Temptations' Whitfield-penned "I Can't Get Next to You" and his own deeply sensual "Tired of Being Alone." The latter featured an amazing desperation-soaked vocal that managed to be restrained, yet commanding and was augmented by sweetly staccato brass punctuation (from the Memphis Horns), placid backing vocals (from the mixed gender trio Rhodes, Chalmers, and Rhodes), and the smooth-as-glass Hi Rhythm Section. Drawing on his gospel roots, Green peppers the song with leaping falsetto improvisations that appear out of nowhere before neatly resolving back into the lyrics. Mitchell's lushly tight production is as crisp as a freshly minted $100 bill, as he seamlessly places Al Jackson's trademark tom-tom on the backbeat rhythm gently over a cozy bed of glistening Hammond organ, low-booming bass, and spare jazzy guitar chords.

A decided counterpoint to the sprawling and busy psychedelic soul experiments undertaken by Whitfield, Mitchell's sound was uncluttered and succinct. Following the sudden heart attack death of Hi founder Joe Cuoghi in 1970, Mitchell had become the label's principal administrator as well as its chief producer. Firmly convinced that the fresh "Tired of Being Alone" was destined for success, Mitchell took to the road himself, wining and dining radio station program directors from New York to Chicago. His exhaustive efforts eventually paid off, and, several months after its May '71 release, the song rose to Number 11 on the pop charts. R&B had a new star and a new silkily romantic sound just in time for the 1970s.

Attempting to sustain the momentum of "Tired of Being Alone," Mitchell called Green into the studio and presented him with a rough musical sketch of a new song that he and Al Jackson had worked up. Due to its laconic metronome-like groove that was even more mellow than "Tired of Being Alone," Green was reluctant to embrace the song. Green still saw himself as an energetic Otis Redding/Jackie Wilson–type shouter and defiantly lobbied to release the up-tempo "You Say It" as the next single. However, Mitchell was adamant, and to get Green more connected to the song he dispatched him to write its lyrics. Fifteen minutes later Green returned with the words to a song he titled "Let's Stay Together." Still not totally convinced that the laid-back style suited him, Mitchell strong-armed Green into softening up on the

Al Green
Let's Stay Together
(1972)

vocals, insisting that he sing certain sections in falsetto and slightly behind the beat, rather than straight on it. Once they had the sound right, Mitchell insisted Green clean up his look by cutting his bushy longhair and abandoning his casual garb for stylish wide-lapelled suits. Green's new dashing lover-man image was now solidified.

Within two weeks of its release, "Let's Stay Together" was in the Top 10 on the R&B charts, and two weeks later it was Number 1, where it remained for the following nine weeks. Even better, it conquered the top spot on the pop charts in February 1972, knocking Don McLean's "American Pie" out of its monthlong residency at Number 1. The horn- and string-sweetened warm and mellow groove was the full embodiment of Mitchell's sublime crossover vision, and it became the benchmark for all romantic soul music that has followed it.

At its core the song was a straightforward appeal for sustained fidelity, but, bathed in the gloriously warm glow of the buoyant Hi Rhythm Section and the tantalizing Memphis Horns, the song suggests something larger to a public wearied by years of strife and division: "whether times are good or bad or happy or sad...c'mon now let's stay together" Green sings backed by the sweet vocals of Rhodes, Chalmers, and Rhodes. There is a rare spiritual reassurance to be found in the song that calmly lets us all know everything's going to be okay.

Catalyzed by the runaway success of "Let's Stay Together," Green and Mitchell embarked on a fabulous run of albums that continued to refine and expand their lushly sensual, mellow sound. As Green's confidence soared, so did his stylistic versatility, and he effectively recorded everything from country weepers like Willie Nelson's "Ain't It Funny How Time Slips Away" and Kris Kristofferson's "For the Good Times," to the Bee Gees' poignant "How Can You Mend a Broken Heart," to Roy Orbison's immortal rocker "Oh, Pretty Woman" with amazing ease. Green's biggest hits were the seductively soaring originals he worked up with Mitchell like "You Ought to Be With Me," "I'm Still in Love With You," "Look What You've Done for Me," "Take Me to the River," and "Love and Happiness."

Mitchell's now-well-honed formula usually involved Jackson and him working up the basic feel of a tune together, then playing it for Green, who would fashion lyrics around the melody. Once that was accomplished, Green would cut his vocals over a spare rhythm with bassist "Flick" Hodges, and either Jackson (who played on the majority of the sure-fire singles) or alternate drummer Howard Grimes (who played on most of the album cuts) on drums. Loyally maintaining his simple double four-track recorder set up, Mitchell rarely treated Green with any type of studio effects other than an occasional pinch of echo. Once the vocals had been recorded, Mitchell would call in the rest of the band and build up the finished version of the song, fitting instruments together like pieces in a jigsaw puzzle.

After solidifying their soul-defining sound on *Let's Stay Together* and *I'm Still in Love With You*, the Green and Mitchell partnership reached its zenith on 1973's *Call Me*. With its amorous combination of sinewy grooves, intimate arrangements, and Green's extraordinarily quiescent vocals, the album was a masterpiece of simmering three-o'clock-in-the-morning blue-light passion. Several of the album's cuts were written by Green himself, including the fragile "Your Love is Like the Morning Sun," the dove-like "Have You Been Making Out O.K.," and its trio of enrapturing velvety hits "Call Me (Come Back Home)," "You Ought to Be With Me," and "Here I Am (Come and Take Me)." The years of hard work had paid off, and *Call Me* achieved the rare combination of commercial and artistic success.

• • • • •

Al Green
Call Me
(1973)

While Motown artists like Marvin Gaye and Stevie Wonder had achieved artistic control and production autonomy by the early 1970s, Norman Whitfield continued to consistently score hits for the label through his total-control approach. In 1970, he co-wrote and produced Edwin Starr's Number 1 hit "War," an anthem that had originally been slated for the Temptations. He was behind white rock band Rare Earth's marvelously driving Top 10 take on the Tempts' "(I Know) I'm Losing You" and helmed its worthy 1973 funk release *Ma*, which was highlighted by the mesmerizing side-long title cut and the clavinet-strutting "Big John is My Name." Whitfield also assembled the Undisputed Truth, a vocal trio originally consisting of Joe Harris, Brenda Joyce, and Billie Rae Calvin.

Working in similar multi-tracked terrain as his Tempts productions, Whitfield freely experimented on a slew of early-1970s albums with the Undisputed Truth. Often he used the group's recordings as a sound laboratory for material he would then refine on Tempts albums, including the landmark pocket-funk opera "Papa Was a Rolling Stone." His greatest success with the group came in 1971 with its doom-laden version of "Smiling Faces Sometimes," a song that uneasily channeled the zeitgeist of powder-keg racial tensions and tenuous urban renewal. Galvanized by a haunting melody, socially relevant themes, a menacing pace, and kitchen-sink production touches, "Smiling Faces Sometimes" was one of Whitfield's most glorious productions.

With the Temptations 1972 album *All Directions*, its first album to feature musician credits, Whitfield's move from psychedelic-soul towards urban funk was complete. He had been injecting social commentary into densely constructed R&B since "Cloud Nine," but it was *All Directions'* Number 1 smash single "Papa Was a Rolling Stone" that brought his vision to its full commercial and artistic fruition. Again co-written with Strong, the song snaked to over eleven completely engaging minutes in its unedited album guise.

The song begins with a hypnotically long instrumental introduction of swishing hit-hat percussion, earth-shaking repetitive bass, lacerating wah-wah guitar, and teasingly devilish strings (fashioned by brilliant Motown arranger Paul Riser). After what seems like an eternity, the extended opening instrumental passage finally gives way to vocalist Dennis Edwards's hard-knock life recollections, before ultimately arriving at the unforgettable pathos-laden chorus: "Papa was a rolling stone/Wherever he laid his hat was his home/And when he died all he left us was alone." Undisputedly a watershed musical moment, the song almost single-handedly ushered in a new era of socially aware R&B. Like wildfire, "Papa Was a Rolling Stone"'s wah-wah-powered frankness permeated everything from Curtis Mayfield's milestone *Superfly* to the regally urban "Sound of Philadelphia" productions for groups like the O'Jays and Harold Melvin and the Bluenotes, undertaken by Gamble and Huff and their baroque arrangement-embracing associate Thom Bell.

Whitfield followed the triumphant *All Directions* with the Tempts' gritty inner-city song-cycle *Masterpiece*. Whitfield had broken with Strong and was now writing all of the group's material himself. As a result, the group had become little more than a vehicle for his increasingly elaborate productions, as evidenced by the nearly sidelong orchestral title track and the meandering but effectively anguished junkie-themed "Hurry Tomorrow." Further solidifying the producer's Svengali-like reputation was the album's back cover, which featured a small image of a white-suit-clad Temptations sprouting from Whitfield's giant afro. The album barely cracked the Top 30, and, while the severely edited title track became a top R&B chart hit, it failed to successfully crossover to the pop charts—a bitter disappointment coming in the wake of the monumentally successful "Papa Was a Rolling Stone."

Whitfield's final Tempts outing with would come in late 1973 with the futuristic *1990*. One of the most underrated funk releases of the entire decade, *1990* not only attempts to predict the future—it actually succeeds. With the scathing indictments of systemic American corruption and racial injustice featured in "Ain't No Justice" and "1990," Whitfield's commentaries were at their most biting and provocative. Even more prescient was the construction of the title track, which used stuttering rhythm machine beats (first introduced to R&B on Sly Stone's chilling 1971 masterwork, *There's a Riot Goin' On*), clipped James Brown-like staccato guitar rhythms, and disembodied snatches of vocal harmony to portend the foundation of modern hip-hop.

Equally astounding was the mind-moonshot "Zoom," which attempted to escape the bleak ghetto environment of the rest of the album for the freedom and equality of zero-gravity outer space. A proto-chillout fifteen-minute masterwork, "Zoom" slowly unfurls over a montage of overlapping vocals, floating orchestral flourishes, an echo-encrusted chorus, and spacious electronic textures. Rather appropriately, the elaborately hedonistic track became the final stop on Whitfield's dazzling Temptations odyssey.

• • • • •

With their addictive sound firmly established, Mitchell and Green continued to successfully apply the formula on top-shelf mid-1970s releases *Livin' for You, Al Green Explores Your Mind*, and *Al Green is Love*. Their in-studio routine had become so well established by that point that Green would cut his vocals and then completely entrust the arrangements and final mix to Mitchell. By the time of 1976's ironically titled *Full of Fire*, the formula had finally begun to run on fumes. Always an enigmatic personality, Green had gone through a spiritual transformation first hinted at on *Call Me*'s benediction-like "Jesus is Waiting" and *Livin' for You*'s cryptic and unwieldy "Beware." Undoubtedly, Green's move towards the Lord was hastened by the infamous 1974 incident where a jilted ex-girlfriend scalded him with a boiling pot of grits before fatally turning his own gun on herself.

Green broke from Mitchell after *Full of Fire* and recorded two redemptive albums (*Belle* and *Truth N' Time*) that marvelously juggled secular and sacred themes. His enormous impact continued to be felt, but by the end of the decade Green had completely turned his back on pop music in favor of the world of gospel and a life in the ministry. Since then, he has intermittently dipped his feet in secular waters, but he continues his life as a Memphis minister.

Mitchell proceeded to run Hi and worked with artists during and after his run with Green. In 1973 he scored a huge hit with Ann Peebles's vibrant "I Can't Stand the Rain," and her album of the same name became a true classic of '70s soul. Mitchell continued to employ the familiar, yet always welcome, Hi sound to great effect on several albums for O.V. Wright, Otis Clay, and Syl Johnson, but by 1980 the Hi Rhythm Section had dissolved. Mitchell reunited with Green in 1985 for the album *He is the Light*, but, despite a few bright spots the album failed to shine. In 2003, the duo re-teamed for *I Can't Stop*, an occasionally spectacular album that sought to build a silky bridge back to their '70s heyday. Mitchell continues to own and operate Royal Studios in Memphis, and he runs the Beale Street nightclub, Willie Mitchell's Legends. Meanwhile, his glorious Al Green productions not only define a decade, they have remained so impossibly fresh and perennially influential that they now border on the immortal.

· · · · ·

Shortly after *1990*'s unfortunately chilly reception, Whitfield left Motown and formed his own label, Whitfield Records. He continued to work with the Undisputed Truth, who, by the time of spacey mid-seventies releases *Cosmic Truth* and *Higher Than High*, had shuffled its members and its image. With the new lineup Whitfield morphed the group into a George Clinton–inspired cosmic funk band outfitted in outrageous spacesuits and glitter wigs, but, despite a few compelling dance-floor booty-shakers, the albums were met with only limited acceptance.

Whitfield scored a huge success for his new self-owned label with the soundtrack to the 1975 Richard Pryor and George Carlin classic *Car Wash*. Featured throughout the double-album soundtrack was Whitfield's newest act, Rose Royce. Whitfield had first formed the group as Total Concept Unlimited to supplant vocalist Edwin Starr back in the early-'70s. The group subsequently changed its name to Magic Wand, and Whitfield began to use them on recordings for vocalist Yvonne Fair and Undisputed Truth (including the disco-space album *Method to the Madness*) and as the live backing band for the Temptations. When Whitfield bolted from Motown, he took the newly renamed Rose Royce with him.

Because Whitfield and Rose Royce were allowed to watch the movie as it was being filmed, several of the songs were actually tailored to coincide with the onscreen scene. With its thin plot, Whitfield's soundtrack was woven unusually prominently into the film, and it often played more like an extended music video than an actual comedy. Initially, Whitfield was less then enamored of the *Car Wash* project, and his disinterest left him stumped for lyrics to the needed title track. With the recording deadline approaching, inspiration fatefully struck Whitfield while playing in a pickup basketball game. Reputedly he raced to the sidelines and jotted down the theme song lyrics on the only thing he could find: a bag of Kentucky Fried Chicken. Amazingly, the song would become a Number 1 smash and a true disco-funk classic.

Car Wash quickly went platinum on the strength of Rose Royce's hand-clapping, watery bass-slapping hit title song. A further highlight was their Temptations-like follow-up single "I Wanna Get Next to You," a soaring gossamer ballad that was easily one of the finest and most subtle productions of Whitfield's career. Several Whitfield-produced Rose Royce albums followed through the end of the decade, most notably on *Rose Royce II: In Bloom*, which was home to the utterly luscious "Wishing On a Star."

Either burned out or passed over by the demise of funk and disco, Whitfield's productivity dropped off significantly by the early 1980s. However, his painstakingly complex productions and socially conscious songwriting helped keep Motown relevant through the changing times and significantly infused a new reality into R&B. His influence continues to be felt strongly through his extended funky album cuts, which helped lay the foundation for both the dance remix and the rise of echo-laden Jamaican dub music. Additionally crucial is his hip-hop harbingering production technique utilized on the Temptations *1990*, an album that remains eerily relevant today. From Prince to Public Enemy, Whitfield's funk revolution has played a pivotal role in soul music's evolution.

KEY RECORDINGS
Willie Mitchell

Bobby "Blue" Bland –	*A Touch of the Blues* (produced half) (Duke 1967)
Don Bryant –	*Doin' the Mustang* (Hi 1991)
Otis Clay –	"Trying to Live My Life Without You" (Hi 1972)
	I Can't Take It (Hi 1977)
	The Complete Otis Clay on Hi Records (Hi 2000)
Al Green –	*Green Is Blues* (Hi 1970)
	Al Green Gets Next to You (Hi 1971)
	"Tired of Being Alone" (Hi 1971)
	Let's Stay Together (Hi 1972)
	"Let's Stay Together" (Hi 1972)
	Call Me (Hi 1973)
	Livin' for You (Hi 1973)
	Al Green Explores Your Mind (Hi 1974)
	Al Green is Love (Hi 1975)
	Full of Fire (Hi 1976)
	Have a Good Time (Hi 1976)
	He is the Light (PSM 1985)
	Love Ritual: Rare and Unreleased (1968–1976) (Hi/MCA 1989)
	I Can't Stop (Blue Note 2003)
Syl Johnson –	*Back for a Taste of Your Love* (Hi 1973)
	Diamond in the Rough (Hi 1974)
Jimmy McCracklin –	*High on the Blues* (Stax 1971)
Willie Mitchell –	*Sunrise Serenade* (Hi 1963)
	It's Dance Time (Hi 1965)
	"Bad Eye" (Hi 1966)
	Ooh Baby, You Turn Me On (Hi 1967)
	"Soul Serenade" (Hi 1968)
	Soul Bag (Hi 1969)
	The Many Moods of Willie Mitchell (Hi 1970)
Ann Peebles –	*This is Ann Peebles* (Hi 1969)
	Part Time Love (Hi 1971)
	Straight from the Heart (Hi 1972)
	I Can't Stand the Rain (Hi 1974)
	Tellin' It (Hi 1976)
Otis Rush –	*Any Place I'm Going* (House of Blues 1998)
Jesse Winchester –	*Talk Memphis* (Bearsville 1981)

O.V. Wright –   *If It's Only for Tonight* (Backbeat 1965)
                "Eight Men, Four Women" (Backbeat 1967)
                Nucleus of Soul (Backbeat 1968)
                A Nickel and a Nail and Ace of Spades
                    (Backbeat 1971)
                Memphis Unlimited (Backbeat 1973)
                Into Something (I Can't Shake Loose)
                    (Cream 1977)

Norman Whitfield

Yvonne Fair –   *The Bitch is Black* (Motown 1975)

Marvin Gaye –   "I Heard it Through the Grapevine"
                    (Tamla/Motown 1968)
                In the Groove (Tamla 1968)
                That's the Way Love Is (Tamla 1969)
                "Too Busy Thinking About My Baby"
                    (Tamla 1969)

Gladys Knight –   "I Heard it Through the Grapevine" (Soul 1967)
    and the Pips   "Friendship Train" (Soul 1969)
                Nitty Gritty (Soul 1969)

Willie Hutch –   *Fully Exposed* (Motown 1973)

The Marvelettes –   "Silly Boy" (Motown 1963)
                "Too Many Fish in the Sea" (Motown 1964)

Rare Earth –   "(I Know) I'm Losing You" (Rare Earth 1970)
                Ecology (Rare Earth 1970)
                Ma (Motown 1973)

Rose Royce –   *Car Wash* (MCA 1977)
                Rose Royce II: In Full Bloom (Whitfield 1977)
                "I Wanna Get Next to You" (MCA 1977)
                Rose Royce III: Strikes Again! (Whitfield 1978)
                "Love Don't Live Here Anymore"
                    (Whitfield 1979)

The Supremes –   *I Hear a Symphony* (Motown 1966)

Jimmy Ruffin –   "Don't You Miss Me a Little Bit Baby?"
                    (Motown 1967)

Edwin Starr –   "War" (Gordy 1969)
                War and Peace (Gordy 1970)
                Involved (Gordy 1971)

The Temptations –   "Girl (Why You Wanna Make Me Blue)"
(Gordy 1964)
The Temptin' Temptations (Gordy 1965)
"(I Know) I'm Losing You" (Gordy 1966)
"Ain't Too Proud to Beg" (Gordy 1966)
"Beauty is Only Skin Deep" (Gordy 1966)
Gettin' Ready (Gordy 1966)
Wish it Would Rain (Gordy 1968)
Cloud Nine (Gordy 1969)
"I Can't Get Next to You" (Gordy 1969)
Puzzle People (Gordy 1969)
"Ball of Confusion (That's What the World is
Today)" (Gordy 1970)
Psychedelic Shack (Gordy 1970)
"Just My Imagination" (Gordy 1971)
Sky's the Limit (Gordy 1971)
Solid Rock (Gordy 1972)
"Papa Was a Rolling Stone" (Gordy 1972)
All Directions (Gordy 1972)
Masterpiece (Gordy 1973)
1990 (Motown 1973)

The Undisputed Truth – The Undisputed Truth (Gordy 1971)
"Smiling Faces Sometimes" (Gordy 1971)
Face to Face (Gordy 1971)
Cosmic Truth (Gordy 1975)
Higher Than High (Gordy 1975)
Method to the Madness (Warner Bros. 1976)

The Velvettes –   "Needle in a Haystack" (Motown 1964)
"He Was Really Saying Something"
(Motown 1965)

THE MINIMALISTS:
BRIAN ENO AND
JOHN CALE

In London, Brian Eno was walking home from a recording session in 1975 when an odd thought popped into his head: "If that song were the last thing I ever record, would I mind having that as my final piece of work?"[1] Quickly dismissing his morbidity, he continued to walk. A hundred yards later, he slipped on the rain-slicked sidewalk and tumbled into the street. He desperately tried to step back in time, but it was too late: A taxi plowed into him at 40 mph, running over his legs and snapping his head back into a parked car like a bullwhip. As blood streamed from his skull all he could think was, "You brought this on yourself."

Eno convalesced in hospital, lucky to be alive. Eventually his recovery led him home, where he laid bedridden and disoriented by painkillers. One soggy afternoon, Eno hobbled over to his turntable and dropped the needle on a record of 18th-century harp music. Exhausted, he barely mustered enough energy to collapse back into bed. As the record started, it became apparent that only one speaker worked and that the volume was too low to for the music to be clearly heard over the din of falling rain. Too weak to get up and increase the volume, he began to drift into a bleary, lenitive sleep.

As the record played on, he drifted off, and something strange happened. While certain louder notes were audible, the rainstorm obscured the quieter passages, and the two sounds seemed to meld seamlessly into a new atmospheric whole.

"This presented what was for me a new way of hearing music— as part of the ambience of the environment just as the color of the light and the sound of the rain were parts of the ambience," Eno wrote.[2]

He had discovered a new musical language; ambient music had been envisaged.

Meanwhile across the Atlantic, in New York, the Bowery-based punk-underground inched towards international visibility as Patti Smith prepared to corral the archetypal ghosts of symbolist poetry and iconic rock 'n' roll into her debut album, Horses. *As the first artist from CBGB signed to a record deal, Smith was hell-bent on injecting a shot of nitro straight into the sickly heart of mid-1970s American rock. All she needed was the proper producer...*

Sitting in her tiny apartment, Smith pondered potential producers without success. Suddenly, a John Cale record caught her eye, and his moon-faced countenance shone like an epiphany: "I looked at the cover of Fear *and I said, 'Now there's a set of cheekbones.'... In my mind I picked him because his records sounded good."[3]*

However, with Cale she got more than she bargained for: "But I hired the wrong guy. All I was really looking for was a technical person. Instead I got a total maniac artist. I went to pick out an expensive watercolor painting and instead I got a mirror," Smith said.[4]

Despite Smith's equation of the recording sessions to "a season in hell," the singular Horses *was a musical milestone, and its hopped-up energy and inspired improvisation were direct results of Cale's unblinking stewardship. As the first warning shot in the impending punk/new wave invasion,* Horses *proved that New York's rock underground could gallop far outside of the grimy stables of Manhattan.*

But breaking boundaries was nothing new for John Cale and Brian Eno.

• • • • •

John Cale could not escape his musical destiny. Highly gifted on piano and violin, his reputation as a child prodigy was solidified after performing an original composition on the BBC when he was only eleven years old. Despite a lack of musical encouragement from his working-class parents, the Welsh-born Cale was well aware where his future resided. "Somebody told me once that when Orpheus gave up music and became a glass cutter, he went crazy. So I sort of bore that in mind," he said.[5]

Cale enrolled at London's Goldsmith's College as an undergraduate classical music student in 1960. Despite the traditional musical curriculum he was being exposed to, his interests began to drift towards modern avant-garde composers such as John Cage and Karlheinz Stockhausen. He was fascinated by their minimalistic, entrancingly repetitious compositions and began to incorporate their philosophies into his own developing theories. Completely dedicated to avant-garde by the early 1960s, Cale was oblivious to the nascent rock-oriented "British beat boom" that was beginning enrapture teens throughout the country.

After earning his classical music degree in London, Cale's talents came to the attention of Aaron Copland. The American composing giant was so taken with his potential that he arranged a Leonard Bernstein scholarship that allowed him to study modern composition in Massachusetts. Once Cale arrived stateside and began working with Copland, though, it was clearly evident that the two did not see eye to eye. Copland was alienated by Cale's penchant for destructive experimentalism, and, fearing for the safety of his piano, he refused to let him perform his violent compositions. Seeking more open minds, Cale headed to New York and promptly fell into a short but memorable association with the legendary John Cage.

Arriving in Manhattan, Cale was immediately enlisted to participate in an eighteen-hour Cage-led piano recital. The marathon performance revolved around an Erik Satie piece that was played exactly 888 times. Part serious statement, part publicity stunt, a photo of Cale performing the piece landed his gaunt mug in *The New York Times*. After his brief tenure with Cage, he began to work with another well-regarded minimalist composer named La Monte Young in his Theater of Eternal Music. The two men shared similarly extreme ideas, and Young persuaded Cale to take up the electric viola for a new quartet he was assembling, soon dubbed the Dream Syndicate.

The newly formed Dream Syndicate featured Cale on customized electric viola, a hand drummer, a violinist, and a vocalist. Soon after assembling, the quartet began to perform Young's open-ended compositions in various art galleries around New York. Often accompanied by surrealistic light projections, Young's heavily amplified modal blues compositions were jet-engine loud and heavily steeped in Indian-derived drone. Undoubtedly, Young's drone pieces predicted the plethora of similar Eastern experiments to appear later in the decade from a number of composers.

Despite the Dream Syndicate's considerable artistic headway, Cale grew frustrated with the limited commercial sphere of avant-garde. Recently, he had developed a voracious appetite for rock 'n' roll and would often spend his post-rehearsal evenings spinning 45s with fellow Dream Syndicate member Tony Conrad. As time went on, Cale found himself increasingly drawn to the urgent energy of rock. By the spring of '65 his mind was made up: He would forsake the rarified avant-garde world for the musical blasphemy of rock.

Cale soon found his unlikely conduit to rock in the guise of a quietly intense songwriter named Lou Reed. Reed was working as an assembly-line songsmith cranking out throwaway novelty tunes by the dozens for Pickwick Records, a hack record company in New Jersey. Reed harbored hopes that one of his latest songs, a pseudo-dance ditty called "The Ostrich" (credited to the fictitious band the Primitives), was going to become a breakout hit for Pickwick. In an effort to promote the single, Reed was recruiting musicians to perform live as the Primitives. Incongruously, he somehow ended up with Cale and other defectors from the Dream Syndicate.

As Reed ran through "The Ostrich," Cale was astonished to discover that all of the guitar strings were tuned to the same note, just as the Dream Syndicate had done with Young's compositions. After a smattering of tepidly received gigs as the Primitives, "The Ostrich" failed to fly. Undeterred, Cale and Reed continued to rehearse together, along with fellow Young expatriates Tony Conrad and Angus MacLise. Cale was duly taken with Reed's unflinching urban dope tales, such as "Waiting for the Man" and "Heroin." Meanwhile, Reed was summarily blown away by Cale's prodigious musical talent. With the subsequent addition of Reed's friend Sterling Morrison and the subtraction of Conrad, the fledgling band began to play chaotic, free-formed shows around New York.

With a lineup of Reed and Morrison on guitars, MacLise on drums, and Cale on viola, bass, and occasional guitar, the group's shows were an aggressive blend of studious minimalism, off-kilter R&B, and primal rock 'n' roll. Performing Reed's gritty taboo-narratives under a barrage of nasty "orchestral chaos," the band was managing to confound and bewilder audiences wherever it played. By the end of 1965 the young female drummer Maureen Tucker had replaced MacLise, and the group christened itself the Velvet Underground.

With a sound predicated on sonic confrontation, the Velvet Underground became the dark-clouded Eastern antithesis to the West Coast's euphoric sunshine daydream. "I had no intention of letting music be anything other than troublesome to people. We really wanted to go out there and annoy people," Cale proclaimed years later.[6]

In early 1967 the band finally released its debut, *The Velvet Underground* and *Nico*. Produced by pop-art mastermind Andy Warhol, the album dynamited the doors off of conventional rock 'n' roll. Warhol had recently taken the band under his pale wing, featuring them in his live multi-media happenings, dubbed the *Exploding Plastic Inevitable*. While Warhol had no real understanding of music production, he did sit behind the board for the album's recording, and the band felt his curious presence. Warhol had recently added the German model Nico to the band, and her deadpan Dietrich-like vocals lent the Velvets a decidedly doomy quality.

Building on Reed's subversive *cinema verité* song stories, gobs of guitar feedback and relentless stone-age percussion, Cale's own musical contributions to the album were crucial. Providing his droning viola virtuosity, fantastically inventive basslines, and pulverizing piano assaults, Cale elevated the band from mere noise dilettantes to sonic futurists. Fatefully, he would last only one more album with the band, the heavily distorted and hastily recorded *White Light/White Heat*. Anchored by the amphetamine-propelled title track, the savage seventeen-minute transvestite-themed feedback opus "Sister Ray," and Cale's macabre spoken-word short story "The Gift," *White Light/White Heat* remains one of the fiercest collections ever recorded.

After the album's prompt commercial failure, Reed grew weary of the band's unrelenting sound. As a response, he began to retreat towards an introspective acoustic songwriting style, quickly landing him at odds with Cale's uncompromising experimental ideals. Convinced that the Velvets had lost sight of its original concept and unable to usurp Reed's leadership, Cale departed the band in late 1968. Freed from the velvet shackles, Cale's next project would see him scurry back towards his avant-garde roots.

• • • • •

Although Nico's Velvet Underground membership was only temporary, the dour German beauty forged a deep bond with Cale. Along with Reed he had already contributed several songs and instrumental backing for her folk-rockish post-Velvets solo album, *Chelsea Girl*. With Cale now exiled from the same band, he was enlisted as the arranger for Nico's second album, the frightening *The Marble Index*. (Although, the album's official production credit was given to Frazier Mowhawk, Cale functioned as its arranger and ostensible producer.)

Cale commenced the sessions by recording Nico's stark harmonium (a droning, reedy Indian instrument) over her trademark soporific monotone. Influenced in part by her then-lover Jim Morrison, Nico's songs were packed full of often-impenetrable lyrics and bone-chilling imagery, exemplified by the harrowing "No One is There" and the arctic "Frozen Warnings." After Cale had completed her haunting tracks, he dismissed Nico from the studio and locked the door behind her. Two days later, he let her back in and played her the completed album.

Fashioning a series of pitch-black arrangements, Cale's production of *The Marble Index* more closely resembled European avant-garde and ancient Teutonic folk than contemporary pop. As Nico sat in the studio listening to the album unfold, she broke out in tears with each new song, totally overcome by its frigid beauty. Completely at odds with the 1969 rock world, the austere album sold virtually nothing. But like the Velvet Underground's oeuvre, *The Marble Index* has steadily grown from a challenging anomaly to puissant touchstone. As the original gothic rock recording, its dark influence pervades through the Cure, to Nine Inch Nails, to the next doleful "goth" band-in-waiting. Cale would continue to develop Nico's similarly monochromatic vision the following year on the barren and unyielding *Desertshore*.

Four years later Cale guided Nico's slightly fuller, although no less demanding '74 release, *The End*. For the album's title track Nico undertakes a spine-tingling, dirge-like rendering of the Doors' "The End" in which she ironically tussles with the Oedipal demons and death of ex-lover Jim Morrison. Aided by Brian Eno's menacing synth, Cale contributed a dizzying array of instruments to *The End*, ranging from glockenspiel to guitar.

Soon after the completion of *The Marble Index*, Cale was paired with four motley rustbelt misfits, appropriately called the Stooges. Sprouting from the same rabble-rousing Michigan scene as the militant MC5 and blue-eyed garage-soul rascals the Rationals, the Stooges were as lewd and crude as a rock band could be. Led by rail-thin, ultra-confrontational singer Iggy Stooge (soon renamed Iggy Pop), the band's brief career had been spent inciting crowds around the college town of Ann Arbor.

Blazing through incendiary half-hour opening-slot sets, the Stooges' relentless aural assault would instantly polarize unprepared audiences. Almost immediately, a shirtless Iggy would antagonize the crowd with nihilistic glee, breaking bottles then cutting himself with their jagged edges, baiting the jocks in the front while trying to steal their girlfriends and climbing atop amps and then stage-diving off them. While Iggy scared the living shit out of anyone within range, the band churned out an ultra fuzzed-out brand of narcotic rock.

Cale sensed a kinship with the Stooges' unblinking mayhem and flew the band out to New York in an effort to trap its raw power at Hit Factory Studios. Once again working at the speed of light, Cale produced the band's explosive self-titled debut in two scant days in June 1969. Shuttling the Stooges' inherent minimalism to the forefront, Cale's production is immediate and uncluttered. Combining Iggy's Jagger-meets-Morrison snarl, Ron Asheton's squalor-toned Stratocaster, and the incessant rhythm attack of Scott Asheton and Dave Alexander, the anomic album wallows in horny desperation and terminal boredom.

From *The Stooges'* scorching, wah-wah run amok opener "1969," to the mopish snot rock of "No Fun," to the pensive slow-burn of "Ann," to the lyrically improvised "Not Right" and "Real Cool Time," Cale allows the album to derive its malevolent power from a minimalistic simplicity. Nowhere is Cale's approach more effective than on the depraved "I Wanna Be Your Dog"—where tangled fuzz-riffs, careening drums, and roily sleigh-bell percussion collide with Iggy's debauched desires. Cementing the disturbing atmosphere is Cale's incessant one-finger piano motif, which tinkles a tension so thickly sinister it almost becomes too much to bear.

The Stooges
The Stooges
(1969)

Like *The Marble Index*, *The Stooges* was another dose of commercial poison, although within five years the aggressive angst-ridden masterpiece would become retrospectively heralded as the original punk rock album. With Cale's own collection of material accumulating, he began to scheme his first step towards a solo album. Anyone who had been following his unrelentingly confrontational career thus far was in for a surprise.

• • • • •

As a boy living in the rural English countryside, Brian Eno was transfixed by the "Martian Music" transmissions he received from his radio. A U.S. Air Force base neighbored his small village of Suffolk, and Eno religiously tuned into its Armed Forces Radio broadcasts, completely mesmerized by the seemingly alien American doo-wop sides it played. By the time he was a teenager, his obsession moved to tape recorders. Mechanically inclined, he was endlessly fascinated by their knobs and buttons, and he began to accumulate a vast array of the machines in various states of disrepair.

Heading off to art school in 1965, Eno was exposed to conceptual painting and the sound experiments of minimalists like Cage, Young, and Terry Riley. Unable to play a traditional instrument, Eno focused on tape recording experiments as an alternative. Attempting to build sound sculptures, he spent countless hours recording random noises, then manipulating the tapes by playing them backwards and at different speeds, fascinated by the endless sonic possibilities. For one early minimalist recording project, he rang a large metal lampshade like a bell and then altered the tape speed to create a fascinating sound collage.

Firmly entrenched in avant-garde by the late 1960s, Eno briefly joined the performance art outfit Merchant Taylor's Simultaneous Cabinet, which was followed by short stints in Cornelius Cardew's avant-garde Scratch Orchestra and the intentionally amateurish Portsmouth Sinfonia. Propitiously, his perspective was forever changed after hearing the seminal noise rock of the Velvet Underground. With its primal, minimalist sound, the Velvets made good on the exciting musical possibilities first introduced to Eno by the Who on their devastating feedback-laden anthem "My Generation." Emboldened by rock's expanding boundaries, he joined the short-lived improvisational Maxwell Demon as a vocalist in 1969.

Soon after the quick demise of Maxwell Demon, Eno relocated to London, where he toiled at a local newspaper pasting up advertisements. Desperate to escape the creatively stifling job, he began to refurbish old speakers and collect second-hand electronics, which he would then deal to various acquaintances around town. One of his customers was a musician friend named Andy MacKay. The lanky saxophonist knew that Eno owned a Revox tape recorder and asked him if would record some demos of his new band, Roxy Music.

When Eno showed up at the embryonic recording session he was thrilled to discover a band awash in an ironic confluence of experimental ideas. With a detached post-modern aesthetic, Roxy Music was seeking to refract old Hollywood glamour and early rock 'n' roll iconography through a prism of space-aged futurism. Eno was intrigued by Roxy's tension-through-technology vision and signed on as its live sound mixer, occasionally supplying backing vocals from an offstage microphone. Soon he found himself onstage as the band's synthesizer player. A self-professed "non-musician," Eno devised an aggressive style that thrived on unexpected mechanical bleats and feral squawks derived from a bank of keyboards and pre-recorded tapes. With his long-flowing blonde hair, garish makeup, velvet corsets, and feathery boas, his on-stage appearance was androgynously alien.

Eno lasted long enough in Roxy to contribute mightily to their first two landmark albums, the wonderfully chaotic *Roxy Music* and the sublimely futuristic *For Your Pleasure*. The releases established the band as searing post-modern visionaries and were largely responsible for shaking the somnambulant early '70s British rock scene to life. However, the lavish onstage attention Eno was receiving for his outrageous getups and squelching synth sounds was clearly stealing the spotlight from suave singer Bryan Ferry. Eventually, Ferry's ego reached a breaking point, and his onstage rival was driven from the band. Far from disappointed, Eno felt liberated.

• • • • •

As Cale's debut solo album, *Vintage Violence*, quickly began to take shape through three days of 1970, it was becoming apparent that its contents were certain to shock his most ardent fans. Belying its title, the album was actually a slyly restrained collection of deftly sketched pop. Drawing on an economical song structure reminiscent of the Band, *Vintage Violence* bursts with memorable melodies and occasionally lush Spectorian production touches. Cale eschewed his viola drone for rollicking piano; the album revolves around Cale's cast of intriguing living and dead characters. With a thin Welsh intonation, Cale reveals a voice that is lilting and frequently poignant, illustrated on the expansive "Big White Cloud," the jaunty "Hello There," and the gripping "Ghost Story."

Cale returned to more challenging waters with *The Church of Anthrax*, a collaboration undertaken with minimalist luminary Terry Riley that was actually completed prior to *Vintage Violence*. The intermittently satisfying recording featured the duo's repetitious keyboard patterns spiraling over a jazz-rock rhythm foundation. He continued to experiment with *The Academy in Peril*, recorded in part with the Royal Philharmonic Orchestra in 1972. Although the predominantly classical album was primarily un-engaging, it succeeded in keeping Cale's solo path unpredictably open-ended.

Harkening back to the tasteful pop construction of his debut, Cale recorded the evocative trip back in time, *Paris 1919*. Produced by the sure-handed Chris Thomas, the stately song-cycle exudes a gentle, sweeping majesty flush with literary references to Dylan Thomas, Graham Greene, and William Shakespeare. Cale's vocals demonstrate a newfound confidence, especially on such tranquil vignettes as "A Child's Christmas in Wales," "Hanky Panky Nohow," and "Andalucia." Unexpectedly, much of the album's restrained musical underpinning comes from members of Dixie-fried boogie kings, Little Feat. Inarguably, *Paris 1919* ranks as one of the finest albums of Cale's career.

With his genre-busting outside productions and four wildly diverse solo albums in less than four years, the artistically restless Cale had successfully skirted all musical pigeonholes. As a daring experimentalist and a sophisticated pop purveyor, he established a rare stylistic duality that would shadow his entire career. Taking note of his versatility and vision, he was hired as an A&R/house producer for Warner Bros. Records in 1971. Shortly after signing on, he returned back behind the mixing board for two rather disparate projects.

Jennifer Warnes was a talented, though obscure, singer, vaguely known for her appearances on the infamous *Smothers Brothers Comedy Hour* television show. Following a stint in the L.A. cast of *Hair*, Warnes recorded two below-the-radar albums of late-sixties rock and pop covers. Warnes was newly signed to the Warner Bros. offshoot Reprise, and Cale was curiously tapped to produce her 1972 label debut, *Jennifer*.

Demonstrating a clear-eyed studio command, Cale crafted a quietly assured soft pop gem for Warnes. Drawing on a strong set of material from songwriters like Jimmy Webb, the Bee Gees, Jackson Browne, Donovan, and Cale himself, the album swims in sympathetic strings, *Dusty in Memphis*–like soul flourishes, and crystal clear vocal turns from Warnes. *Jennifer*'s vulnerable vocal pop was worlds away from *The Stooges'* nihilistic mayhem, dramatically demonstrating Cale's ability to provide the proper touch to each project. *Jennifer* quickly sunk without a trace, but the album remains Cale's most underrated and understated outside production.

Returning to rockier terrain, Cale was farmed out to a Boston band bred on his own musical past. Ironically calling themselves the Modern Lovers, the nerdy quartet was led by a precocious Velvet Underground disciple named Jonathan Richman. With a sound torn from the post-Cale Velvets songbook, Richman's songs mercilessly skewered the hypocrisies of '60s counter-culture idealism through a teetotaler's perspective. In

Richman's contrarian view, the hippie youth was just as conformist as the establishment they were rebelling against.

By the early-1970s, the Modern Lovers began to attract unlikely attention around Boston. Shortly after, the estimable David Geffen signed on as manager, and the group quickly garnered interest from Warner Bros. At Richman's request, Cale was dispatched to produce a slew of demos for the nascent band in April 1972. Seeking to preserve the band's raw honesty, Cale left the arrangements skeletal, allowing the adenoidal Richman to whine such anti-rock rants as heeding parents and not getting stoned, over a backdrop of furiously strummed guitars, discordantly shrill keyboards, and pounding drums.

Eventually the band's spirited back-to-basics defiance would become a key component of the English punk blueprint, but the Anglo explosion was still four years away. In the interim, Cale's appropriately minimal document languished in the can. Frustrated by Warner's unceremonious dismissal of the demos, the Modern Lovers attempted to re-record the songs with the infamous rock Svengali Kim Fowley. But the results paled in comparison to Cale's originals, and Fowley's demos were awarded the same unceremonious fate.

Finally, in 1976, the original Cale-produced Modern Lovers demos were released as the band's eponymous official debut album. "Roadrunner," the album's joyously infectious ode to AM radio, promptly became one of rock's greatest anthems, bolstered by an endless string of cover versions that included a famous stab by the early Sex Pistols. Despite its widespread influence, soon after *The Modern Lovers* release, the band called it quits. Original keyboardist Jerry Harrison would soon charter new territory as a Talking Head, while drummer David Robinson would fortify Boston new wave heroes the Cars. Richman formed a new acoustic version of the Modern Lovers before embarking on a solo career. Meanwhile, Cale's production vision had set another proto-punk cornerstone. It would not be his last.

· · · · ·

Recently extricated from Roxy Music, Eno put the finishing touches on a collaboration with King Crimson guitar intellectual Robert Fripp. After an introduction, the two discovered that they shared the same minimalist sensibilities and began to collaborate on *No Pussyfooting*. The album consisted of two curiously titled side-long pieces, "The Heavenly Music Corporation" and "Swastika Girls." For its innovative construction, Eno processed Fripp's mathematical electric guitar patterns through several custom delay treatments, then ran the signal through two separate Revox recorders to create a technique later anointed "Frippertronics." The end result was a trailblazing foray into tape-looping that multiplied Fripp's lone guitar into a swelling orchestra of demonic guitar noise.

Significantly, Eno's newly formulated sound processing technique enabled him to break down the barriers between producer and musician. *No Pussyfooting* was revolutionary in the fact that it was two people making one combined sound. With its pioneering utilization of studio-facilitated tape-looping, the album portended sampling techniques later widely used in hip-hop and electronica. "That got me into the idea of the studio, not as a place for reproducing music but as a place for changing it, or re-creating it from scratch," Eno said, looking back on *No Pussyfooting*.[7]

Eno's career as a formal solo artist began with a bang on 1973's feverish *Here Comes the Warm Jets*. Attempting to expand the dynamic tension of Roxy Music, Eno assembled a group of seemingly incompatible musicians with the hope of creating a series of happy studio accidents. Using warped glam-rock and surrealist pop as jumping-off points, the album filtered Eno's snotty, fey vocals and bizarre stream-of-consciousness lyrics through a myriad of processed sounds and electronically treated instruments. Twisted but catchy songs such as "Dead Finks Don't Talk," "The Paw Paw Negro Blowtorch," and "Baby's On Fire" all overflowed with what Eno deemed an "idiot glee" and helped make *Warm Jets* an auspicious debut.

Eno skewed his vision even further with 1974's monumental *Taking Tiger Mountain (By Strategy)*. Inspired by a series of postcards depicting a Chinese revolutionary opera, the enigmatic album plays like a poppy-fueled fever dream full of absurd lyrical twists and unexpected sonic detours. Avant-pop classics such as "Burning Airlines Give You So Much More," "Mother Whale Eyeless," and "The True Wheel" brim with ebullient splendor, while the menacing "The Great Pretender" and hypnotic "Third Uncle" are rendered in considerably darker tones.

Seeking to further court the random possibilities of the recording studio, Eno began to develop a set of tarot-like instructional oracle cards dubbed Oblique Strategies. Each card contained a so-called "worthwhile dilemma," a suggestion intended to inject spontaneity and harness serendipity. The first card he created read: "Honour thy error as a hidden intention." At various stages of recording *Tiger Mountain*, he would consult one of the strategies, which would dictate an otherwise unconsidered action. In a sense, Eno was constantly striving to forget what he had already learned about recording. Eventually he refined and expanded the Oblique Strategies to 64 cards (each one was illustrated by artist Peter Schmidt), and they became a key component of nearly all of his future recordings.

Soon after releasing the crazed proto-punk single "Seven Deadly Finns," Eno embarked on a 1974 UK tour as front man for the mutant pub rockers the Winkies. In ill health, he suffered a collapsed lung a week into the scheduled performances. Once recuperated, he began to shift his focus almost exclusively to studio-based pursuits. Removed from the grind of touring, Eno remodeled himself from a flamboyant rock icon into a behind-the-scenes session man, contributing unorthodox synthesizer and sound treatments to artful albums for Cale, Nico, Robert Wyatt, 801, Phil Manzanera, Quiet Sun, Genesis, and others.

With his services highly in demand, Eno found himself running from session to session. But everything changed that stormy London evening when, returning from a Phil Manzanera recording date, he skidded off the sidewalk and catapulted headfirst into a moving taxi. He would never see things the same way again.

• • • • •

Obliterating the quaint nostalgia of *Paris 1919*, Cale embarked on a series of albums that simultaneously embraced his defiant Velvets past while grasping towards the impending punk future. Soaked in a dipsomaniacal fervor, 1974's *Fear* and the following year's *Slow Dazzle* and *Helen of Troy* formed a thematic trilogy of doom. All three of the textural albums featured Eno and benefited immensely from his treatments and unorthodox studio strategies.

Cale and Eno had first worked together on the classic *June 1st, 1974* concert album (recorded with Nico and ex–Soft Machine eccentric Kevin Ayers), and the two kindred minimalists would subsequently contribute to each other's recordings throughout the decade.

Cale mined diverse territory on the doom trilogy, which is rich in dangerous, paranoiac hard rock like "Fear is a Man's Best Friend," "Gun," and "Leaving it Up to You" and expansive Brian Wilson-derived pocket symphonies such as "Mr. Wilson," "The Man Who Couldn't Afford to Orgy," and "China Sea." He also revealed admirable skill as a heartfelt balladeer through a slew of exquisitely touching songs, including "Ship of Fools," "Cable Hogue," "I'm Not the Loving Kind," and "I Keep a Close Watch." In fact, the latter was so awash in boozy sentimentality and emotional eloquence that Cale earnestly dreamt of Frank Sinatra covering it. However, his dream would remain unrealized. In fact, his next project would be about as far as one could get from the Chairman of the Board.

Patti Smith believed in the transcendent power of rock 'n' roll, at a time when it displayed very little of it. She was a disciple of Baudelaire and Rimbaud's symbolist poetics, a student of Morrison's leather enshrouded spiritualism, a mirror of Jagger's androgynous magnetism, a fellow passenger on Hendrix's cosmic astral plane, and a descendant of all the garage rock primitives. Accompanied by guitarist Lenny Kaye, Smith performed her hopped-up, Beat-influenced poetry at cafes around New York City through the early '70s. By mid-decade the two had formed the full-fledged, rather green Patti Smith Band.

In August 1975, Cale and the Patti Smith Band assembled in New York's Hendrix-built Electric Ladyland studio to begin recording the band's debut, *Horses*. Immediately, the band and the producer assumed their respective roles as petulant students and wizened taskmaster. For Cale's first act, he miffed the band by confiscating its beat-up, out-of-tune instruments. Methodically, Cale tuned each one himself. He then returned them and told the band to begin playing—but there was a problem.

According to Cale, "the band sounded awful."[8] Despite vehement protests from the group, Cale insisted on procuring an entirely new set of instruments. "I handed all these guys who were sensitive musicians completely new axes to do what they're used to doing. But the results were estimably better," he said.[9]

Patti Smith
Horses
(1975)

Cale quickly began to dissect the songs and alter their construction by sharpening up some of the more rambling numbers while stretching out others to afford them greater purpose. In doing so he established what Lenny Kaye called "a psychological aura in the studio."[10] With Cale's often-radical reworking, tempers quickly began to flare between band and producer. However, out of the tumult, Cale was extracting rare genius.

"It was really like 'A Season in Hell' for both of us. But inspiration doesn't always have to be someone sending me half a dozen American beauty roses. There's a lot of inspiration going on between the murderer and the victim,"[11] Smith contended.

From its street-corner cool, free-verse update on the garage nugget "Gloria," to the reggae-fied lesbian suicide tale "Redondo Beach," to the searing emotional wasteland of "Break it Up," *Horses* revels in a rudimentarily rocking, loosely structured defiance. Cale's improvisational influence permeates throughout, notably on the sprawling "Birdland" and the epic "Land." In the latter, Chris Kenner's "Land of a Thousand Dances" is merged with Smith's stream-of-consciousness meditations on urban violence, archetypal teenage rebellion, symbolic stallions, and Hendrix's final mortal moments. Smith's album storms the future by way of the past, but ultimately it resides in the visceral here and now.

Horses rode into the U.S. Top 50 in November 1975 and introduced Smith's firebrand poetic punk to the outside world. She would continue to record several stirring songs, although she was never able to recapture the loose primitivism that Cale conjured on her debut. As a result, subsequent Smith releases were often marred by overly slick production and stilted arrangements. But *Horses* remains a high-water mark of volatile artistic expression and reckless rock 'n' roll abandon. Cale had done it again.

• • • • •

Recovering uncomfortably at home after his taxi accident, Eno listened, amazed, as a barely audible harp record melded with the din of falling rain to form its own unique environmental ambience. Realizing that music contained similar attributes as light and color, he had inadvertently stumbled onto a new way of not only hearing music, but seeing it as well. Thrilled by the newly discovered textural possibilities, his approach to recording would never be the same again.

Once fully recuperated from the accident, Eno began to explore his new ambient theory on the escape themed *Another Green World*. Boldly, or perhaps naïvely, he entered the studio without any written material and suffered through four frustratingly fruitless days of recording. In desperation he turned to his Oblique Strategies, and, almost magically, the Oblique Strategies cards immediately triggered a deluge of fertile ideas. Each uninhibited studio experiment led Eno in a different fantastical direction, from the extemporized choppy Farfisa organ that sparked "Golden Hours," to the treated "snake guitar" that slithers around "Sky Saw," to Robert Fripp's gloriously kinetic guitar solo in "St. Elmo's Fire." Cale was a significant contributor, performing devilishly hypnotic viola on two of the album's key cuts. Where Eno softened the edges around Cale's dread-laden recordings by adding texture and color, Cale imbued Eno's album with starkly sublime menace.

Bowing in November 1975, *Another Green World* was a moody masterpiece. By toning down the absurdist whimsy of his earlier albums, Eno forged a minimalistic mix of laconic childlike pop and seductive ambience that approximates a hypnogagic mind trip filled with secret soundscapes. Sonic discoveries abound on such aptly imagistic titles as "In Dark Trees," "Sombre Reptiles," and "Spirits Drifting." By essentially painting with sound, Eno furthered the promise of studio pioneers Phil Spector and Brian Wilson. He had dramatically transformed the recording studio into a singular instrument and succeeded in inventing a new musical language of mood, texture, and form.

Bolstered by his recent studio achievements, Eno made his first attempt at wholly environmental music with *Discreet Music*. Revisiting his early interest in tape experiments, he manipulated a string group recording of Johann Pachelbel's baroque "Three Variations on the Canon in D major" by slightly slowing the pitch down and processing it through a customized digital delay/echo unit. The crafty tape treatments altered the recording into pulsing patterns of soft sound. Released on his own avant-garde Obscure Records in 1975, the quiescent *Discreet Music* was a harbinger of fascinating ambient experiments to come.

Eno returned to *Another Green World*'s pop structure two years later with the inventive *Before and After Science.* By pairing sprightly nonsense pop songs such as "Backwater" and "No One Receiving" alongside wondrously warm drifting sketches such as "Julie With" and "Spider and I," the album was another triumph of textural innovation. Demonstrating his increasingly assured studio mastery, Eno playfully allows the album's subtle sonic skin to be peeled back one layer at a time, richly revealing hidden depths with each new listen. The captivating release would mark Eno's last attempt at song-oriented pop until an early 1990s collaboration with John Cale.

Beginning with 1978's *Music for Films*, Eno's solo work focused almost exclusively on the development of his ambient music theories. Consisting of several atmospheric vignettes, and again featuring viola work from Cale, the collection relied heavily on muted synthesizers and subtle studio treatments. Remarkably, the mood pieces maintained a humanistic soul at its core, and with its unlikely alliance of textured electronics and palpable emotion, *Music for Films* solidified the framework for Eno's future environmental endeavors.

Later that year, the somber *Music for Airports* was the first album to officially market itself as "ambient." Partially intended to calm the frazzled nerves of weary travelers in actual airports, its sparse construction and somnolent choir rendered a drowsy mood to the album's four long cuts. Twenty years after its original release, the New York experimental collective Bang on a Can re-recorded *Music for Airports* with live musicians and a female choir. The deftly executed album became a surprise triumph, while illuminating the inherent humanity that is crucial to Eno's ambient music.

• • • • •

Ironically, as Eno's own work continued to drift farther from the pop mainstream, his services were more in demand than ever. With the upstart New York and London punk scenes stripping the bloat from flabby '70s rock, a new crop of rule-defying artists began to covet his refreshing recording theories. With his serendipitous studio approach and favoring of genuine expression over technical craft, Eno was the perfect ally for artists looking to escape the rote state of rock. One of the first artists to come calling for an escape plan was another old glam rock refugee.

David Bowie had made a career out of making chameleon-like persona and stylistic musical changes. After his most recent incarnation as the coke-inhaling, plastic-soul-purveying "Thin White Duke" had run its course, Bowie bottomed out in Berlin. Seeking to again shed his skin, he sought Eno's aid. Working closely with Eno, Bowie released a trilogy of groundbreaking albums that transformed him from R&B dilettante into experimental auteur. While the estimable Tony Visconti received the actual producing credits, Eno's fingerprints are omnipresent on the inspired trilogy.

With 1977's cathartic *Low*, Eno stripped down Bowie's grandiose pretensions into a lean collection of chilly futurism, bleak atmospherics, and boxy rhythms. Half the record was taken up with meditative keyboard-heavy instrumentals like "Warszawa" and "Subterraneans"; the remainder was rooted in fractured electronic rock such as the dysfunctional "Breaking Glass" and the desperate "Be My Wife." For the shimmering single "Sound and Vision," Eno consciously toyed with pop conventions by withholding Bowie's crooning lead vocal from the mix until the song was more than half over. The unconventional strategy worked, and the early synth-pop song became Bowie's biggest hit in two years.

Although the duo enjoyed a budding friendship, their studio approaches were diametrically opposed. Bowie was impatient but

David Bowie
Low
(1977)

clear-eyed, preferring to cut a song in one take and then rush off to the next party. Conversely, studio-rat Eno was determined to patiently pursue results that could only be achieved through deliberate trial-and-error studio experiments. Fortunately, their clashing recording styles sparked a winning creative tension, and, despite weak album sales, *Low* succeeded in pushing Bowie to the forefront of new rock's cutting edge.

The duo continued in the same vein for 1978's *Heroes*, which again juggled icy instrumentals like "Sense of Doubt" and "Moss Garden" and jarring electronic rock like the pounding crucifixion tale "Joe the Lion" and the mysterious "Sons of the Silent Age." The album's most memorable cut was the soaring *Frippertronic*-powered title track. The elegy of doomed Cold War love became an international hit single and one of Bowie's career-defining anthems. For 1979's *Lodger*, Eno and Bowie drew from a larger palette of international and pop styles than they utilized on their first two outings. Unfortunately, its daring song structures and lack of a hit single on the order of "Heroes" spelled commercial disappointment for the frequently far-reaching album. More importantly than its commercial failings, the Eno trilogy transmogrified Bowie from rock dinosaur to enigmatic new wave icon.

As the punk groundswell gathered momentum, Eno embarked on a succession of productions, beginning with Ultravox's 1977 eponymous first album. With its early coupling of a drum machine with a live drummer, the record's mumpish mood was best characterized by the cybernetic "I Want to Be a Machine." Slightly too early to catch the new wave, and too late for glam, the curiosity's standout track was the affectedly stark, Eno-influenced "My Sex." With singer John Foxx's overt rever-ence for the Bowie/Roxy Music axis, *Ultravox!* precipitated the post-glam "new romantic" movement, soon furthered by gender-bending synth bands like Japan and Duran Duran.

Eno was behind the controls for the Cologne, Germany–based recording of Devo's '78 debut, *Q: Are We Not Men? A: We Are Devo.* Devo had risen through the procreant mid-1970s Ohio punk scene, tightly winding bizarre rants on de-evolution around a tension-without-release sound. Among the first rock albums to rely heavily on synthesizers, *Are We Not Men?* bursts with herky-jerky time signa-tures, sandpaper guitars, and robotic musical contortions. A new wave call-to-arms, the abrasively infectious album is highlighted by a gnarled deconstruction of the Stones' "Satisfaction," the frantic, too-many-chromosomes tale "Mongoloid," and the fevered de-evolution manifesto "Jocko Homo." Surprisingly, the sessions were frustrating for Eno. Once he got Devo in the studio, he was shocked by the group's stubborn unwillingness to deviate from its earlier demos, and as a result many of his ideas were dismissed out of hand.

"They were a terrifying group to work with because they were so unable to experiment," he recalled.[12] Nonetheless, the album estab-lished Devo as progenitors of American new wave, and its electronic undercurrent opened the floodgates for the ensuing onslaught of quirky '80s synth-pop acts.

Taking up residency in the revitalized New York scene of the late '70s, Eno caught wind of a noisy performance-art movement perco-lating on the SoHo periphery that primarily revolved around a coterie of four key bands: the Contortions, Teenage Jesus and the Jerks, Mars, and DNA. Each group specialized in "no wave," a dissonant and atonal style of art-damaged punk. Keenly aware that the move-ment was fleeting, Eno arranged to produce *No New York*, a compila-tion album to document the no wave scene.

Released in 1978, the combative compilation featured contribu-tions from the four no wave bands. Eno's instincts were proven correct, and the truculent movement imploded shortly after the album's release. Despite its brief existence, no wave's cerebrally punky, noise-encrusted improvisations became a guiding light for future alternative music titans such as Sonic Youth, Mission of Burma, Big Black, and the Pixies.

• • • • •

Seeking to inhabit the punk promised land he helped pioneer, in the late-1970s Cale's music took a turn for the maniacal. Literally donning a hard hat, and backed by a musically sleazy support band, Cale's live performances turned viscously martial and full of rambling political hectoring. Drinking heavily, Cale's onstage personality often turned erratic and recklessly theatrical. During one performance of the song "Chicken Shit," he shocked a crowd by decapitating a chicken (it was already dead). His vegetarian band members were so outraged by the stunt that they quit that night. All the feedback-drenched madness and nasty depravity of songs such as the ironically fascist "Mercenaries (Ready for War)" and the mutinous "Captain Hook" are captured on *Sabotage/Live*, which Cale recorded at CBGB's in 1979.

In hindsight, the period proved cathartic for Cale, and following the angry *Honi Soit*, he retreated towards more low-key terrain. His dramatic about-face was demonstrated on the spartan 1982 release *Music for a New Society*. A bleak minimalist cousin to Nico's *The Marble Index*, the album is full of Eno-esque ambience and disquieting classical motifs, exemplified on "Taking Your Life in Your Hands" and "Chinese Envoy." With its desolate arrangements and unnerving themes, the album remains the most unnerving in Cale's solo canon.

Cale continued to sporadically produce artists through the late-'70s, including Squeeze's 1978 debut album, *U.K. Squeeze*. Recorded during his soused period, an ornery Cale rejected all of the band's existing material, insisting that it formulate a new set of songs on the fly and inexplicably suggesting it call the album "Gay Guys." Oddly quirky and somewhat rag-tag, the release had little in common with Squeeze's future as one of new wave's classiest pop acts. The unrepresentative album would become Cale's most glaring misstep as a producer and the most uncharacteristic of Squeeze's frequently pleasing pop career.

• • • • •

With the "new wave" cresting, Eno embarked on a memorable three-album odyssey with New York's twitchy Talking Heads. As one of the early CBGB's bands, the Talking Heads helped resuscitate the lifeless mid-'70s Manhattan rock scene with a spare, nervously nerdy aesthetic. The group's first album, *Talking Heads '77,* begot a minor hit in the paranoiac anthem "Psycho Killer," but its dry production was largely lackluster and constricting.

Coming on board for its sophomore release, *More Songs About Buildings and Food,* Eno immediately chartered a more textured studio-based sound. Unlike Devo, the band openly embraced his experiments, and Eno quickly gelled with likeminded Dadaist frontman David Byrne. By bringing the Heads' limber rhythm section closer to the forefront, Eno downplayed some of the band's quirkier aspects in favor of a looser, funkier sound. The strategy soon paid dividends when the album and its engaging cover of Al Green's "Take Me to the River" both landed in the U.S. Top 30 in late 1978.

Buoyed by the success, the Eno/Heads collaboration continued a year later with the transitional *Fear of Music,* recorded at the loft of married Heads Tina Weymouth and Chris Frantz. With Eno exerting an increasing songwriting and arrangement influence, he steered the band towards denser, more electronic waters on such cuts as the difficult "Life During Wartime," the coke-frazzled "Drugs," and the African-influenced "I Zimbra." For the first time, much of the band's material was derived from studio jams rather than through live performances, which lent a thematic quality to the album. "They had lots of bits and pieces, like modules which we would try and to fit together," Eno recalled of the album.[13]

By the time of 1980's luminescent *Remain in Light,* Eno had essentially become a fifth Talking Head, sharing writing credits with Byrne on all but one of its songs. Steeped in complex, interlocking African and Caribbean polyrhythms, echo-laden ambience, and dense sermonic wordplay, the luxuriously spacious tracks featured several session players and were almost entirely composed in the studio. The album benefited from a meticulous studio-based experimentation, exemplified by the laboriously overdubbed "Born Under Punches," which utilized no less than six basses. "Instead of having a few instruments playing complex pieces, you get lots of instruments all playing

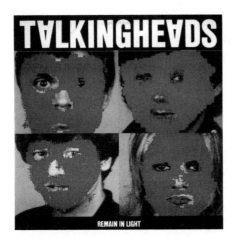

Talking Heads
Remain in Light
(1980)

very simple parts that mesh together to create a complex track," Eno revealed.[14]

A future-funk tour de force, *Remain in Light* remains one of rock's most startling accomplishments. Despite its genre-stretching results, Eno's increasing songwriting presence became too rankling for the rest of the band, and the outing would be his last with the Talking Heads. Nonetheless, Eno and Byrne continued to work together, soon returning to complete an unfinished musical collage, *My Life in the Bush of Ghosts*, that they had begun before *Remain in Light*. Disenchanted with traditional song structures, the duo constructed the album around a visionary use of audio snippets culled from such diverse sources as an indignant radio call-in show host, a Lebanese mountain singer, an exorcist, and a vitriolic radio evangelist. Eno and Byrne then layered the recordings like disembodied ghosts over a shape-shifting bed of electronics and "found" percussion coaxed from garbage cans and ashtrays.

"What we wanted was to create something more mysterious, and by taking voices out of context, but featuring them dominantly as the main vocal performance, you can go on to create meaning by surrounding the voice with a musical mood. In a way it was an experiment to see if you can create fairly sophisticated moods with voices outside their linguistic meaning," Eno said shortly before the album's release.[15]

Released in 1981, Eno/Byrne's *My Life in the Bush of Ghosts* is a prescient album, astoundingly still ahead of the curve more than two decades later. Its exotic rhythms and ethnic music cross-pollination opened the door for future fusions mined by artists ranging from Peter Gabriel and Paul Simon, to Senegalise singer Youssou N'Dour and Qawwali master Nusrat Fateh Ali Khan. Additionally, the album's trailblazing audio snippet sound collages served as a direct antecedent to the menacing hip-hop sampling technique utilized by the Bomb Squad's Hank Shocklee on seminal recordings for Public Enemy and Ice Cube.

Through the early '80s, Eno continued to explore ambient music through autumnal endeavors with minimalist pianist Harold Budd, experimental ethnic music fusions with avant-garde trumpeter Jon Hassell, and immaculate electronic forays with austere German technocrats Cluster. Ultimately, it was Eno's own 1982 release, *On Land*, that truly crystallized his vision of "listening to the world in a musical way." By masterfully blending natural noises, such as croaking frogs, shifting sand, and rubbed stones with synthetically treated sounds into a serene "drifting music," Eno was suggesting nothing short of a new type of musical possibility.

Drifting away from land towards space, 1983's celestial *Apollo: Atmospheres and Soundtracks* was yet another ambient achievement. The wondrously ethereal album was recorded with large assistance from Eno's brother Roger and frequent Acadian collaborator Daniel Lanois. Eno's ambient works proved highly influential and somewhat dubiously spawned the frequently vapid and consistently soulless '80s music genre New Age and several mood music record labels like Windham Hill. A decade later, Eno's same recordings would wield an enormous impact on the studio technology-driven electronica movement purveyed by artists like Aphex Twin, the Orb, and Moby, among numerous others. Eno had managed to forge revolutionary change while operating on pop's periphery. However, he would soon find himself on its frontlines.

• • • • •

By the mid-1980s, Cale had successfully dried out from booze. Replacing drinking for healthier pursuits like playing squash, he continued to record unpredictable solo albums while taking on the occasional

John Cale schemes his "Music for a New Society," early '80s

outside production gig. In 1987, he entered the studio with Manchester, England's notorious Happy Mondays for its debut, *Squirrel and G Man 24 Hour Party People Plastic Face Carnt Smile*. Led by thuggish front-man Shaun Ryder, Happy Mondays spearheaded the notorious "Madchester" scene, a drug-fueled, pulsating dance-rock movement that essentially invented hedonistic rave culture. Corralling the band's woozy mix of off-key party funk, throbbing house music, garage-psych, and attitude-copping post punk proved to be a challenge for Cale. While the band's best work was yet to come, the album's loopy "24 Hour Party People" quickly became Madchester's anthem of debauchery.

For the first time since *White Light/White Heat*, Cale reunited with Lou Reed in 1989 for *Songs for Drella*. A tribute to the recently deceased Andy Warhol, the speedily written album is a frequently rewarding song-cycle revolving around the life and death of the famed pop artist. Four years later, the two would participate in a full-blown Velvet Underground reunion, which spawned a European tour and subsequent live album. Unfortunately, ego clashes between Cale and Reed re-surfaced, and the re-formed band was unable to hold things together long enough for any U.S. appearances. Sadly, the '95 death of Velvets guitarist Sterling Morrison permanently quashed the possibility of any future reunions.

• • • • •

Back in spring 1984, the young Irish band U2 was rising up the rock ranks. The stridently political band had been gaining momentum on the strength of its unifying live performances and passionate mélange of energetic post-punk and anthemic rock. With its reputation swelling, the band took a daring left turn when it recruited Eno to helm its fourth album. When U2 informed its label, Island Records, of its seemingly incongruous intention, the company panicked. Desperately afraid that Eno was going to turn its promising cash cow into artsy navel-gazers, management begged U2 to reconsider. Even Eno himself was initially unsure about the pairing.

"I don't know what I could offer you," the producer said to U2's Bono.[15] Eno made it clear that he would drastically alter U2's sound, but the band assured him that was exactly what it wanted. "We could carry on being the same kind of rock 'n' roll band forever, and we'd do well at it, but we want to go somewhere else," Bono assured Eno.[16]

Eno took the job and invited fellow producer/engineer Daniel Lanois along with him. Bringing another producer onto the project was something of an insurance policy for Eno; he figured that, if things did not work out between he and the band, Lanois could finish the project himself. As the U2 sessions got under way in May '84, a division of labor was quickly established between the two producers. Lanois focused on the more practical aspects such as selecting a certain drum and making the sessions comfortable for the band, while Eno was left to sit back and make executive decisions, evaluating song ideas and pragmatically steering the album's overall direction.

Recorded in a cavernous Irish castle, the atmospheric *The Unforgettable Fire* was expectedly moodier than anything U2 had previously attempted. From the thundering compressed drums and slashing echo guitar of the impassioned Martin Luther King tribute "Pride (In the Name of Love)," to the twinkling textures of "A Sort of Homecoming" and "Bad," the impressionistic album is delicately

U2
Achtung Baby!
1991

enveloped in a late afternoon haziness. While its experimentation confounded certain fans more accustomed to the band's earlier fist-pumping anthems, its blurry song structures and heavy reliance on sequencers pointed towards a new direction for modern rock.

Three years later, the Eno/Lanois produced *Joshua Tree* made good on the promises of its predecessor and promptly catapulted U2's popularity to the stratosphere. Coupling the band's politically anthemic tendencies with more mature personal themes, the album was swathed in lushly warm tones, hypnotic rhythms, and harmonic hooks. On the strength of emotional breakout hits "I Still Haven't Found What I'm Looking for," "With or Without You," and "Where the Streets Have No Name," *Joshua Tree* became U2's first U.S. Number 1 release and resonated as a decade-defining album. The fact that U2 had reached this plateau with Eno makes their enormous success sweetly ironic.

U2 retained Eno and Lanois for its early '90s albums *Achtung Baby!* and *Zooropa*. Both releases succeeded in morphing the band's sound into a futuristic mix of Madchester-influenced electro-dance rhythms and post-modern irony. *Achtung Baby!* was a particular triumph of eclectic experimentation and calculated commercialism. The multi-platinum 1991 album won the Grammy for Best Rock Album By a Duo or Group and bore Eno and Lanois Producers of the Year Grammys.

"If you manage to get the four of them in one room with instruments in their hands, you're going to get results. That has a lot to do with my job—just getting them in the room and playing," Eno said, summing up his U2 work. With a colossal debt to Eno and Lanois's innovative studio ideals, U2 has retained a freshness that has allowed the band to remain among the rock 'n' roll elite for over two decades.

• • • • •

In 1990 Eno and Cale finally attempted their first official collaboration, *Wrong Way Up*. After frequently guesting on each other's albums throughout the '70s, the minimalists went in different directions through most of the '80s. When the duo rekindled their working relationship with Eno's appearance on Cale's 1989 album *Words for the Dying*, they decided to finally cut a formal album together.

Recording in the seclusion of Eno's 100-year-old Suffolk, England house dubbed "The Wilderness," the sessions did not run smoothly. Disagreements erupted over lyrics and song directions. Cale preferred lyrics sung in the first person, but Eno had always shied away from using words such as *I* and *you*, opting to rely on a more arbitrary phonetically derived approach. Cale temporarily stormed off the project, but cooler heads prevailed and the outstanding album was finally released in the fall of 1990. The inspired results proved that Eno still had a magical vocal presence and that Cale was still capable of penning resonant pop songs. Cuts such as "Spinning Away," "Lay My Love," and "Cordoba" contained a buoyant mix of atmospheric mystery and pleasing avant-pop that helped make the album a satisfying affair.

Cale continues to record when the mood strikes him, including 1994's *Last Day on Earth*, an ambitious thematic album cut with cult hero Bob Neuwirth, and 1998's *Nico*, an elegy to his old Velvet Underground compadre who died of a brain hemorrhage in 1988. In recent years he has continued to work with a typically diverse set of artists including goth stalwarts Siouxsie and the Banshees, Celtic music legend Alan Stivell, indie noise merchants Jesus Lizard, and Welsh avant-popsters Super Furry Animals.

Eno has remained busy, working on a number of ambient-techno releases and occasional soundtracks along with a clutch of outside productions, including a reunion with Bowie on his 1995 release

"Meeting of the minimalists," John Cale and Brian Eno, 1990

Outside. He has also undertaken a number of vertical video experiments, created several multi-media installations, and forayed into audio computer software. Perhaps Eno's widest ranging contribution is also his most subtle. In 1995, he created the "Microsoft Sound," the ubiquitous synthesizer crescendo that accompanied the Windows 95 operating system each time a computer was booted up—a musical watermark that has undoubtedly become imbedded in the collective subconscious.

KEY RECORDINGS
Brian Eno

Laurie Anderson –	*Bright Red* (Warner Bros. 1995)
David Bowie –	*Low* (RCA 1977)
	Heroes (RCA 1977)
	Lodger (RCA 1979)
	Outside (Virgin 1995)
Michael Brook –	*Hybrid* (Editions E.G. 1985)
Harold Budd –	*The Pavilion of Dreams* (Obscure 1978)
Harold Budd and – Brian Eno	*Ambient 2: The Plateaux of Mirror* (Editions E.G. 1980)
	The Pearl (Editions E.G. 1984)
John Cale –	"The Soul of Carmen Miranda" (Words for the Dying) (Warner Bros. 1989)
Cluster and Eno –	*Cluster and Eno* (Skyclad 1977)
Cluster –	*After the Heat* (Skyclad 1979)
Devo –	*Q: Are We Not Men? A: We Are Devo* (Warner Bros. 1980)
Edikanfo –	*The Pace Setters* (Editions E.G. 1981)
801 –	*801 Live* (E.G. 1976)
Brian Eno/ – David Byrne	*My Life in the Bush of Ghosts* (Sire 1981)
Brian Eno/John Cale –	*Wrong Way Up* (Opal 1990)
Brian Eno/ – J. Peter Schwalm	*Drawn From Life* (Astralwerks 2001)
Brian Eno/Jah Wobble –	*Spinner* (Gyroscope 1995)
Brian Eno –	*Here Comes the Warm Jets* (Island 1973)
	"Seven Deadly Finns" (Island 1974)
	Taking Tiger Mountain (By Strategy) (Island 1974)
	Another Green World (Island 1975)
	"The Lion Sleeps Tonight" (Island 1975)
	Discreet Music (Discreet 1975)
	Before and After (Island 1977)
	Music for Films (E.G. 1978)
	Ambient 1: Music for Airports (E.G. 1978)
	Ambient 4: On Land (E.G. 1982)
	Apollo: Atmospheres and Soundtracks (E.G. 1983)
	Thursday Afternoon (E.G. 1985)
	My Squelchy Life (Opal 1991)
	Nerve Net (Opal 1992)
	The Shutov Assembly (Opal 1992)
	Neroli (Gyroscope 1993)

The Drop (Thirsty Ear 1997)

Roger Eno –   *Voices* (E.G. 1985)

Robert Fripp/ –   *No Pussyfooting* (Antilles 1973)
    Brian Eno   *Evening Star* (Antilles 1975)

Jon Hassell/Brian Eno – *Fourth World Vol. 1: Possible Musics* (E.G. 1980)

Jon Hassell –   *Fourth World Vol. 2: Dream Theory in Malaya*
         (E.G. 1981)
     Power Spot (ECM 1986)

Laraaji –   *Ambient 3: Day of Radiance* (E.G. 1980)

James –   *Wah Wah* (Mercury 1994)

Passengers –   *Passengers: Original Soundtracks* (Island 1995)

Portsmouth Sinfonia – *Plays the Popular Classics* (Columbia 1974)
     Hallelujah (Antilles 1976)

Roxy Music –   *Roxy Music* (Reprise 1972)
     For Your Pleasure (Reprise 1973)

Talking Heads –   *More Songs About Buildings and Food* (Sire 1978)
     Fear of Music (Sire 1979)
     Remain in Light (Sire 1980)

U2 –   *The Unforgettable Fire* (Island 1984)
     Wide Awake in America (Island 1985)
     The Joshua Tree (Island 1987)
     Rattle and Hum (Island 1988)
     Achtung Baby! (Island 1991)
     Zooropa (Island 1993)

Ultravox –   *Ultravox!* (Island 1977)

Various Artists –   *No New York* (Antilles 1978)

Robert Wyatt –   *Ruth is Stranger than Richard* (Virgin 1975)

John Cale

Kevin Ayers/ –   *June 1st 1974* (Island 1974)
    John Cale/
    Brian Eno/Nico

Brian Eno/John Cale – *Wrong Way Up* (Opal 1990)

John Cale –   *Vintage Violence* (Columbia 1970)
     The Academy in Peril (Reprise 1972)
     Paris 1919 (Reprise 1973)
     Fear (Island 1974)
     Slow Dazzle (Island 1975)
     Helen of Troy (Island 1975)
     Animal Justice (EP) (Illegal 1977)
     Sabotage/Live (I.R.S. 1979)
     Honi Soit (A&M 1979)

John Cale (cont.) –	*Music for a New Society* (Ze 1982)
	Caribbean Sunset (Mango 1984)
	Artificial Intelligence (Beggars Banquet 1985)
	Words for the Dying (Opal 1989)
	Fragments for a Rainy Season (Hannibal 1992)
	Seducing Down the Door (Rhino 1995)
	Walking On Locusts (Hannibal 1996)
John Cale/Terry Riley –	*The Church of Anthrax* (Columbia 1971)
John Cale/ – Bob Neuwirth	*Last Day on Earth* (MCA 1994)
The Dream Syndicate –	*Inside the Dream Syndicate Vol 1.: Day of Niagara* (Table of the Elements 2000)
	Inside the Dream Syndicate Vol. 2: Dream Interpretation (Table of the Elements 2002)
	Inside the Dream Syndicate Vol. 3: Stainless Steel Gamelan (Table of the Elements 2002)
Happy Mondays –	*Squirrel and G-Man 24 Hour Party People Plastic Face Carnt Smile, White Out* (Factory 1997)
Jesus Lizard –	*The Jesus Lizard* (Jetset 1998)
David Kubinec –	*Some Things Never Change* (A&M 1978)
Nico –	*The Marble Index* (Elektra 1969)
	Desertshore (Reprise 1970)
	The End (Island 1974)
	Camera Obscura (Beggars Banquet 1985)
Lou Reed/John Cale –	*Songs for Drella* (Warner Bros. 1990)
The Modern Lovers –	*The Modern Lovers* (Beserkley 1976)
Siouxsie and – the Banshees	*The Rapture* (Geffen 1995)
Patti Smith –	*Horses* (Arista 1975)
U.K. Squeeze –	*U.K. Squeeze* (A&M 1978)
Alan Stivell –	*1 Douar* (Dreyfus 1998)
The Stooges –	*The Stooges* (Elektra 1969)
Jennifer Warnes –	*Jennifer Warnes* (Reprise 1972)
The Velvet – Underground	*The Velvet Underground and Nico* (Verve 1967)
	White Light/White Heat (Verve 1967)
	VU (Polygram 1985)
	Another View (Polygram 1986)
	Live MCMXCIII (Warner Bros. 1993)

7

THE THIRD WORLD'S REVENGE: KING TUBBY, LEE "SCRATCH" PERRY, AND THE RISE OF DUB

"We liked to record drums and bass first, to get them perfect. The other instruments would be put on afterwards. But sometimes the rhythm track would be so fucking perfect that we'd just forget about the other parts and just play about with the drums and bass. So what started as a technical thing became a creative thing,"[1] recalled Lee "Scratch" Perry, recounting his dubwise awakening during the King Tubby collaboration Blackboard Jungle Dub.

• • • • •

O sbourne Ruddock was a natural-born tinkerer, seduced by the science of sound. By the late '50s, the Kingston-bred teenager had parlayed his technical proficiency into a living as an electrical engineer and a radio repairman. Nicknamed King Tubby, because of his mother's maiden name (Tubman) and his particular expertise with radio tube circuitry, he began to drift towards Jamaica's magnetic music scene.

By 1962 Jamaican bands were moving away from their derivative American R&B and Big Band jazz aping towards a new homegrown sound called "ska." A tropically spirited sound, ska synthesized sweet soul, jump blues, Big Band, and Afro-Cuban with "mento," an indigenous Jamaican musical form that merged Caribbean calypso rhythms with traditional British Isles folk. Predicated on the second and fourth beats, ska was played at a rhythmically choppy, frenetically shuffling tempo, peppered by a playfully loopy horn section that often emphasized a freewheeling trombone. With its novel infectiousness and inherent danceability, the tough new music swept over the

King Tubby
Meets Rockers Uptown
(1976)

island like a tropical storm and dominated Jamaica through the mid-1960s.

Capitalizing on Jamaica's fervent devotion to music and remarkably deep local talent pool were three producers: Clement "Coxsone" Dodd, Leslie Kong, and Duke Reid. Each had opened his own recording studio and complementing labels and competition between the rivals was fierce. It was at reigning kingpin Duke Reid's Treasure Isle Studio that King Tubby got his first break, overseeing the production of test-pressing acetates as a "disc cutter." Legendarily fastidious and inherently technical, Tubby's quality control methods were methodical and rigorous, as he invariably went to extreme lengths to ensure that a song sounded as good as it possibly could. The fact that the equipment at Treasure Isle was unimaginably primitive only heightened the challenge of Tubby's labor.

It was during one particular disc-cutting session that Tubby accidentally excluded sections of a vocal track from the mix of one of the recordings. As he played the errant mix, he was taken aback by what he heard: rather than an expected disaster, the song was actually improved by the mistake. Far different than a standard recording, the fractured mix considerably opened the recording and the song was unexpectedly energized with a refreshing spaciousness. The first flower of dub music had sprouted.

As the wildly popular, tight-quartered Jamaican dance halls swelled far past capacity, music promoters began moving the clubs outside to street corners around Kingston to accommodate the throngs of insatiable partygoers. Essentially gigantic block parties, these weekend celebrations were stoked by booming sound systems that kept everybody moving to the current local dance hits long into the steamy tropical nights. Competition was stiff and often violent between rival sound system operators (known as "selectors") and their "rude boy" henchmen, and as a result equipment was frequently sabotaged and speakers were often damaged. With his electrical expertise and repairman pedigree, Tubby became the go-to man to fix the ravaged sound systems.

Often armed with Tubby's own instrumental remixes, each rival selector engaged in an ongoing game of one-upmanship with its competition. Because of this, Tubby was perpetually customizing each sound system to be more powerful than the one before. Although the early sound systems were relatively small and benign, the new set ups were equipped to play at increasingly rump rumbling volumes—clearly, louder was better. Finally, Tubby embraced the inevitable and began to construct his own super mega-watt "Home Town Hi-Fi" sound system.

By 1968 Tubby had demolished the competition with his soupped-up sound system. Utilizing his technical engineering expertise and keen understanding of sound dynamics, the Home Town Hi-Fi was outfitted with a multitude of customized circuitry, transistor technology, sound filters, and industrial-strength speakers (which he strategically placed high in trees and away from harm's way). Utilizing a relatively advanced "weight and treble" wiring system, Tubby was afforded the luxury of a separate valve amplifier that allowed the all-important bass to boom loudly and melodically; a transistor treble amplifier gave the system a crisp high-end clarity that was clearly lacking from the other systems. However, Tubby's true secret weapon was the heavy-duty echo and reverb capacities arming the Home Town Hi-Fi—sonic artillery that would soon become staples of his dub revolution.

Along with the selector (the designate responsible for choosing the music and actually playing the records), many of the sound systems featured live DJs who worked in a style called "toasting," which improvised rhyming jive boastings over the instrumental passages of spinning records. (Undoubtedly, this block-party toasting style would become a clear antecedent to the embryonic rap style that would begin cropping up around the New York streets by the mid-seventies.) Jamaica's greatest toaster was the nimble-voiced "Originator," U-Roy, a thoroughly engaging personality and gifted rhymer who would often appear with Tubby's Home Town Hi-Fi system. Tubby had first seen the charismatic U-Roy perform at an outside dance in Spanish Town, Jamaica, in 1968, and he immediately recruited him for his own sound system. Powered by Tubby's advanced effects, U-Roy's jivey reverb-saturated proclamations instantly stood out from the other less-sophisticated sound rigs.

Utilizing the technique he had accidentally stumbled onto while disc-cutting, Tubby capitalized on the emerging toasting style. By eliminating the vocals from A-side singles and remixing them into instrumental "versions," he stripped the records down to their rawest bass and drum rhythmic essence. Perfectly tailored for DJs like U-Roy to rhyme over, the versions quickly became a sound system mainstay. While fellow Treasure Isle engineer (and competing sound system operator) MC Ruddy Redwood had first pioneered the concept of the bass-heavy version, it was Tubby's visionary use of custom-built sound effects like echo, phasing, and reverb that elevated his own versions into an unbeatable toasting platform. With his version blueprint drawn, Kingston's top toasters—including U-Roy, Big Youth, and I-Roy—helped enable Tubby's Home Town Hi-Fi to tower high above its competition. Jamaican music was changing.

$$\bullet \quad \bullet \quad \bullet \quad \bullet \quad \bullet$$

"I'm still a child in my mind."—Lee "Scratch" Perry[2]

Not even five feet tall, Lee Perry's riot of imagination transcended Jamaica's shores to wash over the world. Like many in his small Jamaican country town, Perry grew up dirt poor. His father was a road repairman, and his mother spent her days toiling in the hot island fields. As a boy, Perry was prone to escapism, and he often drifted into a fantasy world of comic books and cartoons—imagery that would frequently crop up throughout the course of his recordings. As a teenager, Perry haunted the local dance halls, mesmerized by the horn-stoked jazz and rhythmic blues sounds that propelled his tightly

Lee Perry
Roast Fish Collie Weed
Corn Bread
(1976)

wound, attention-getting dance steps. When not stepping in the clubs, Perry was playing dominoes, which he found particularly useful for gleaming psychological insights into people: "Through dominoes I practiced my mind and learned to read the minds of others," he said.[3]

After a stint as a bulldozer driver, Perry headed to Kingston, the Island's nefarious center of sin and salvation, determined to break into Jamaica's fledgling music industry. By the early '60s he had settled in Vineyard Town, a densely populated ghetto in West Kingston. The displaced musical neophyte began to linger around various mutant R&B recording sessions run by Duke Reid at Treasure Isle Studios. An aspiring songwriter, Perry freely offered up his songs to Reid. However, Perry quickly grew adversarial with the Treasure Isle honcho after discovering he was receiving virtually no credit for his ideas. Competing underdog producer Clement "Coxsone" Dodd had also become familiar with the wiry and animated Perry. In a move indicative of the cutthroat and competitive Jamaican music business, Dodd stole Perry from under Reid's nose and hired him to work at his Downbeat sound system.

Originally working as an errand boy, Perry's fireplug energy and bizarre dance steps helped endear him to Dodd and his cronies, who dubbed the diminutive country boy "Little Lee." Once accepted into Dodd's inner circle, Perry's duties were expanded to include shuttling recording materials between studios, talent-scouting new blood, and studio production assistance. Finally, after tireless persistence, he was given a chance to cut his own tune. Titled "Chicken Scratch," Perry

based the song on the dance craze of the same name that was currently delighting the country. Supplanted by several members of the
soon-to-be legendary Skatalites, Perry cut the twitchy R&B–based
"Chicken Scratch" at Federal Studios in 1961. After the session, Perry
was awarded a five-year contract with Dodd and a second nickname
that would last a lifetime: "Scratch." Never officially released as a single, the funky shuffle became a popular and exclusive mainstay of
Dodd's Downbeat sound system for years to come.

Despite his slight frame, Perry was fearless and, as violence
between rival sound systems began to escalate, he became one of the
primary protectors of Downbeat. Also helping to keep the sound system safe from Reid's pernicious saboteurs was fellow bodyguard and
aspiring songwriter Prince Buster. Like Perry, Prince Buster was also
creatively suffocating under Dodd's stranglehold, and in a move for
independence he defected from the Downbeat crew. Forming his own
Voice of the People sound system and record label, Prince Buster
soon became ska's top star.

Witnessing Prince Buster's success, Perry was itchy to record
more of his own bouncily risqué ska songs. But the eternally stubborn
Dodd resisted, insisting that Perry's rural semi-spoken vocals were
still not polished enough for proper recording. Although Dodd didn't
care for Perry's croaky voice, he liked his feisty and salacious songs
(especially the lyrics), and he began to fork them over to other
Treasure Isle artists, like burgeoning vocalist Delroy Wilson. After
penning a clutch of combative tunes for Wilson to counterpunch rival
Prince Buster, Perry continued to languish on the sidelines. "Coxsone
never wanted to give a country boy a chance. No way. He took my
songs and gave them to Delroy Wilson. I got no credit, certainly no
money. I was being screwed," Perry remarked years later.[4]

In an effort to consolidate his record labels, Dodd moved all his
assets under the umbrella of Studio One in early 1964. Installing
prodigious rhythm and horn champs the Skatalites as the label's devastating house band, Dodd mounted an aggressive campaign to swal-
low up all of the island's top young vocal talent. Acting on Perry's
keen advice, Dodd signed the soulful singer Toots Hibbert (who would
later form the seminal Maytals) and a scruffy quintet from the Trench
Town ghetto of Kingston called the Wailers. The Wailers had already

cut a few slight singles for pop-savvy Chinese-Jamaican producer Leslie Kong, but Perry sensed something unique buried deep within the group. Especially intriguing was one of its vocalists, a fiery, fellow country boy named Bob Marley. Dodd saw the promise as well and gave the restless Marley a tiny room adjacent to the studio to keep him out of trouble. As Dodd's top promo man, Perry received his marching orders: make the Wailers the biggest group in Jamaica.

While Perry continued to cut a number of songs for Studio One, Dodd curiously continued to balk at officially releasing most of them locally. Ironically, exclusive acetates of Perry's lascivious dance songs like "Pussy Galore" and "Rub and Squeeze" were regularly spun on Dodd's Downbeat sound system and had proved to be enormously popular among the revelers. In the ensuing years since Perry was hired, Studio One had grown from pugnacious upstart into Jamaica's most esteemed and powerful label. Rightly considering himself a key factor in the label's ascendance, Perry was out of patience with Dodd and broke with Studio One.

As ska began to give way to the less horn-reliant and airier guitar and piano-dominated rocksteady sound, Perry hooked on with fledgling promoter/producer Joe Gibbs in 1966. Working as an arranger for Gibbs's WIRL studios, Perry began to take over many of the sessions, barking musical instructions to the band and frequently assisting on percussion. With a large debt to Perry's efforts, WIRL quickly came out of nowhere to become a major player within the Jamaican music industry. Although once again feeling under-appreciated and under-compensated, Perry soon torched his bridges with WIRL, as he had done at Studio One.

Now a free agent, Perry took to recording a number of venomous tracks directed at his former miserly employers. Among these stinging indictments was the anti-Dodd "The Upsetter" (a song that provided Perry with yet another new nickname), and the savage "People Funny Boy," a rhythmically jittery attack on Gibbs that was independently released as a single in 1968. Framed by Perry's growlingly incensed vocals, stuttering electric bass, drum-heavy beats, and disconcerting overdubs of his crying infant son, "People Funny Boy" became a huge local hit and cemented Scratch as an important new school producer. The song's rebel defiance, roughly quickened pace (in comparison to the more languid Rocksteady), and emphasis on imaginative engineering made "People Funny Boy" arguably the first true reggae single.

King Tubby
Creation Dub
(1995)

• • • • •

Meanwhile, King Tubby's groundbreaking versions were gaining prominence. A crop of new breed of producers, including Scratch, Bunny "Striker" Lee, and Glen Brown, hired the engineer to lend his distinctive rhythm and reverb remix treatment to their recordings. Moving away from the percussive piano and scratchy guitar rocksteady style, these producers were pushing towards a sophisticated new sound that emphasized offbeat "riddims"—a Jamaican rhythm pattern that elevated bass and drums from its traditional backing support role to lead instruments. Derived from Jamaican street slang, this new genre was called reggae.

Continuing to operate out of Treasure Isle's archaic studio, Tubby began to outfit the recording equipment with his customized filters and echo units. Generously applying his array of sound-stretching gimmicks, Tubby created his surrealistic remixes totally on the fly. Demonstrating an innate mixing ability akin to a master conductor, Tubby deftly dropped out vocals, effortlessly faded up bottomy bass and swishing hi-hat drums passages, and colorfully panned horns and organs from speaker to speaker. Tubby was forging nothing less than a new musical language, the remix culture was born.

With the dominating sound system in Kingston and his remix skills in top demand, Tubby finally opened his own recording studio in 1971. Located on Dromilly Avenue in the rough-and-tumble Waterhouse ghetto of West Kingston, the studio was small, but its acoustics were warmly conducive to his emerging sound. No longer just a remixer, Tubby had become a full-fledged recording engineer, as he skillfully squeezed the most from the studio's rather limited two-track recorder. When Kingston recording studio mainstay Dynamic Studios upgraded to a new console, Tubby secured financial assistance from producer (and overall fix-it man) Bunny Lee to purchase Dynamic's discarded four-track recorder. Despite its relative obsolescence, having four tracks was a true luxury to Tubby, and he immediately went to work on tinkering with the board. Constantly re-configuring the set-up, the studio came to resemble a Frankensteinian laboratory bursting with parts scrounged from various makes and models. Utilizing the spare parts, Tubby created customized reverb machines, makeshift equalizers, and homemade delay units. His most important enhancement involved replacing the board's four worn-out sliding volume faders with newer, more resilient sliders that afforded him far greater command and control of the mixing levels.

By improving the flexibility of the faders, Tubby was given a clear advantage over competing engineers like Errol Thompson, whose more modern mixing board relegated him to punching buttons to control volume levels. As a result, Tubby's competitors' mixes were often jerky and sporadic. At last comfortable in his own immaculately kept studio, Tubby continued to hone his recording techniques. Wizened by his disc-cutting time at Treasure Isle, where he meticulously recorded multiple quality-control test-pressings for each track, Tubby discovered that certain sections could be elevated to greater resonance by simply isolating a melody or vocal phrase. Although his sound was inherently sparse, after the individual sections were swaddled in echo, delay, and reverb and then mixed together, a hypnotically spaced-out whole would be forged. Moving far past the original instrumental version style, Tubby had perfected an entirely new genre called "dub."

By 1972 Tubby had his dub technique down to a science. First, he would allow the song's melody to be introduced before promptly fading out the music and thus leaving the singers to sing the opening bars *a capella*. Then he would invert the mix and abruptly drop out the vocals to "cool" (sometimes before the lyric line was even completed) while leaving the music to float by instrumentally for a section: "During the *a capella* vocals the abdomen is not being resonated by the bass, and the head is occupied by the singing. When the band track drops back in, the awareness of the listener is quickly diverted down towards the abdomen for a moment and the cerebral stimulus of the singing ceases," Tubby explained.[5] A gloriously disorienting approach, the recordings were imbued with an air of suspenseful intrigue, leaving the listener to wonder when a vocal or instrumental part would glide back into the song.

By now, all of the island's greatest musical and producing talent descended on the Dromilly Avenue studio, looking to get the Tubby dub treatment for their songs. Tubby worked non-stop with a variety of artists and producers that included Scratch, Augustus Pablo, and Bunny Lee and his remarkably elastic backing band, the Aggrovators. With his unerring drive for perfection, Tubby would often cut up to a half-dozen different mixes of the same song before finally deciding on the best take. This exacting approach not only said a lot about his recording methods, but about his overall approach to life. A neat freak, everything from his freshly pressed clothes and spotlessly shined shoes, to the immaculately polished chrome on his studio amplifiers reflected his obsession with cleanliness and order. Considering the supremely stoned-out sound of his recordings, it was almost unfathomable that he personally eschewed ganja smoking. Ganja was a sacrament of the prevailing Rastafarian lifestyle taken up by many in the reggae fraternity, but Tubby vehemently banned it from being smoked within his studio.

• • • • •

With the runaway success of the proto-reggae "People Funny Boy," Scratch Perry was rapidly cultivating a reputation as a feisty and idiosyncratic innovator. To aid in his developing set of sonic ideals, he assembled a musically tough-minded backing group of young Kingstonians called the Upsetters. Capitalizing on the brutal outlaw spirit of Italian Spaghetti Westerns movies (which they frequently attended), Perry and the Upsetters released several driving instrumentals that merged ricocheting gunfire and sundry Western movie sound effects with warbley organ, choppy guitar, and clipped proto-reggae bass and drum riddims. Occasionally, the songs would be punctuated with Perry speaking the song title, but usually cuts such as "For a Few Dollars More," "Dig Your Grave," "Clint Eastwood," and "Return of Django" appeared strictly as loose homage. Several of the Upsetters' singles found their way onto the British charts, and the group successfully toured the country for six weeks in 1969. With its captivating island rhythms and bad-ass desperado appeal, the group was significantly responsible for kick-starting Britain's lasting reggae obsession and for planting the first insurgent seedlings of '70s political punk rock.

Crucial to the early Upsetters' sound was the group's astonishing rhythmic foundation, which came courtesy of Barrett brothers: bassist Aston and drummer Carlton. Originally known as the Soul Mates, then (along with singer Max Romeo) the Hippy Boys, the young siblings had been so inspired by the ska rhythms of the Skatalites that they taught themselves to play music on homemade instruments. Nicknamed "Family Man" (because of his several out of wedlock children), Aston had made his first bass out of a plywood board, a curtain rod, and a string. Carlton first developed his percussive "one drop" inverted riddim technique by practicing on a drum set made out of empty paint cans and old pots.

By 1969 Perry had opened the Upsetter umbrella to cover a sound system, a record label, and a Kingston record shop. It was at the Upsetter record shop that Perry was reunited with the Wailers, the group he had spent so much time and energy promoting for Dodd back at Studio One. With Bob Marley elevated to lead singer, the group recorded more than 70 songs for Studio One, and several were released as successful singles, including the seminal "Simmer Down" in 1964. The members of the Wailers had gone their separate ways in 1966 but recently reassembled with a core trio of Marley, Peter Tosh, and Bunny Livingstone.

Desperate to replicate Perry's British chart success, the newly Rastafarian-embracing Wailers sought Scratch's tutelage, not to mention back-up support from the supremely musically endowed Upsetters. However, Perry was focusing on fostering the killer instrumental rhythms of the Upsetters to the exclusion of everything else, and as a result he was hesitant to take on a vocal group. Nonetheless, he gave the group an impromptu tryout and promptly reconsidered after hearing its remarkable new material. With Perry producing and co-writing most of

*Bob Marley and
the Wailers*
African Herbsman
(1973)

the songs, the Wailers cut two album's worth of archetypal reggae over an astoundingly productive six-month stretch between late 1970 and early 1971. Included in the fruitful sliver of time were several tautly spare and spooky powerhouses like "My Cup," "Duppy Conqueror," "Small Axe," "400 Years," and "Soul Almighty"—ghostly songs that juggled allegorical folklore and disenfranchised political outrage.

Influenced by R&B's expanding funk innovations and socially conscious themes of American producers like Sly Stone and Norman Whitfield, Perry steered the band towards a lean, sinewy sound built on the Wailers' mighty mixture of personal spirituality, Rasta mysticism, and ghetto-spawned militancy. Perry worked closely with Marley on his vocal phrasing, chiding him to ratchet up his energy and intensity while discouraging his predilection for laziness and the unnecessary falsetto leaps that marred some of the Wailers' earlier material. Although Perry did not possess a traditionally accomplished voice himself, his method of slowly enunciating lyrics to inject a passionate conviction into the words became a lifelong influence on Marley.

Unfortunately for Perry, the union of the Upsetters and the Wailers was too perfect, and, when Marley's group signed on with Chris Blackwell's Island Records in 1972, it took the Barrett brothers with it as full-time band members. By the following year, the Wailers parlayed its skanking Perry-derived sound into international superstar status and became the group most responsible for transforming reggae into a musical phenomenon. Perry would continue to sporadically lend his mercurial magic to Marley (often behind the scenes), most

Upsetters
Blackboard Jungle Dub
(1973)

notably on the spunky mid-1970s B-side, "Punky Reggae Party," until the icon's death in 1981.

Recovering from the loss of his core Upsetters, Perry formed a new lineup, and his sound began to enter a new phase. Diving headfirst into experimental waters, Perry's work was increasingly marked by ganja-addled arrangements, unpredictable multi-layered overdubs (of everything from traffic noise to falling rain to broken glass), and scattershot mixes, which were typified on releases like the proto-dub *Cloak and Dagger* and the invigorating *Rhythm Shower*. As Perry continued to sharpen, skew, and scramble his recording skills, he began to delve into King Tubby's emerging dub style. Heavily reliant on nimble on-the-fly mixes and over-flowing buckets of bouncing echo, ricocheting reverbed rhythms, and serendipitous studio ambience, Perry took to the sonically lawless dub experimentation like a duck to water.

In 1973, Perry and Tubby began working together on *Blackboard Jungle Dub*, an epochal recording that would ostensibly become the first real dub album. With its stripped-down smorgasbord of primal melodies, ultra-echoed stop-and-go rhythms, free-floating horns, and Scratch's disquieting array of sinister growls, guttural moans, and siren-like wails, *Blackboard Jungle Dub* was the ultimate amalgamation of Tubby's technocratic minimalism and Perry's ganja-clouded anarchy. The release launched the dub genre into space, and it would continue to orbit around Jamaica through the end of the decade. Moreover, with its recycled rhythms, dub helped introduce the concept of musical sampling, a technique that remains a bedrock component of hip-hop and electronica.

• • • • •

Bolstered by the addition of a second four-track recorder that allowed him to record vocals in the studio, Tubby enjoyed a breakthrough hit with Roy Shirley's danger-courting "Stepping Razor." Following the watershed *Blackboard Jungle Dub* came additional dub milestones *Dub from the Roots* and *King Tubby Meets the Aggrovators at Dub Station*, which were both recorded with Bunny Lee. The two would frequently work together with the Aggrovators throughout the decade, mining Lee's "flying cymbal" rhythm (a variation on the "Philly-bump" American soul beat) on scores of remixes.

Tubby's dub vision scaled new heights with his work on Augustus Pablo's Far Eastern–influenced *King Tubby Meets Rockers Uptown*, a masterful recording that elevated the art of dub into a mysterious, pathos-laden, classical form. Included on the Pablo record was the title track, a melodic version of Jacob Miller's "Baby I Love You So." An infinitely echoing bass and drums tour-de-force, the song garnered international notoriety and crystallized the seductively dark and alluring underpinning of dub.

Remixing non-stop, Tubby's name was so coveted by the mid-1970s that many bought records simply based on his name alone—an amazing and unprecedented achievement for an engineer! Rapidly becoming ubiquitous, Tubby's name appeared on an endless stream of recordings for producers like Winston "Niney the Observer" Holness and master orchestrator Harry Mudie. He also teamed up with Vivian "Yabby You" Jackson, most notably on his landmark roots releases, *Conquering Lion* and *Wall of Jerusalem.*

Always eager to impart his wisdom and foster new talent, the patriarchal Tubby mentored several young talents who would soon come to production prominence, including Mikey Dread, Scientist, Prince (later King) Jammy, and Prince Phillip Smart. By freely divulging his multi-track recording methodology, techniques of achieving his trademark thunderclap sound effects, and secrets of equalization and microphone placements, Tubby revealed nothing less than his lifelong amassed theories of *sound.* In doing so, Tubby generously strove to pass the baton in order to keep the dub dynasty thriving.

• • • • •

However, Scratch Perry was far too restless to strictly remain a dub purveyor. Although he would re-visit the genre later in the decade on albums like *Revolution Dub*, the beastly *Super Ape*, and its sequel *Return of Super Ape*, his take on dub was more cluttered and vocal-dominant than the minimalist formula typified by King Tubby and his disciples. Perry further defined his herb-roasted rhythm sound on a number of productions for reggae vocalists including Leo Graham, Dave Barker, and, most importantly, Junior Byles. Working with the gifted, but disturbed, Byles, Perry produced a number of politically searing tracks such as the nursery rhyme-like "Pharaoh Hiding" (a swipe at the ruling Jamaican Labour Party) and "Beat Down Babylon" (a scathing protest song that overdubbed a cracking bull-whip on top of an anguished refrain of "whip them, whip them lord!") that helped further embolden reggae's rebel music reputation. Conversely, his biggest hit with Byles was "Curly Locks," a poignant love song in which Perry restrained his over-the-top tendencies in favor of a effervescently gauzy backing track.

With money accrued from a run of successful productions, Perry sought to hole up even further into his own warped imagination. Inspired by a vivid dream he had while napping in front of a tree in his backyard, he opened his own label and home studio called the Black Ark in 1974. Taking its name from the Ark of the Covenant, Perry called the studio a "power plant of righteousness."[6] With a great deal of help from magnanimous wiring wizard King Tubby, the Black Ark was outfitted with the best equipment available, including a four-track Soundcraft board, a TEAC recorder, a Conn Rhythm box drum machine, an Echoplex delay unit, and a Roland space echo rigged to a Mutron phaser device.

With his costly sonic playroom finally finished, Perry worked around the clock, hatching floating underwater dubs over bubbling backwards beats, elliptical horns, and abstruse toastings—all the while dancing around the tiny studio like a tank-top-clad whirling dervish. Enshrouding the sessions was an ever-present thick fog of Colombian ganja, which he would blow on the recording tape in a sacramental effort to bless the music. Perry would often leave the stu-

The Congos
Heart of the Congos
(1977)

dio doors open, courting natural ambience as the music and smoke wafted out towards the neighborhood. Laying down the skittering, inside-out rhythms was a revolving cavalcade of Jamaica's top session men, including an indomitable team of horn players, the amazing rhythm section of bassist Boris Gardiner and drummer Michael Richards, guitar stalwarts Earl "Chinna" Smith and Ernest Ranglin, and dubwise keyboardist Augustus Pablo.

Somehow with Perry's endless rhythm deconstructions, distorted volume meter-pinning mixes and multitudinous overdubs of flushing toilets and mooing cows, the early Black Ark sound managed to be feathery light, pillowy soft, and, of course, higher than the sun. Defining production achievements of the early Black Ark period included The Congos' mythical *Heart of the Congos*, Keith Rowe's buoyant "Groovy Situation," Junior Murvin's gravity-defying "Police and Thieves," the Heptones' flanged beat-box sweetened "Party Time," Max Romeo's politically conscious "War Ina Babylon," Dr. Alimantado's severely cock-eyed "Best Dressed Chicken in Town" and Perry's own mixologist manifesto, *Roast Fish Collie Weed & Cornbread*.

Twisting elastic tracks into sweet sonic taffy, Perry's demands to artists were often cryptic and confounding. Whether it was the unorthodox way he demanded a rhythm played, a specific lyric phrased, or even a cymbal crashed, artists were usually more confused *after* they asked Perry to explain why he wanted something done. Indeed, much of Scratch's genius resided in his wonderfully warped, generally improvised arrangements that emphasized the mercurial spontaneity of the live performance. This method was in direct contrast to post-production specialists like King Tubby and Prince Jammy, who achieved all of their magic long after the original tracks had been cut.

Further contributing to the mystically blurry Black Ark sound was Perry's rule-defying track construction, which sometimes entailed splicing up to three different rhythms together. Because the studio was equipped with only a four-track recorder, Perry was constantly relegated to dumping tracks onto each other ("bouncing down") in order to clear additional recording space for more tracks. With each "bounce down," an additional recording generation was spawned, and each time the sound would get a little fuzzier—but somehow, a little deeper. Rather than detracting from the overall sound, Perry's endlessly bounced-down tracks seemed to benefit with each new murky layer.

As the decade wore on, Perry's productions became weightier and increasingly unpredictable. Consequently, some his productions were akin to failed soufflés that were either half-baked or entirely too dense to rise. Perry, who had been revered in England since the Upsetters' 1968 tour, began to work outside of the reggae environs with a diverse range of British artists including political punks the Clash, atmospheric-folkie John Martyn, fellow ganja lover Paul McCartney, and white-boy soulster Robert Palmer.

As one of the only pop artists to actually record at Black Ark, Palmer was exposed first-hand to the studio's bizarre atmosphere: "These guys come around wearing robes and they've got magic wands and shit. I'm doing vocals and one stands in front of the mic and starts doing this weird dance. It was very strange, and Lee didn't do a thing to try to stop it. He was very amused by my reaction," Palmer said.[7]

Always unusual and idiosyncratic, by the late '70s Perry began to court the mad genius tag more aggressively than ever. Apocryphal legends abound of constant LSD tripping, rampant coke snorting, an inhuman intake of industrial-strength weed and rum, tape-head cleaning fluid drinking, walking backwards on sidewalks for hours on end, obsessions with children's rubber balls, eating money, bowing to bananas, and bonking around the studio with a hammer while looking for Caesar's ghost. Through neglect, Black Ark began to fall into disrepair, compounded by water damage and Perry's perplexing practice of scrawling graffiti over the studio walls and then painting over all of the vowels with black Xs.

While fact and fiction around this period are as intoxicatingly blurry as one of Perry's trademark mixes, it is certain that some sort of massive breakdown gripped the producer in 1983, causing him to inexplicably torch his beloved Black Ark Studio. Although faulty wiring has sometimes been blamed for the accident, most likely the tragedy was precipitated by the combination of a Satan-fearing acid freakout, acrimonious marital problems, and the unsavory presence of extortion-demanding gangsters. Perry was held in jail for several days on arson suspicion, but local authorities were unable to collect sufficient evidence, and he was eventually released.

· · · · ·

Branching out into straight production work in the '80s, King Tubby worked with much of Jamaica's new generation vocal talent, including Sugar Minott, Gregory Isaacs, Anthony Red Rose, and Ninjaman. Despite his success, Tubby kept his studio in the tough neighborhood of Waterhouse. It was there that he was shot and killed in what is widely considered to be a robbery gone wrong in February 1989—yet another victim of the senseless violence that has cost several reggae icons their lives

Relocating to England in the mid-eighties, Perry rebounded with the manic 1986 release, *Battle of Armagideon (Millionaire Liquidator)*, an oddball collaboration with producer Mad Professor. Even better were teacher/mentor recordings with British producer (and Scratch-disciple) Adrian Sherwood and his Upsetters-inspired house band, the Dub Syndicate, including the darkly demented *Time Boom X De Devil Dead* and the ranting *From the Secret Laboratory*. Perry moved to Switzerland in 1989 and still manages to occasionally dispatch his bulletins from outer space.

King Tubby and Scratch Perry's paradigm-shifting studio-as-an-instrument sound collages, early sampling forays, and visionary dub remix experiments continue to swell in importance. Today, the two

Jamaicans are rightly regarded as the forefathers of mixology—a beat science that has significantly influenced punk pioneers (the Clash and the Slits), post-punk deconstructionists (the Fall and Public Image Ltd.), trip-hop/jungle/drum and bass mavens (Massive Attack, Tricky and Squarepusher, et al.), turntablists (DJ Spooky and Cut Chemist), and hip-hop innovators (from Grandmaster Flash, to the Beastie Boys, to Timbaland) and beyond. Thanks to Jamaican dub's continued pervasive influence, the eternally marginalized third world has finally exacted its revenge.

KEY RECORDINGS
Lee "Scratch" Perry

Junior Byles –   *Beat Down Babylon* (Dynamic 1973)
     "Curly Locks" (Heartbeat/Munich 1974)

Susan Cadogan –   *Hurt So Good* (Trojan 1975)

The Clash –   "Complete Control" (U.S. version of The Clash)
     (Epic 1977)

The Congos –   *Heart of the Congos* (Black Art 1977)

Doctor Alimantado –   "The Best Dressed Chicken in Town"
     (Greensleeves 1978)

Dub Syndicate –   *Research and Development* (On-U Sound 1996)

George Faith –   "To Be a Lover" (Island 1977)

The Gladiators –   "Ungrateful Girl" (Heartbeat 1976)

Danny Hensworth –   "Mr. Money Man" (*Build the Ark*) (Trojan 1990)

The Heptones –   "Sufferer's Time/Sufferer's Dub" (Island 1976)
     Party Time (Mango 1977)

Carlton Jackson –   "History" (Black Art Records 1977)

Jah Lion –   *Columbia Colly* (Mango 1976)

Bob Marley and –   "Duppy Conqueror" (Shelter 1970)
  the Wailers   *Soul Rebels* (Trojan 1970)
     African Herbsman (Trojan 1974)
     Rasta Revolution (Trojan 1974)
     "Punky Reggae Party" (Island 1977)
     Early Years 1969–1973 (Trojan 1993)

Junior Murvin –   *Police and Thieves* (Mango 1977)

Lee Perry –   "People Funny Boy" (Doctor Bird 1968)
     The Upsetter (Trojan 1969)
     Africa's Blood (Trojan 1972)
     Rhythm Shower (Trojan 1972)
     Kung Fu Meets the Dragon (Justice League 1975)
     "Dreadlocks in the Moonlight" (Mango 1976)
     Roast Fish Collie Weed & Cornbread
     (Lion of Judah 1976)
     Revolution Dub (Anachron 1979)
     Battle of Armagideon (*Millionare Liquidator*)
     (Trojan 1986)
     Time Boom X De Devil Dead (ON-U Sound 1987)
     From the Secret Laboratory (Mango 1990)
     Arkology (Polygram 1997)
     Live at Martime Hall (Martime 1998)

Prince Jazzbo –   "Croaking Lizard" (Mango 1976)

Prodigal –   "4 and 20 Dread Locks" (Seven Leaves 1982)

Max Romeo –   *War in a Babylon* (Mango 1976)

Keith Rowe –   "Groovy Situation" (Black Swan 1977)

Leroy Sibbles –   "Garden of Life" (Trojan 1979)

The Silvertones –   "Silver Bullets" (Trojan 1973)

The Upsetters –   *Return of Django* (Trojan 1969)
                         Eastwood Rides Again (Trojan 1970)
                         The Good, the Bad & the Upsetters (Trojan 1970)
                         Double Seven (Trojan 1972)
                         Blackboard Jungle Dub (Clocktower 1973)
                         Super Ape (Island 1976)
                         Return of Super Ape (Island 1980)

King Tubby

The Aggrovators –   *Johnny in the Echo Chamber (Dubwise Selection
                         1975–1976)* (Attack 1994)
                         *Creation Dub (King Tubby Meets the Aggrovators
                         at Dub Station)* (1973–1977) (Lagoon 1995)

Ken Boothe –   *You're No Good* (Burning Bush 2003)

Dennis Brown –   *Some Like it Hot* (Heartbeat 1992)

Glen Brown –   *Way to Mt. Zion* (ROIR 1995)
                         Termination Dub (Blood and Fire 1996)

Dillinger –   *3 Piece Suit* (Lagoon 1993)

Mikey Dread –   *African Anthem Dubwise* (Ras 1979)
                         Mikey Dread at the Controls Dubwise
                         (Trojan 1979)

I-Roy –   *Don't Check Me With No Lightweight Stuff
                         (1972–1975)* (Blood and Fire 1997)

King Tubby –   *Dub From the Roots* (Jet Set 1974)
                         *King Tubby & Friends: The Rod of Correction
                         Showcase* (1974–1979) (Abraham/Clocktower
                         1994)
                         King Tubby's Special (1973–1976) (Trojan 1989)
                         King Tubby Meets the Upsetters
                         (Reggae Best 1993)
                         If Deejay Was Your Trade (1975–1979)
                         (Blood and Fire 1994)
                         Dub From the Roots (Jetset 1998)
                         Roots of Dub (1973–1975) (Clocktower 1995)
                         *Yah Congo Meets King Tubby and Professor at
                         Dub Table* (ROIR 1995)

King Tubby (cont.) –	*Dub Gone Crazy: The Evolution of Dub at King Tubby's '75–'77* (Blood and Fire 1995)
	Dub Explosion (Trojan 1996)
	King Tubby Meets Roots Radics: Dangerous Dub (Greensleeves 1996)
	Dub Like Dirt (1975-1977) (Blood and Fire 1999)
	Best of King Tubby: King Dub (1973–1977) (Music Club 2000)
King Tubby and – Prince Jammy	*Dub Gone 2 Crazy* (Blood and Fire 1996)
King Tubby and – Soul Syndicate	*Freedom Sounds in Dub* (1976–1979) (Blood and Fire 1996)
The Observer All-Stars –	*Dubbing with the Observer* (Observer 1975)
Augustus Pablo –	*King Tubby Meets Rockers Uptown* (Shanachie 1976)
	Rockers Meets King Tubbys in a Fire House (Yard 1980)
Carlton Patterson –	"Watergate Rock" (Black and White 1974)
The Upsetters –	*Blackboard Jungle Dub* (Clocktower 1973)
Yabby You – (Vivian Jackson)	*King Tubby's Prophesy of Dub* (Prophet 1976)
	Jesus Dread (1972–1977) (Blood and Fire 1997)
	Dub it to the Top (1976–1979) (Blood and Fire 2002)

THE QUIET CHAMELEON:
CHRIS THOMAS

In September 1968, Chris Thomas, a 22-year-old bass player, was learning the ropes of record production from the ground up in London. Hired as an apprentice at the AIR music production company, Thomas was basically a glorified messenger boy, running errands and fetching tea for the bosses. In his down time he was also permitted to attend and quietly observe various recording sessions.

Having just returned from a vacation, Thomas read a note left on his desk. He could not believe what it said:

"Dear Chris, hope you had a nice holiday—I'm off on mine now. Make yourself available to the Beatles."

Signed, George Martin[1]

Dressed in the standard suit and tie, Thomas reluctantly made his way downstairs to the Abbey Road studio like a convict tentatively walking to the electric chair. His first-ever assignment was to helm a recording session for the world's biggest rock band, and all the nerve-wracked Thomas could think was "Don't puke in the control room." The night's session was to be devoted to a recklessly crazed screamer about a child's slide, titled "Helter Skelter."

• • • • •

C hris Thomas was brainwashed by Buddy Holly's horn-rimmed rock twang. By the time he was fifteen, he dropped out of the junior program at the London's Royal Academy of Music and ditched his respectable violin for an uncouth guitar. Swept away in the first tide of Beatlemania in late 1962,

Thomas discovered that his classical violin training made learning the guitar confusing, so he soon switched over to bass. First forming the bluesy rock combo Black Cat Bones, and later Second Thoughts, Thomas toiled anonymously on the bottom rung of London's swingin' pop scene.

It was a thrilling time to be playing rock around town, and the jovial Thomas struck up friendships with several emerging stars, from Pete Townshend, to Ron Wood. Despite his frequent brushes with greatness, none of it seemed to rub off on his own bands. Thomas began to dread the instability that came with being in a rock band that seemed destined for obscurity. Especially frustrating was the reliance on shady managers and fly-by-night promoters that entailed making it big. Fed up with performing live to indifferent audiences, all he wanted to do was hole up in the studio and make great-sounding records.

Spellbound by the Beatles' immaculately produced records, Thomas decided to march straight to the source of his worship, George Martin, right in the middle of the band's *Help!* heyday. Martin was still an employee at the monolithic EMI at the time, and, because he lacked the clout to hire an employee, Thomas was turned away. By the end of 1967 Martin had finally slipped away from EMI to form AIR London, England's first independent record production company. Hearing the news of AIR's formation Thomas again queried Martin, and this time he was called in to interview. Earnest and eager, Thomas impressed the AIR team and was hired on as a messenger runner/tea boy for a six-month trial period.

While Thomas was primarily engaged in the menial responsibilities that come with starting on the bottom, the job did have considerable perks. Specifically, he was permitted to observe a number of recording sessions that ranged from pop heartthrob Engelbert Humperdick to rock bluebloods the Hollies. Naturally, when the completely inexperienced Thomas received Martin's understated request to "make himself available to the Beatles," he was scared shitless. He spent the next two hours fretting away in an upstairs office. Finally, he gathered his nerve and queasily entered Abbey Road Studio Two for the Martin-less session. Fatefully, the first person he bumped into was Paul McCartney:

"What are you doing here then?" the Beatle asked bluntly.[2] Notoriously leery of interlopers, the Beatles made up the world's most exclusive club, and McCartney gleefully took to hazing the studio rookie.

"Didn't George tell you anything about this?" Thomas stammered back.[3]

"No," McCartney said disingenuously.

Much to McCartney's amusement, Thomas began to squirm as he nervously explained the instructions Martin had given him. Sensing that Thomas was sufficiently worked up, the Beatle went in for the kill: "Oh well, if you want to produce us, you can produce us, but if you're no good, we'll just tell you to fuck off," he said in his famous Liverpudlian accent and stalked out.[4]

Not surprisingly, Thomas was "destroyed" by McCartney's comment, literally so scared that he "couldn't speak for hours."[5] The minutes passed like hours to Thomas, but eventually he made it to 7 p.m. It was time to cut "Helter Skelter." Easily the Beatles' most unabashedly hard rocking song ever attempted, the band had already recorded a rather sprawling 27-minute version of it a few months earlier. Clearly a more succinct take was needed, and it became Thomas's job to reign in the song's joyfully malevolent madness.

From the onset, the Beatles regarded Thomas as if he was nothing more than a substitute teacher behind the board. With the band members out of their heads on a medicine cabinet full of substances, mischievous schoolboy-like chaos quickly reigned. During one take, George Harrison darted around the studio with a flaming ashtray on his head distracting McCartney from screaming his blood-curdling vocal. "All in all a pretty undisciplined session, you could say!" Thomas said, recalling the session.[6]

Throughout the constant hijinks, Thomas was unable to loosen up. Still far too frightened to speak up, he remained mute through the first half of the session. Eventually, the band adjourned to discuss some sticky matters regarding its flagging money-pit of a company, Apple. As the band sat Indian-style on the studio floor, Thomas walked by and caught the tail end of John Lennon muttering something along the lines of: "He's not really doing his job is he?"[7] Lennon could have been talking about anybody, but Thomas assumed the comment was directed at him. Thomas figured this was it, the moment of truth: He had better assert himself during the second-part of the session, or he was destined for to shortest producing career in music history.

Eventually the band reconvened, tuned up, then launched into another super-charged, ear-splitting take. Only this time, as it slid into the song's chorus, Thomas rang a loud buzzer that rattled the studio. "Start again, there was a mistake," he said calmly.[8] The band was stunned, indignant to be called out by the scrub behind the board. Summarily, all four of them defiantly marched towards the control room to have a listen. As they approached, Thomas's heart threatened to pop out of his chest. He prayed that he hadn't imagined the gaffe— fortunately, he hadn't.

Listening to the playback, the band heard the mistake. The men nodded their shaggy heads in acknowledgement, and ambled nonchalantly back into the studio like nothing had happened. Thomas was buoyed as he called for a new take. Officially indoctrinated into Beatledom, he began to grow more confident as the long night wore on. Seventeen draining takes later, the "Helter Skelter" session was over. Thomas had not only survived the ordeal, he had become a legitimate music producer in the process.

Thomas continued to be closely involved with the "White Album" sessions in Martin's absence over the next three weeks, which included work on sardonic Lennon songs "Happiness is a Warm Gun," and "Glass Onion." For Harrison's "Piggies," Thomas suggested using a harpsichord that had been set up in the studio for an upcoming classical recording date. Harrison not only agreed, but he insisted Thomas play it himself. Thomas also wrote the peppy horn arrangement for Harrison's "Savoy Truffle" and played droning keyboards on his yearning "Long, Long, Long." When it came time to press the album, it was none other than Lennon who insisted that Thomas be credited for his assistance. Apparently Thomas had done his job after all.

· · · · ·

After his baptism by flaming ashtray, Martin encouraged Thomas find his own band to shepherd. As a result, he found himself in a precarious position. Although he had served as an ostensible

Beatles producer, his overall lack of experience was a hindrance towards cultivating a proven band. Since nearly every capable rock group in London had already been gobbled up by a recording contract, Thomas trekked out to the country in search of a hidden gem. Eventually, he stumbled upon the Climax Chicago Blues Band, a scruffy outfit who primarily gigged around the pubs of Stafford.

Just a week removed from his Beatles stint, Thomas began to produce their eponymous debut. Without a background in engineering, Thomas's knowledge of studio technology was severely limited. Fortunately, Climax was a warts-and-all British blues band in the mold of John Mayall and early Fleetwood Mac, which enabled him to cut a relatively no-frills document of the band. Thomas encouraged the group to write a few new originals to help distinguish the record from being a mere collection of blues covers, and the group obliged. Two days later the album was completed—a far cry from the Beatles seemingly endless five-month "White Album" endeavor. The release performed modestly well, and Thomas continued with the Climax Blues Band ("Chicago" was eventually dropped from the name) for three more albums, culminating with 1971's taut *Tightly Knit*.

Soon after he began to work with the unknown Climax, Thomas received an opportunity to polish his studio skills with a band that had already tasted the big time. In the early summer of 1967, Procol Harum released the evocative, classical-rock hybrid "A Whiter Shade of Pale." On the strength of Gary Brooker's cathedral-like organ and Keith Reid's burnished vocal, the enigmatic song quickly became one of the most heralded singles of the decade. After three innovative, early progressive rock albums that combined guitarist Robin Trower's limber blues workouts with Brooker's lofty classical concepts, the band was searching for a hungry new producer to bring a fresh edge to its sound.

Through his affiliation with AIR, Thomas was paired with Procol Harum for its 1970 release, *Home*. The album was somewhat of a transitional affair for the band, hard rocking but somewhat aimless. However, Thomas was learning on the job, and he quickly re-teamed with the band for its more realized follow-up, *Broken Barricades*.

With *Broken Barricades'* exciting dynamics, studio experimentation, and mountain-stream clarity, Thomas's airy production hallmarks first began to appear. Building a solid foundation on crisply recorded percussion, a multitude of colorful keyboards, inventively lean strings, and distorted guitar leads, Thomas transformed songs like "Simple Sister" and "Power Failure" from potentially lumbering indulgences into artfully invigorating winners. Thomas crafted one of his first arrangements for the title track and split the song into two parts, ingeniously shuttling chords to one side of the mix while leaving the arpeggios to gently tinkle away on the other. When the song arrived at the line "glittering sand," he bounced a keyboard sound off the phrase to make the music mirror the lyric, a trademark device that he would utilize throughout his career.

Thomas continued with Procol Harum for a live album recorded with the 52-piece Edmonton Symphony Orchestra and a 25-piece vocal choir. The original plan was to record the rehearsals as well as the actual performance (for backup in case the concert did not go as expected). Although unforeseen time constraints did not allow for this luxury, and Thomas and the band scrambled to get the concert right or risk disaster. Thomas suggested that the group perform some of its earlier material, including the stirring "Conquistador," which was given a dramatic classical Spanish arrangement. Fortunately, the concert went off without a hitch, but Thomas was still forced to make several tricky edits to the final album. "By the time the tape was actually mixed, it looked like a zebra crossing, but fortunately, virtually every single edit that we tried worked," Thomas said.[9]

Among the many taking note of the elegant symphonic recording was the iconoclastic John Cale. Impressed with Thomas's flowing arrangements, Cale drafted him to produce his Europe-in-decay song-cycle, *Paris 1919*. Cale and Thomas worked well together from the onset. However, after the two received word during one of the sessions that a mutual friend had died, the album's tone took a decided turn for the darker. With the startling news a disturbing atmosphere of morbidity began to haunt several of the recordings, especially the ghostly "Hanky Panky Nohwow." Ultimately, with its combination of regal string arrangements, elegant ambience, and palpable pall of death, *Paris 1919* became one of the most intoxicating albums of the decade.

Now on a roll, Thomas was recruited to supervise the final mix of Pink Floyd's long overdue concept album, *Dark Side of the Moon*. Plagued by the pursuit of perfection, the psychedelic luminaries had been laboring for so long in the studio that they had lost nearly all perspective on the project. In need of some much-needed objectivity, they turned to Thomas. An admirer of Floyd's enigmatic previous release *Meddle* (especially its sprawling sidelong head-trip "Echoes") Thomas was eager to attempt something similarly experimental. Although after concluding that the album "was just a bunch of songs," he became somewhat disillusioned with the project.[10]

By the time Thomas was finally able to get his hands on the console he found that the band had already recorded and sequenced almost the entire record. However, it continued to obsessively fiddle with new overdubs and re-recorded solos. After reviewing the tapes, Thomas lobbied to restore many of the original solos, along with several other discarded ideas from earlier versions of the album. Ironically, he did not think much of the finished product at the time, never imaging that the hallucinatory headphone trip would become one of the most beloved releases of all time. Much to his surprise, the seamlessly stony *Dark Side of the Moon* eventually remained for an unfathomable 723 weeks on Billboard's Top 200 album charts from 1973 to 1988. Again, Thomas had somewhat accidentally stumbled into rock history.

• • • • •

Meanwhile, Thomas's role continued to expand with Procol Harum on *Grand Hotel* and *Exotic Birds and Fruit* (released in 1973 and 1974, respectively). Although the band's material was becoming increasingly lackluster, both releases enabled the producer to sharpen his increasingly silky studio sound. Picking up the slack for the band, Thomas began to take over the albums, meticulously crafting a plush atmosphere for each song. Rather than focusing on control room trickery, he was more eager to coax unusual sounds from the actual instruments. His experiments included recording out-of-tune pianos to sound like they were under water and positioning a twelve-string guitar to reverberate inside an old piano that was doubling the same riff. After the scrupulous releases were met with commercial indifference, Thomas parted ways with the band.

With the demand for his colorful productions growing, Thomas began literally working day and night. While juggling the recording of *Grand Hotel* with the mixing of *Dark Side of the Moon*, he proceeded to take on yet another band, Roxy Music. Roxy had asked Cale to produce its second album, *For Your Pleasure*, but he was unable to commit to it and referred the group to Thomas. Propelled by the creative tension generated from the dueling egos of Bryan Ferry and Brian Eno, Thomas found the futuristic glam rock band bursting with unusually fresh and fertile ideas. Completely enthused, he immediately went to work on its frenetic single, "Do the Strand." The pairing to proved to be inspired as Thomas skillfully provided the ironic dance ditty with an impressive gloss and heft.

Stewarding the rest of *For Your Pleasure* proved to be an unusual experience for Thomas. Unlike the traditional rock bands he was used to, Roxy's members preferred to work individually, creating backing tracks on their own, then subsequently merging their parts with Ferry's bizarre imagery and mannered vocals. Thomas's role was to record the modernistic songs as cleanly as possible, and his spacious approach allowed plenty of room for inspired improvisation. Casting the album in chromium sheen, Thomas's lavish sound was a perfect companion to Roxy's decadent vision. Encouraged by the seamless symbiosis achieved on *For Your Pleasure*, Thomas was retained for the band's next three albums.

Following Eno's departure after *For Your Pleasure* (Thomas would subsequently mix his solo debut, *Here Come the Warm Jets*), Ferry became the band's unrivaled leader. Roxy continued to work in the established mode of its predecessor with 1973's inspired *Stranded*. First the members would record formless keyboards, bass and drums backing tracks for each song; then a number, rather than a name, would be assigned to it. Only after the guitar overdubs were added would the song truly begin to take shape. This was Thomas's cue to spring into action, and he would excitedly build up the tracks and then flesh them out through ingenious, unsullied mixes. Finally, Ferry added his vocals to complete such esoteric delights as the heavily edited, sectional pastiche "Mother of Pearl" and the wistfully faux-Parisian "Song for Europe."

After ceding control of much of Roxy's pleasing *Country Life* to engineer John Punter, Thomas took back the reigns for the

Roxy Music
Siren
(1975)

band's impeccable 1975 album, *Siren*. Sharply veering away from the unflinching experimentalism of earlier releases, Ferry had mutated into a tuxedo-clad crooner, and the album's air of ardent sentimentality perfectly complemented his sophisticated jet-set charm. Thomas turned in one of his most sleekly grand productions, evidenced by the clarion drum sound and robust backing tracks that power standouts like the irresistibly slinky "Love is the Drug" (the band's biggest U.S. hit), the incessantly rhythmic "Both Ends Burning," and the luscious ballad "Sentimental Fool."

Roxy had come a long way from its disjointed, chaotic early sound to the sterling sensuality of *Siren*. But the journey had netted several rewards along the way. From new wave and new romantic, to Britpop and beyond, Thomas's sumptuous Roxy Music albums rank among the most influential and rich sounding recordings in pop's pantheon.

Working in a more straightforward power-pop mode, Thomas took on star-crossed Beatles protégés, Badfinger. By 1973 the band's early run of gloriously bittersweet radio hits had ended, and the band found itself plagued by complicated contracts, avaricious managers, and debilitating personal problems. After stepping in to help complete the atypically hard-rocking *Ass*, Thomas and the band returned to the studio a scant six weeks later for the hastily forced follow-up, *Badfinger*.

With the band relegated to making songs up on the spot in the studio, Thomas was given greater leeway than with Roxy Music. His sun-kissed production touches warmed cuts like the catchy "Shine On" and the heartbreaking "Lonely You." Ultimately, the band's bitterness crept into *Badfinger*, and, with the confusion of two albums released so closely together, the record flopped. Fortunately, its outlook was decidedly rosier on the Thomas-produced 1974 release, *Wish You Were Here*. One of Badfinger's finest albums, Thomas's painstaking production sparkles throughout buoyant mini-masterpieces such as "Know One Knows," "Just a Chance," and "Dennis." This release was completely ignored; it should have restored the band to radio prominence. Instead, it became just another sad chapter in their tragic history.

• • • • •

In the summer of 1975, a manipulative British manager named Malcolm McLaren approached Thomas to produce a latter-day New York Dolls album. Thomas expressed interest, but the pioneering gutter-glam band soon broke up. Thomas heard nothing more from McLaren until the manager reappeared the following year, this time offering a brazen new punk rock band called the Sex Pistols.

The group had recently recorded a clutch of chaotic demos with guitarist Chris Spedding, who had raved to Thomas about its ferocious sound shortly after McLaren's offer. Coincidentally, on the same night that Spedding had mentioned the band, Thomas caught the group performing on TV's *So It Goes*. Spedding's assessment had not been exaggerated; Thomas saw through the shambling chaos to spy a damn good rock band. Thoroughly impressed by its anarchistic abandon, Thomas called McLaren and agreed to produce the Sex Pistols.

In October 1976, Thomas and the Sex Pistols entered Wessex Studios to cut the caustic punk treatise "Anarchy in the U.K." Contrary to the band's perceived, bash-it-out style, Thomas laboriously orchestrated over a dozen layers of guitar, double-tracking certain riffs and separating other sections to build the song into a raging monstrosity of noise. When it finally came time for the pimple-faced frontman Johnny Rotten to record his snarling vocal, he appeared dumbfounded. Seemingly confused, he either stood under the microphone doing nothing, or he proceeded to scream the lyrics throughout the entire take. Thomas needed to take control, and eventually he persuaded Rotten to ease up on the screaming. Rotten was a defiant personality, at odds with all means of authority, but somehow Thomas's persuasion won out. Consequently, he was able to extract the vitriolic final take that soon woke rock from its mid-1970s siesta.

While the Sex Pistols courted controversy through a run of devilishly outrageous publicity stunts, Thomas was busy working with the man who had scared him speechless eight years earlier: Paul McCartney. The ex-Beatle had just completed a massively successful worldwide tour with Wings, and he brought Thomas in to assist with organizing the heaps of live tapes. At one point the chameleon-like Thomas was essentially splitting his time between McCartney and the Sex Pistols. Working on totally opposite ends of the musical spectrum, Thomas's colleagues were left baffled. Eventually, Thomas would produce the final Wings album, *Back to the Egg*, but first he returned to the studio to record the Pistols' full-length album.

The Pistols had recently ousted original bassist Glen Matlock for such unthinkable offenses as fancying Beatles chords and washing his feet. In Matlock's place was a spike-haired/spike-loving Sid Vicious. While the new member looked the pasty punk rock part (when not nodding out), he possessed virtually no bass-playing skills. Because of this not-so-minor detail, the band was in a quandary, and it invited Matlock to contribute to the album as a session man. Not shockingly, the freshly snubbed ex-member never showed. Thomas was quickly running out of options. He tried to make do with some of Vicious's bass parts by garbling them low in the mix, but it simply wasn't working.

Finally, with the exception of the bass parts, all the tracks had been recorded. In a desperate move, Thomas asked the Pistol guitarist Steve Jones to try to play the bass himself. Although he didn't know how to play bass, Jones was game. Winging it, he proceeded to play the simple root notes of the song's guitar chords on a bass. Magically, it turned out to be the explosive missing ingredient—and the revolutionarily rumbling Sex Pistols sound was born! Instantly, inflammatory anthems like "God Save the Queen," "Pretty Vacant," and "EMI" had been emboldened with the blitzkrieg force of an invading Panzer tank division.

Released in the fall of 1977, *Never Mind the Bollocks Here's the Sex Pistols* shocked the world with its power-chorded punk rock nihilism. Choosing the pop-savvy Thomas over a traditional hard-rock producer

The Sex Pistols
Never Mind the
Bollocks Here's the
Sex Pistols
(1977)

turned out to be a boldly propitious and inspired move by McLaren. With Thomas's massive go-for-the-jugular production empowering the Pistols' venomous indictments, the album became one of rock's most fundamental recordings. "I was never really interested in the Pistols as a social phenomenon. I thought I could make a good rock 'n' roll record with them, and as such I thought they were fantastic," Thomas said.[11]

• • • • •

In 1979, Thomas was putting the exhausting finishing touches on Wings' *Back to the Egg* when he got a call from a singer named Chrissie Hynde. Thomas had first met ex-rock scribe Hynde when she lent backing vocals to his production of Chris Spedding's album, *Hurt*. Thomas had sensed her latent talent and seductive charm during the sessions, and he had encouraged her to form her own band. Three years later she had one, called the Pretenders, and she asked Thomas to consider producing its debut album. Thomas agreed to listen to the band's four demos, which included "Private Life," "The Wait," "Up the Neck," and "Brass in Pocket," and was walloped by their attitude and stylistic diversity.

Recording the album was made easy by Hynde's remarkable collection of punchy yet poppy material. After quickly identifying the slow-moving "Brass in Pocket" as the song's first single, he fortuitously suggested picking up its tempo to give it "a little bit more bounce"[11] and making it into "an almost Al Green–type thing, with Al

Jackson drums on it."[12] Enormously contributing to the album's distinctive sound was James Honeyman-Scott's inventively searing guitar, which Thomas colorfully treated with a variety of phasing effects. By skillfully adding a myriad of textures to Honeyman-Scott's guitar, Thomas imbued depth to pugnacious rockers like "Precious" and "Tattooed Love Boys" and gentle nuance to restrained ballads like "Kid" and "Brass in Pocket."

Released in January 1980, *The Pretenders* immediately rose to Number 1 on the U.K. charts and went as high as Number 9 stateside. Meanwhile, the smoldering "Brass in Pocket" became the band's first U.S. hit and a true rock classic. The eponymous album immediately became a 1980s benchmark and introduced Hynde as one of the most gifted and original women in rock.

After the twin drug overdoses of Honeyman-Scott and bassist Pete Farndon that followed the band's sophomore release, *Pretenders II*, the doubly snake-bitten Hynde (along with drummer Martin Chambers) eventually garnered the strength to regroup for the aptly titled 1984 release, *Learning to Crawl*. Again produced by Thomas, the album was the biggest of the band's career and was capped by modern rock staples "Back on the Chain Gang" and "Middle of the Road." Ten years later, Thomas reunited with the band for "I'm a Mother," which appeared on *Last of the Independents*, a return to form for the band that had somewhat lost its way in the interim.

• • • • •

Thomas remained sedulous throughout the '80s and '90s, producing a slew of commercially winning INXS albums, including *Listen Like Thieves*, *Kick*, *X* and *Disappear*. Additional noteworthy turns came with his spot-on productions for Pete Townshend's passionate early-1980s solo releases, *Empty Glass* and *All the Best Cowboys Have Chinese Eyes*. Aided by Thomas's sympathetic, spacious production, the releases allowed Townshend to slip away from the Who's estimable shadow.

He also embarked on a long working relationship with old friend Reg Dwight, a gap-toothed pianist who he first met back at the Royal Academy of Music. By the time Thomas began to work on his

1981 album, *Fox*, Dwight was known the world over as Elton John. Thomas has since produced more than a dozen John albums that have netted a large cache of latter-day hits including "I'm Still Standing," "I Guess That's Why They Call it the Blues," and the Grammy-winning "Can You Feel the Love Tonight?"

Remaining contemporary, in 1995 he produced disciples of Roxy Music, Pulp's Britpop breakthrough *Different Class*, a record that Thomas considers among the best he has ever made. One of the most acclaimed releases of the year, the immaculately produced, often theatrical album established literary bandleader Jarvis Cocker as one Britain's new musical leading lights. Thomas continued to work with the band on its troubled, combatively eclectic 1998 album, *This Is Hardcore*. Taking over eighteen arduous months to record, Thomas found himself completely drained by the time of its completion.

Almost certainly, Thomas's startling versatility, sparkling sound, and sympathetic workman-like approach guarantee more surprises. A quiet chameleon content to exist in rock's shadows, in almost Zelig-like fashion Thomas has been a frequent participant in rock history—assisting in the assemblage of several of its weightiest cornerstones, including "The White Album," *Dark Side of the Moon*, *Never Mind the Bollocks Here's the Sex Pistols*, and *The Pretenders*. Good thing he made it through that first night at Abbey Road without puking in the control room....

KEY RECORDINGS
Chris Thomas

Badfinger –	*Badfinger* (Warner Bros. 1974)
	Wish You Were Here (Warner Bros. 1974)
The Beatles –	*The Beatles* (assistant produced) (Capitol 1968)
John Cale –	*Paris 1919* (Reprise 1973)
Climax Blues Band –	*The Climax Chicago Blues Band* (Sire 1969)
	Tightly Knit (Sire 1971)
Brian Eno –	*Here Come the Warm Jets* (mixed) (Island 1973)
Bryan Ferry –	*Let's Stick Together* (Atlantic 1976)
INXS –	*Listen Like Thieves* (Atlantic 1985)
	Kick (Atlantic 1987)
	X (Atlantic 1990)
Elton John –	*Too Low for Zero* (Geffen 1983)
	"Can You Feel the Love Tonight"
	(Hollywood 1994)
	Big Picture (Mercury 1997)
Ronnie Lane –	*One for the Road* (mixed) (Island 1975)
Pink Floyd –	*Dark Side of the Moon* (mixed) (Capitol 1973)
The Pretenders –	*Pretenders* (Sire 1980)
	Pretenders II (Sire 1981)
	Learning to Crawl (Sire 1984)
	"I'm a Mother" (*Last of the Independents*)
	(Sire/Warner Bros. 1994)
Procol Harum –	*Broken Barricades* (Chrysalis 1971)
	Live in Concert with the Edmonton Symphony
	Orchestra (Chrysalis 1972)
	Grand Hotel (Chrysalis 1973)
	Exotic Birds and Fruit (Chrysalis 1974)
Pulp –	*Different Class* (Island 1995)
	"Help the Aged" (*This is Hardcore*) (Island 1998)
Roxy Music –	*For Your Pleasure* (Atco 1973)
	Stranded (Atco 1973)
	Siren (Atco 1975)
Sex Pistols –	"God Save the Queen" (Virgin 1977)
	"Holidays in the Sun" (Virgin 1977)
	Never Mind the Bollocks, Here's the Sex Pistols
	(Virgin/Warner Bros. 1977)
Chris Spedding –	*Hurt* (Rak 1977)
Tom Robinson Band –	*Power in the Darkness* (EMI 1978)

Pete Townshend –   *Empty Glass* (Atco 1980)
    All the Best Cowboys Have Chinese Eyes
        (Atco 1982)
    White City (Atco 1985)

Wings –   *Back to the Egg* (Columbia 1979)

THE ORDER OF DISORDER:
MARTIN HANNETT, FLOOD,
AND STEVE ALBINI

"Right, I want you to play that again...only this time make
it faster but slower"
—Martin Hannett's in-studio instructions to
A Certain Ratio bassist Jeremy Kerr

*In 1980, trained chemist Martin Hannett had moved from con-
ducting professional chemical experiments in a science lab in
Manchester, England, to conducting personal chemical experiments
in a recording studio. The sonic architect of post-punk, Hannett
helmed more than fifteen releases in 1980 alone.*

*But drugs soon doused the flurry, and he would produce virtu-
ally nothing for the next four years. After briefly returning in the late
1980s to help morph the monochromatic Manchester sound into the
kaleidoscopic "Madchester" rave juggernaut, Hannett's victory
proved to be short-lived. By 1991, the stubbornly combative recording genius would be dead, only a year removed from the decade he
helped shape.*

· · · · ·

Martin Hannett grew up in perpetually drab-skied,
industrial Manchester thrilled by the open-ended possibilities of sound. Haunting the local fairgrounds, he would
stand under giant Wharfdale speakers and allow himself to be swept
away by the invigorating rush of Spector's Wall of Sound records at
full volume. By the time he was in college, he subsisted on a steady
diet of Kinks, Beatles, and Small Faces before succumbing to the

dark Hollywood arts of the Doors (he was blown away by its compressed treble drum sound) and the unsettling cotton-candy surrealism of Love. Eventually, Hannett glommed onto the Velvet
Underground, often playing the same noise-encrusted cuts over and
over, for hours on end.

By the early 1970s Hannett had earned a degree from
Manchester Polytechnic and began taking work as a low-level
chemist. Far more enthused by music than chemistry, Hannett spent
much of his free time absorbing the technical nuances of record production. Scientifically analyzing the inventive recording techniques
of things like Captain Beefheart's *Clear Spot* and Steely Dan's *Katy
Lied*, Hannett's true calling was becoming too strong to suppress.
Finally, he gave up the straight world of chemistry for music and
began stints in various go-nowhere Manchester bands as a soundman
and occasional bassist. As the glittery British musical underground
began to slouch towards mid-decade anarchy, Hannett became energized by local proto-punk Bowie obsessives, Slaughter and the Dogs.
Determined to showcase the group's talents, he co-founded Rabid
Records, a tiny indie label based in Manchester. In short order, the
label became the early home of bushy-haired punk poet, John Cooper
Clarke and new wave jokester Jilted John (a.k.a. Graham Fellows).

As the punk rock fallout from the Sex Pistols' explosion began
to settle over Manchester, Hannett shrewdly viewed the musically
rudimentary movement as an opportunity to enforce his sonic will.
Leading the Manchester punk insurgency was a smart-alecky group
of collegians called the Buzzcocks. Formed by bookish vocalist
Howard Devoto and Krautrock-influenced guitarist Pete Shelley, the
band cemented its reputation after opening for the Pistols' second
Manchester gig in July 1976. Hannett immediately gravitated to the
Buzzcocks' snotty punk-pop and began to arrange a slew of local gigs
for the band. Eventually, he convinced the Buzzcocks to let him produce its 1977 debut, *Spiral Scratch*.

Released as a 7" EP on the Buzzcocks' own New Hormones
label (in a picture sleeve that featured a blurry black-and-white band
photo and stark lettering), *Spiral Scratch* was the first independent
British punk single and an instant landmark. The rules of rock had
changed; suddenly, a few chords, a couple of bucks, and a reservoir

of moxie were all that was required to release a record. The DIY floodgates had been opened.

Billed as Martin "Zero," Hannett produced *Spiral Scratch* as an unvarnished document of the foursome's feisty, bash-and-pop live sound. Appalled by Chris Thomas's painstakingly overdubbed Sex Pistols productions, Hannett's recording was intentionally tinny, defiantly muffled, and joyously unbridled. Contrasting the nihilistic London punk of the Pistols and the political crusading of the Clash, the Buzzcocks' sound sulked in adolescent angst and deceptively melodic pop, as distilled on confused teen anthems like "Breakdown" and "Boredom." The first 1,000 copies pressed of *Spiral Scratch* disappeared in an instant, but the Manchester scene was just beginning to breathe.

Further giving to life to the Manchester scene were Hannett's cartoon-like productions for John Cooper-Clarke, commencing with his Rabid-released debut single, "Psycle Sluts," in 1977. A year later came his charmingly quirky *Disguise in Love*, a loopy Hannett-arranged pastiche of percolating electronics and avant-pop that served as a playful backdrop to Cooper-Clarke's mirthful "talking in tune" musical poetry. Hannett also helmed Jilted John's 1978 dèbut, *True Love Stories*, an unabashedly catchy and blissfully absurd album that was immortalized by the DIY novelty classic of spurned teenage lust, "Jilted John."

Seizing Manchester's momentum was the infamously opportunistic Tony Wilson, an upstart music promoter and the host of a BBC TV show that frequently showcased underground local bands. Fancying himself an impresario, Wilson created Factory, a combination club and record label that was named in homage to both Andy Warhol's decadent New York coterie and Manchester's billowing smokestacks. Needing a principal engineer and producer for Factory, Wilson inevitably solicited Hannett, the only one with any real recording expertise in town. Hannett, whose appetite for substance consumption was voracious, simply saw Wilson's offer as a means to afford better drugs and signed on with the label.

Self-consciously stepping away from the rigid boundaries of London punk, Factory sought to distinguish Manchester by building a roster predicated on stylistic diversity and genre-busting unpredictably.

After Hannett produced tracks for a Factory sampler EP, he was paired with the Durutti Column for his first full-length label production. The band had been recently decimated by personnel attrition and was essentially reduced to swan-necked Vini Reilly and his digital-delayed Les Paul guitar. Unlike the crude and cacophonous musicianship that typified most Manchester acts, Reilly was an accomplished guitarist who deftly sketched melancholic, jazz-inflected soundscapes.

Hannett was thrilled to traipse the Durutti Column's textural terrain, and in preparation he packed Manchester's tiny Cargo Studio full with boxes of recording gizmos, digital effects (much of it imported from the United States), and cumbersome synthesizers. As the sessions began, Hannett fell into what would become his trademark tunnel-vision recording approach. Scarcely uttering a word to Reilly, he spent the first two days fashioning a haunting array of atmospheric electronic noise and primal drum machine patterns. Expectedly, Reilly grew bored and frustrated as he searched for openings to insert his own guitar parts. Hannett remained oblivious to Reilly's aggravation. So focused was he in his own world of narcotized atmospherics, he barely even noticed the guitarist skipping out after the second day. Undeterred by Reilly's hasty departure, Hannett completed the record by himself the following day.

Debuting in 1979, the ironically titled, totally instrumental *The Return of the Durutti Column* was a delicate, shimmering counterpoint to punk's crass riot. Tucking Reilly's dreamy guitar figures into sheets of atmospheric electronics and mechanical clip-clop rhythms, Hannett's starkly impressionistic production helped Factory establish its recalcitrant identity. The decision to release the album in a sandpaper sleeve (cleverly designed to scratch other covers it came in contact with) helped to further underscore the Durutti Column's against-the-grain loveliness.

Just as Wilson had hoped, the unpredictable and adventurous Manchester scene was beginning to dismantle the increasingly straitjacket-like constraints of punk. Following Factory's lead, harbingers of change began to appear everywhere. After imploding in the wake of its disastrous 1978 U.S. tour, the Sex Pistols gave way to the experimental dubwise offshoot Public Image Ltd. Concurrently, the Clash began to detour from rabble-rousing punk towards a path paved with rockabilly, soul, and reggae. Further indicating a sea change was an onslaught of musically uninhibited "post punk" British bands seeping from every crevice of the country: Liverpool had acid-influenced psychedelic bands Teardrop Explodes and Echo and the Bunnymen; Leeds begat the abrasive Marxist-funk band Gang of Four and lo-fi avant punks the Mekons; Birmingham was home to fashion-oriented new romantics Duran Duran and ska-revivalists the (English) Beat. Even the rural hamlet of Swindon got in on the action, spawning herky-jerky melodicists XTC.

The talent-rich London scene was also evolving. Highlighted by art-school sophisticates Wire, lovable mopes the Cure, second-gen mods the Jam, gothic ghouls Siouxsie and the Banshees, and unconventional, P.M.S.–powered acts like the Slits and the Raincoats, seemingly, new bands were forming daily. However, it was Hannett's next Factory production for Joy Division that crystallized the industrial Manchester sound and most succinctly symbolized the alienated post-punk era.

• • • • •

Originally known as Stiff Kittens and then Warsaw, the band finally organized as Joy Division in January 1978. Possessed with manic, epileptic lead-singer Ian Curtis, Joy Division had a tortured, mesmerizing frontman to offset the blank onstage presence of the rest of the band. Enshrouding Curtis' brooding songs of personal pain and social isolation within a Velvet Underground–influenced onslaught of minimalist noise, Joy Division became one of Manchester's most devastating live acts. It was during one particularly intense gig that Tony Wilson glimpsed a special look in their eyes and offered the group a contract with Factory. Quickly paired with Hannett, Joy Division cut two songs, "Digital" and "Glass" (included on a Factory sampler EP) and then reconvened at Strawberry Studios to begin recording its 1979 debut, *Unknown Pleasures*.

Hannett was completely uninterested in recording a pop album, and his predilection for untamed in-studio experimentation ran rampant throughout the sessions. Hippie-like, disheveled, and ornery, Hannett's recording theory entailed loading up on hash and heroin

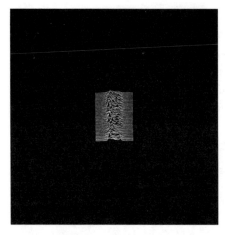

Joy Division
Unknown Pleasures
(1979)

(and anything else he could find), holing up in the studio for days on end and openly courting mercurial serendipity at every turn. Residing on his own personal planet, Hannett's confounding recording instructions to the band were almost always indiscernibly muttered. Most often the speed-addled band simply had no idea what the hell he was talking about. A Spectorian-like studio control freak, Hannett would antagonistically shout the band down if it dared to disagree with any of his cryptic instructions. Often, his decisions were obstinately based on doing the exact opposite of what the band wanted.

"In the studio, we'd sit on the left, he'd sit on the right," Joy Division bassist Peter Hook recalled.[1] "If we said anything like, 'I think the guitars are a bit quiet, Martin,' he'd scream 'Oh my God! Why don't you just fuck off, you stupid retards!' It was alright at first, but gradually he started to get weirder and weirder."

Hannett was unhealthily obsessed with drum sounds and their infinitely variable tinges. Early on in the sessions he commanded drummer Stephen Morris to completely tear down and then reassemble his drum kit in pursuit of the perfect tone. After Hannett spent an eternity tinkering with the tuning of the kit and crawling on the floor in search of the perfect mic placements, he finally got the pulverizing percussion sound he was after. Regarding themselves as a brazen noise rock act, the band was reticent to betray its raw live sound and vehemently protested Hannett's insistence on utilizing embryonic synthesizer technology. Willfully, the producer won the battle and ended up playing most of the spare Kraftwerkian synth lines himself.

As a testament to his skills, Hannett's synth work successfully enhanced rather than overwhelmed the band's natural identity.

There was truly a resolute method to his madness, and *Unknown Pleasures'* terrifyingly barren atmosphere of urban-decay and chilling isolation transformed Joy Division from thrashy punk neophytes into leaders of the new school of textural gloom. From the album's darkly tribal opener, "Disorder," to the slowly churning heavy metal deconstruction "New Dawn Fades," to the kinetically moody, echo-plexed "She's Lost Control," Hannett maps the doom and drone, post-punk blueprint—plaintive, flanged single-note bass, loud, highly-compressed drums, angular guitar shards, and austere synthesizer tape loops. Never has an album been so viscerally cathartic, bleakly harrowing, and slyly rocking as *Unknown Pleasures.*

Hannett and Joy Division continued to refine their post-punk vision with the transcendent singles "Transmission" and "Love Will Tear Us Apart," the latter becoming one of the most glorious and enduring songs of the post-punk era. Dichotomously poppy and doom-laden, "Love Will Tear Us Apart" soars in on a crystal clear acoustic guitar strum, Hannett's trademark compressed drum slam, a moody bassline, and one of the hookiest synthesizer lines ever recorded. Perfectly solidifying the song were Curtis's gleefully fatalistic, monosyllabic vocals, which sadly suggested that there was no solace to be found for the singer, not even in love. Hannett knew there was greatness in the song and assiduously experimented with different mixes for months. The time was well spent, and it eventually became the only hit single of his career.

Hannett and Joy Division followed up *Unknown Pleasures* with a 1980s case study of claustrophobia, *Closer.* Again seizing control over the sessions, Hannett placed even greater emphasis on frozen synth settings and unnerving atmospherics. Perpetually stoned, Hannett's unorthodox improvisational recording methods included shattering glass for jarringly percussive overdubs, running the studio air conditioner full blast for sub-zero bass ambience, blatantly disregarding volume meters, randomly adding tape hiss, reconstituting melodic passages into gnarled fragments, and tailoring tricky false song endings. In a sense, Hannett's pursuit of spontaneous studio magic and emphasis on drums and bass were akin to the anything-goes ethos of dub, although his layered sound was ultimately more subtle and disciplined than the impishly scattershot Jamaican productions.

While Joy Division was reaching musical maturity, Curtis was plummeting further into a demon-plagued abyss, excruciatingly illustrated on *Closer*'s "Atrocity Exhibition," "Isolation," and "Twenty Four Hours." By emphasizing the troubling push-and-pull dynamic between the industrially rhythmic music and supremely tortured lyrics, Hannett channeled a kabalistic atmosphere that dangerously teetered on the brink of emotional collapse. Tragically, the collapse was only momentarily postponed; on a blue Manchester Monday before the band was to leave for its first U.S. tour, the 23-year-old seizure-ridden Curtis hung himself in his apartment.

Devastated, the group eventually mustered the strength to reform as New Order, bowing with its Hannett-produced 1981 debut single, "Ceremony," and ensuing album, *Movement*. Clearly, the band was still shell-shocked by Curtis's death, and both releases were only tentative steps towards breaking away from its sullied past. Fortunately, the band rallied on the single "Everything's Gone Green." With Hannett cleverly mixing real drums and robotic rhythm machines, along with reverberating bass, sequenced synths, and sparsely dour vocals, the song introduced New Order's pervasive electro-dance thump. An antecedent to its immortal 1980s club classic "Blue Monday," the song proved that Hannett could acquiesce to a more overtly accessible sound without compromising his singular vision. New Order had learned a lot from Hannett. With the transition to its new musical identity complete, the band permanently parted ways with the producer.

Hannett's work with Joy Division and New Order was only one part of the incredible flurry of activity he undertook around 1980. Particularly noteworthy was his production of Magazine's thrilling album *The Correct Use of Soap*. Featuring ex-Buzzcock vocalist Howard Devoto, and John McGeoch (one the era's greatest guitarists), along with bassist (and future Bad Seed) Barry Adamson, the album was a loftily obtuse amalgamation of post-punk dynamics, skewed pop savvy, and driving, brittle rhythms.

Additional defining post-punk productions turned in by Hannett included O.M.D.'s twinkling synth-pop debut "Electricity" and "11 O'Clock Tic Toc," an early, atypically brooding single by U2. He also helmed several early recordings for the Psychedelic Furs' self-titled debut, along with sessions for industrial funksters A Certain Ratio and an album for dub futurists Basement Five (*Basement Five in Dub*). He then reunited with the (now Pete Shelley–led) Buzzcocks for a triumvirate of singles released between August and December 1980.

After falling out with Tony Wilson and Factory Records (which included a lawsuit over royalties), Hannett retreated into five years of heroin hibernation. Ironically, his influence continued to swell. By the early 1980s elements of his echoing, compressed sound were prevalent in a myriad of trailblazers like the Cure, Pere Ubu, the Birthday Party, Cabaret Volitare, the Fall, Mission of Burma, Big Black, and the Jesus and Mary Chain.

Hannett finally awoke late in the decade to discover that Manchester's perennially gloomy sound had transformed into the cheerfully hedonistic "Madchester" rave scene. Finally back in action, Hannett brought his echoing, trebly disorder to a new crop of drug-gobbling Manchester bands. His first return effort came with the Stone Roses' psych-pop-influenced 1985 debut single "So Young." Three years later, Hannett settled his differences with Tony Wilson and Factory and took on Manchester's leading lights, Happy Mondays.

Spelling John Cale (who produced the band's first album), Hannett took the controls for Happy Mondays' eclectically shambling, ecstasy-fueled classic *Bummed*. With cavalier frontman and resident troublemaker Shaun Ryder feeding Hannett an endless stream of "E," the wildly indulgent sessions featured a crazed, segmented mix of house music rhythms, spacey dub, swirling '60s psychedelia, '70s party funk, and '80s hip-hop. Against all odds, near genius was extracted out of the chaos. With Hannett's cavernous, beat-crazed sound lending an infectious, off-the-cuff swagger to loosely formed songs like "Mad Cyril" and "Wrote for Luck," *Bummed* became a U.K. phenomenon and the definitive Madchester release.

• • • • •

Ultimately, Hannett's return was to be as short-lived as Madchester's destructively fleeting heyday. Less than three years after the joyous triumph of *Bummed*, he was discovered slumped in his chair at home, dead after a lifetime of legendary drug consumption. However, his motley shadow continued to loom over the emerging alternative music scene. Among his disciples was fellow Mancunian, Flood, an enigmatic sound architect who got his first break as a second engineer to Hannett on New Order's debut, *Movement*.

After paying his dues engineering electronic havoc-wreckers like Psychic TV, Cabaret Volitare, and U2's *The Joshua Tree*, Flood graduated to producing, bringing his own resounding beats, echoing ambience, and lush synthesizer sequencing to acts ranging from noir-gothics Nick Cave and the Bad Seeds, to the disco-synth duo Erasure. By the early 1990s his larger-than-life, densely electronic aesthetic significantly shaped the decade via productions for industrial gate-keepers Nine Inch Nails (*Pretty Hate Machine* and *The Downward Spiral*), synth-pop kings Depeche Mode (*Violator*), platinum mope-rockers the Smashing Pumpkins (*Mellon Collie and the Infinite Sadness*), and U2's post-modern euro-trash releases (*Zooropa* and *Pop*).

Also taking up a portion of the Hannett mantle was prickly, naturalist "engineer" Steve Albini. After making a name in the mid-eighties while leading Chicago-based abrasive noise bands like Big Black and Rapeman, Albini began to court freelance recording assignments. Although his studio responsibilities were essentially those of a traditional producer, the fiercely independent Albini stubbornly insisted on only receiving engineer or "recorded by" credit. His breakthrough came on the Pixies' monumental 1987 album of "lazy evil," *Surfer Rosa*, a record that expanded Hannett's pioneering loud/soft dynamic.

With his parched, heavily miked sound, Albini helped ride *Surfer Rosa* to shore on the turbulent waves of mangled guitar noise and deafening drums and bass. Further adding to the chaos was singer Black Francis's (Frank Black) frenzied choruses that tempestuously shifted from disconcerting acoustic quiescence to bone-rattling sonic eruptions on songs like "Bone Machine" and "Where is My Mind?" A revolution in sound dynamics and song structure, the album bridged '80s post-punk to the forthcoming '90s alternative rock of acts like Sebadoh, Smashing Pumpkins, Radiohead, and especially Nirvana.

Smashing Pumpkins
Mellon Collie and the
Infinite Sadness
(1995)

Acutely influenced by *Surfer Rosa*, Nirvana borrowed its loud/soft dynamic for their pop-paradigm shifting 1991 album, *Nevermind* and its grunge smash hit, "Smells Like Teen Spirit." Sucker-punched by their improbable overnight success, Nirvana reacted against *Nevermind*'s Butch Vig-produced glossiness by hiring Albini to oversee its 1993 follow-up, *In Utero*. A stickler for documenting the way a band truly sounds without recording gimmicks and post-production trickery, Albini strove to make *In Utero* the anti-*Nevermind*.

Recording the sessions blazingly fast, and punishingly raw, Albini used up to 30 microphones (many of them vintage German models, taped to the walls and the ceiling) for Dave Grohl's drum kit and employed a battered, partially broken Fender Quad tube amp for distortion. Successfully injecting an ominous starkness into tormented Cobain songs like "Rape Me," "Pennyroyal Tea," and the particularly Pixies-ish "Scentless Apprentice," Albini exiled *In Utero* to a barren and brutal world of sonic menace. *In Utero* hit Number 1 in the fall of 1993 and, almost impossibly, simultaneously restored the band's indie credibility.

Albini worked steadily throughout the 1990s with a variety of artists, ranging from the platinum British grunge-pop act Bush, to twisted country-roots purveyor Robbie Fulks. Included among his noteworthy endeavors were the Breeders's *Pod*, PJ Harvey's raw-nerved thrill ride *Rid of Me*, Palace's Appalachian gothic releases *Viva Last Blues* and *Arise Therefore*, and Mogwai's entrancing, noise-laced, 20-minute single "My Father My King." Albini also formed

Nirvana
In Utero
(1993)

Shellac, a band that thrives on his penchant for atonal noise, odd time signatures, and dour humor. He continues to field a steady stream of unflinching recording assignments.

• • • • •

Well into the early 2000s, Martin Hannett's furtive ambience and visceral, industrial sound continues to resonate. Along with divergent descendents Flood and Albini, traces of Hannett appear in the works of widely imitated shoe-gazers My Bloody Valentine, electronica pacesetter Moby, slow-core kings Low, lo-fi bedroom genius Stephin Merritt's Magnetic Fields, Trent Reznor's industrially processed Nine Inch Nails recordings, Bright Eyes' opened-minded emo, and the post-rock of Jim O'Rourke and Sonic Youth. As alternative rock continues to regenerate via recycling, more and more its future seems to reside in its post-punk past.

KEY RECORDINGS
Martin Hannett

A Certain Ratio –   "The Thin Boys/All Night Party"
                       (Factory/London 1979)
                       "And Then Again" (Factory/London 1980)

Basement Five –   *In Dub* (Island 1980)

The Buzzcocks –   *Spiral Scratch* (EP) (New Hormones 1977)
                       "Are Everything/Why She's a Girl From the
                       Chainstore" (IRS 1980)
                       "Strange Thing/Airwaves Dream" (IRS 1980)
                       "What Do You Know?/Running Free" (IRS 1980)

John Cooper Clarke –   "Psycle Sluts" (Rabid 1977)
                       Disguise in Love (Epic 1978)
                       Snap, Crackle and Bop (Epic 1980)

Crispy Ambulance –   "Live on a Hot August Night"
                       (Factory Benelux 1981)

Durutti Column –   *The Return of the Durutti Column* (Factory 1979)
                       "For Belgian Friends" (Factory/London 1980)
                       "Lips that Would Kiss/Madeleine"
                       (Factory Benelux 1981)

E.S.G. –   "You're No Good/Moody/U.F.O." (99 Records 1981)

Happy Mondays –   *Bummed* (Elektra 1988)

The Heart Throbs –   *Cleopatra Grip* (Elektra 1990)

Jilted John –   "Jilted John/Going Steady" (Rabid 1978)
                       True Love Stories (Rabid 1978)

Joy Division –   "New Dawn Fades" (Factory/London 1979)
                       Unknown Pleasures (Factory 1979)
                       Closer (Factory 1980)
                       "Transmission/Novelty" (Factory 1979)
                       "Love Will Tear Us Apart" (Factory 1980)

Magazine –   *The Correct Use of Soap* (Virgin 1980)

Pauline Murray and –   *Pauline Murray and the Invisible Girls*
  the Invisible Girls   (RSO 1980)

New Order –   "Ceremony" (Factory 1981)
                       "Everything's Gone Green" (Factory/London 1981)
                       Movement (Factory 1982)

Orchestral Manoeuvres – "Electricity" (Factory 1979)
  in the Dark

Psychedelic Furs –   "Susan's Strange" (Columbia 1980)
                       "Soap Commercial" (Columbia 1980)

Slaughter and –
  the Dogs
	"Cranked Up Really High/The Bitch"
	  (Rabid 1977)

Stone Roses –	"So Young" (Thin Line 1985)
U2 –	"11 O'Clock Tick Tock" (Island 1980)

Flood

Nick Cave and – the Bad Seeds	*The Firstborn is Dead* (Mute 1985) *The Boatman's Call* (Mute/Reprise 1997)
Charlatans U.K. –	*Between 10th and 11th* (Beggars Banquet 1992)
Curve –	*Doppelgänger* (Anxious 1992)
Depeche Mode –	*Violator* (Sire 1990)
Erasure –	*Wonderland* (Sire 1986)
PJ Harvey –	*To Bring You My Love* (Island 1995)
Nine Inch Nails –	*Pretty Hate Machine* (TVT 1989) *The Downward Spiral* (Nothing/Interscope 1994)
Nitzer Ebb –	*Showtime* (Geffen 1990)

The Smashing –
  Pumpkins
	Mellon Collie and the Infinite Sadness
	  (Virgin 1995)

U2 –	*The Joshua Tree* (engineered) (Island 1987) *Achtung Baby!* (engineered/mixed) (Island 1991) *Zooropa* (Island 1993) *Pop* (Island 1997)

Steve Albini

The Auteurs –	*After Murder Park* (Hut 1996)
Big Black –	*Atomizer* (Homestead 1986) *Songs about Fucking* (Touch and Go 1987)
The Breeders –	*Pod* (4AD/Elektra 1990)
Cheap Trick –	"Baby Talk/Brontosaurus" (Sub Pop 1997)
The Danielson Famile –	*Fetch the Compass Kids* (Secretly Canadian 2001)
The Dirty Three –	*Ocean Songs* (Touch and Go 1998)
Edith Frost –	*Wonder Wonder* (Drag City 2001)
Robbie Fulks –	*Country Love Songs* (Bloodshot 1996) *Couples in Trouble* (Bloodshot 2001)
Godspeed You – Black Emperor!	*Yanqui U.X.O.* (Constellation 2002)
PJ Harvey –	*Rid of Me* (Island 1993)

The Jesus Lizard –	*Head* (Touch and Go 1990) *Goat* (Touch and Go 1991)
Jon Spencer – Blues Explosion	*Jon Spencer Blues Explosion* (Caroline 1992)
Low –	*Transmission* (EP) (Vernon Yard 1996) *Secret Name* (Kranky 1999)
Mogwai –	"My Father, My King" (Matador 2001)
Nirvana –	*In Utero* (DGC 1993)
Palace Music –	*Viva Last Blues* (Drag City 1995) *Arise, Therefore* (Drag City 1996)
The Pixies –	*Surfer Rosa* (Rough Trade 1988)
The Poster Children –	*Daisychain Reaction* (Twin/Tone 1991)
Rapemen –	*Two Nuns and a Pack Mule* (Touch and Go 1989)
Scrawl –	*Velvet Hammer* (Simple Machines 1993) *Travel on Rider* (Elektra 1996)
Shadowy Men on – a Shadowy Planet	*Sport Fishin'* (Cargo 1993)
Shellac –	*At Action Park* (Touch and Go 1994)
Silkworm –	*In the West* (C/Z 1994)
The Wedding Present –	"Brassneck" (RCA 1990) *Seamonsters* (First Warning 1991)

10

THE BEAT SCIENTISTS:
ARTHUR BAKER,
THE BOMB SQUAD, AND DR. DRE

In the early 1980s bushy-afroed funk bands and polyestered disco groups had boogied themselves into exhaustion. The new decade gave birth to a new electronic sound; synthesizers and drum-machines had begun their dance-emporium mutiny. Tuning into the frequency of change was a nascent engineer/producer named Arthur Baker. On a lunch break from his Long Island day job, Baker sat in a nearby park eating and watching a clutch of young b-boys break-dance to the ghetto blaster powered sounds of Kraftwerk's syntheti-cally chilly Teutonic travelogue, "Trans Europe Express." As the kids athletically spun on their heads and swiveled on their palms, Baker was jolted by an idea; why not wed the austere synth melody to the hyper-electronic beat of his new favorite toy, a Roland TR-808 drum machine?

Soon after his brownbag brainstorm, Baker ran into rapper and pioneering turntablist DJ Afrika Bambaataa at the fledgling hip-hop label Tommy Boy Records. Recently, the two had worked together on Bambaataa's hip-hop predicting paragon "Jazzy Sensation," a clap-ping beat-box reworking of Gwen McRae's '70s dance staple "Funky Sensation." Baker detailed his idea to Bambaataa, and the duo banded with co-producer Shep Pettibone to cut the paradigm-shifting, origi-nal electro-funk recording "Planet Rock." By simply dropping rap rhymes over the new technology of the TR-808 drum machine and Fairlight synthesizer, it was now official: Machines, in the right hands, could actually be funky.

• • • • •

Boston-bred and born in 1955, Baker was weaned on the usual Jefferson Airplane, Allman Brothers, and James Taylor records of the day. By the early 1970s Baker became an R&B freak, hooked on Norman Whitfield's funky space reincarnation of Motown, Willie Mitchell's lusciously sexy Al Green productions, and Gamble and Huff's elegant Philly soul bump. After a turn as a popular club DJ around Boston led to a debut production of Northend's "Happy Days," Baker headed to New York at the end of the 1970s.

Fascinated by the emerging grassroots hip-hop movement, Baker briefly teamed up with Salsoul Records and Nu Yorican Latin soul maestro Joe Bataan. The Spanish Harlem-born Bataan had been cutting fantastic dance sides since the late 1960s boogaloo craze, and by the mid-1970s he had moved on to a sublime brand of orchestrated Latin funk he called "Salsoul." Always innovative and street-wise, Bataan had become intrigued by the street-corner rapping he witnessed cropping up around various Bronx neighborhoods. "Joe said 'yo man, you got to come up to the Bronx and see this. There's guys talking over records. Someone's going to make a million dollars out of this,'" Baker recalled.[1]

Placed over a Chic-like snaky guitar rhythm, simple synthetic drum track, and disco-derived female backing vocalists, Bataan delivered the Baker-produced "Rap-O Clap-O." Arguably the first modern-style rap cut, the novelty-oriented song is a fascinating snapshot in time as Bataan's proto-rap passed the baton from disco's last sweaty night to the new morning of electro-funk. Unfortunately, "Rap-O Clap-O" languished in the can for quite some time. Fatefully, in the interim, the Sugar Hill Gang's "Rapper's Delight" and the Fatback Band's "King Tim" were released, and the two proceeded to duke it out over the title of "original rap song." Frustrated by his lack of success, Baker briefly returned to Boston, only to be drawn back to the belly of the beast for another go-round. It was during his return New York stint that he and Bambaataa stumbled onto the electro-funk formula.

Following Baker's revolutionary mixture of synthesized melodies and synthetic beats pioneered on "Planet Rock," a Number 4 R&B chart hit in 1982, he re-teamed with Bambaataa's Soul Sonic Force. Aided by keyboardist John Robie, Baker's production of Soul Sonic Force's electrifying "Looking for the Perfect Beat" significantly expanded the electro-funk palette. Unlike its predecessor, the song was denser, swaddled in sequenced synthesizers, with aggressive kinetic drum machine programming, resulting in an overall richer sound. Highly notable was Bambaataa's nimble record-scratching technique, which he employed over the freestyle party delivery of rappers G.L.O.B.E. and PowWow. One of the cornerstones of electro-funk, "Looking for the Perfect Beat"'s influence rumbled through several subsequent electronic dance genres, including Detroit techno, Miami bass, Chicago house, and Manchester acid house. With its indefatigable freshness, Baker's technology-embracing electro sound changed the rules of dance music. Subsequently, "Looking for the Perfect Beat" has formed the rhythmic foundation of everything from Bomb the Bass's pioneering 1987 house music sound-collage "Beat Dis" to 95 South's influential early-nineties Miami bass mega-hit "Whoot (There It Is)."

Seeking autonomy, Baker and fellow producer Maurice Starr broke from Tommy Boy and formed Streetwise Records. Continuing to mine virgin electro-funk territory, Baker's pounding, programmed 808 drumbeats and robotic washes of synthesized melodies became the sonic fuel for the budding break dance juggernaut. Reinforcing the break-dance music trend was Baker's endlessly echoed production of Rocker's Revenge "Walking on Sunshine" and his own hyperactive "Breakers Revenge" (which was featured in the 1984 break-dance film *Beat Street*.)

Baker's jittery electro-funk dance rhythms not only resonated in the Triborough dance emporiums and local street corners, but they also made a significant impact on synth embracing DIY English bands. Still in the later stages of new wave, British artists like Gary Numan, Yazoo, Depeche Mode, Human League, and Soft Cell had virtually abandoned guitars and human percussion for the brave new world of frosty synths and mechanical drum machines. Inspired by Baker's sequenced synthesizer and TR-808 sound, British groups began to flock to his studio with hopes of building hits on his man-meets-machine electro-dance blueprint. The first U.K. visitors to his New York studio were Freeze, whose percolating "IOU" was written by Baker in a cab on the way to the session. Framed by a catchy female vocal ("A, E—A, E, I, O, U…and Sometimes Y") and fleshed

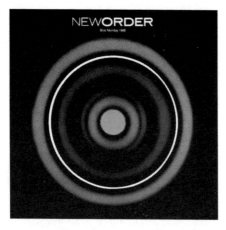

New Order
Blue Monday
(1983)

out with bleepy keyboards, grandiose Fairlight flourishes, and tumbling synth-pad drums, it became a dance floor smash. Tweaking the song further, Baker's eight-minute extended remix allowed the grammar lesson to squawk long into the night.

Next in line was New Order, a gloomy group of Mancunians recently entranced by the groundbreaking electronics of "Planet Rock." Originally shepherded into post-punk immortality by producer Martin Hannett as Joy Division, the band re-christened itself New Order in 1981 (following the suicide of lead singer Ian Curtis) and had begun to gingerly move towards an alternative dance direction. With Baker giving its dourly infectious "Blue Monday" a hypnotic, trance-like extended remix treatment, the song was released as a 12" single (in a sleeve appropriately designed to resemble a computer diskette). Lavished with shimmering layers of sequenced synthesizers, brittle beats, and sparse vocal interludes, "Blue Monday" quickly became *the* dance song of its era. Eventually moving over 3 million copies, it has become the biggest selling 12" single of all-time. The emergence of the 12" single was significant, instead of relegating dance songs to the constrictive running times of the 7" single, the newly favored format allowed remixes to churn for up to 20 minutes. Baker's remix revolution was now in full soul sonic force.

Baker and New Order re-teamed for the collaborative "Confusion," another cutting-edge alternative dance stalwart that reached the lower reaches of the American R&B charts in 1983. With Baker's impenetrable, cataclysmic mix, "Confusion" is a throbbing assault of pulsating electronic squawks, jackhammer beats, and Bernard Sumner's robot-mimicking vocals. The fact that New Order (a white English new wave act) was able to cross over to the R&B charts offered further proof that the anonymous machine age of synth-dance had arrived.

Simultaneously, Streetwise Records' fortunes were cresting, thanks to the signing of a black teen group known as New Edition. Led by the pre-pubescent lead-singer Bobby Brown, the group's Baker-mixed debut *Candy Girl* was a guilty-pleasure '80s update on Jackson Five kiddy-pop bubblegum. Lending his commercially cunning dance sound to pop giants like Bruce Springsteen, Cyndi Lauper, Jeff Beck, and Diana Ross, Baker had become music's most highly sought remixer by the mid-1980s. Notable among his high-profile jobs was a heavily electronic remix of the Rolling Stones' gory "Too Much Blood," whose alacritous rhythms and disconcertingly sequenced sound swarmed straight towards the pullulating British house and Detroit techno scenes.

Baker's visibility reached its zenith with the Artists Against Apartheid charity rock offering *Sun City*, which he co-produced in 1985 with the E Street Band's Little Stevie Van Zandt. More stridently political and inherently musical than other albums of its ilk, the humanitarian release featured a heavyweight list of contributors, including Miles Davis, Bob Dylan, Bruce Springsteen, U2, Keith Richards, Peter Gabriel, Run DMC, Pete Townshend, and Lou Reed. Four years later, Baker released his first official solo album, *Merge*, a dance record brimming with cameos that was marked by the hit Al Green collaboration "The Message Is Love."

In 1985, Baker also masterminded his alter ego, the Criminal Element Orchestra. Under that moniker, Baker released the seminal "Put the Needle to the Record," an intricate song pastiche that built on editing methods first introduced by producer Teo Macero on mid-1970s Miles Davis albums and dub alchemists King Tubby and Scratch Perry. Another watershed, "Put the Needle to the Groove" telegraphed the forthcoming cut 'n' paste recording techniques of electronica.

While his profile has lowered in recent years, Baker continues to mine dance music in much the same way as his early electro-funk days:

> The spirit of making dance records is exactly the same to me as it's always been. You have more control now in the studio, that's the whole new thing. But the spirit in which people make dance records is still DJs and the kids who want to go to clubs and hear their own records. I've never made a great dance record that wasn't the direct result of being in a club the night before. Never. When you make a dance record the objective is clear—to make people dance and have a good time. You really can't take it too seriously.[2]

• • • • •

By the early 1980s many of the nation's inner cities, from New York, to L.A., were in turmoil. As the wealth gap became a chasm and racial tensions threatened to boil over at any moment, increasing urban strain had begun to spark a new round of street level anger. Further packing the powder keg was the double-whammy ascendance of crack and AIDS and the unholy trinity of guns, gangs, and violence. It was in the middle of this shaky urban ground that Adelphi University radio DJ and graphic arts student Carlton Ridenhour met wannabe hip-hop producer and fellow collegian Hank Shocklee at a New York party in 1982.

As part of the party promotion crew Spectrum City, Ridenhour made an announcement at the gathering. As he spoke, his deep baritone voice boomed through the room, commanding Shocklee's attention. After a mutual introduction, Shocklee brought Ridenhour over to his pal Bill Stephney who was the host of a college radio show that specialized in rap. Immediately, the three men forged an alliance built on a passionate love of rap and a shared sense of cultural and political outrage. Ridenhour soon began to appear on Stephney's "Mr. Bill" radio show, where he developed his new politically conscious, rapping alter ego, Chuckie D. Eventually, it was shortened to Chuck D., and he and Shocklee were given their own radio slot, dubbed the "Super Spectrum Mix Show."

Public Enemy

Having a radio show platform was just what the would-be mix-master Shocklee had hoped for. Already a bedroom beat scientist, he had been crafting crude but inventive sound collage rhythm tracks influenced by James Brown's minimalist Afro-centric funk and the jarring industrial proto-sampling of Eno and Byrne's *My Life in the Bush of Ghosts*. It was over these experimental backing tracks that Chuck D. began to rap. One of the earliest songs the duo recorded was fortuitously called "Public Enemy No. 1."

The unusually fierce demo began to circulate and soon found its way to up-and-coming Def Jam music mogul Rick Rubin, who had recently hired Stephney to work at the label. While the demo's aggressive sound and political approach somewhat confounded Rubin and label co-honcho Russell Simmons, neither could deny its sheer power. Eventually, Chuck D., Shocklee, and Stephney (in the role of publicist) were signed to Def Jam. Rounding out the group was rapping foil Flava

Flav, an outrageously comical figure with a predilection for wearing large clocks around his neck (a symbol that informed the audience that they knew "what time it was"), dexterous DJ, Terminator X, and controversial dance choreographer Professor Griff. Public Enemy was now on the loose, determined to unleash its "mind terrorism" on the masses.

With its lineup solidified (and a new group logo of a beret-wearing black militant within a rifle sight), Public Enemy recorded the Rubin-assisted *Yo Bum Rush the Show* in 1987. Cast in a mold similar to recent Rubin-produced rap-rock crossover monoliths for the Beastie Boys (*License to Ill*) and Run DMC (*Raising Hell*), the album was impelled by venomous raps, wailing guitar samples and metallic hard rock rhythms. An undeniably auspicious debut, it was actually the non-album B-Side "Rebel Without a Pause" that first lit Shocklee's explosive Bomb Squad fuse.

The seminal cut begins with an opening spoken sample from the film *Wattstax*: "Brothers and sisters, I don't know what the world is coming to," and then explodes into a raw kick-kick-snare beat and a shrill whistling teapot-like JB's horn loop, which perpetually shrieks around Chuck D.'s pissed-off pontifications. Fleshed out by Shocklee's adroit "cut 'n' paste" editing techniques, which turned music samples into shards of sound and twisted rhythms, and Terminator X's mind-boggling scratching skills, this was the angry aural embodiment of New York's Reagan-era mean streets.

By the time of 1988's lethal follow-up, *It Takes a Nation of Millions to Hold Us Back*, Public Enemy's production duties had been completely passed off to Shocklee and his "Bomb Squad" production crew, which now included his brother, Keith Shocklee, Carl Ryder, and Eric Sadler. Utilizing the Bomb Squad production gadflies was highly significant, as their self-containment afforded Public Enemy unprecedented control over its own sound. Soon rap camps became the rage, and by the early 1990s production crews from Master P's No Limit, to Puff Daddy's infamous Bad Boy team, became standard hip-hop operating procedure.

Seeking to disturb, disconcert, and provoke as "music's worst nightmare," the Bomb Squad's insurgent recipe of hard and heavy drum loops, thunderous bursts of sampled distortion, nods to heavy funk, squawking free jazz, and avant-garde *musique concrète* furiously catalyzed Chuck D.'s

Public Enemy
It Takes a Nation of
Millions to Hold
Us Back
(1988)

incensed political diatribes. Notably interspersed between tracks were short vocal interludes and jokes, a concept that transformed hip-hop from a singles-driven medium into an album-oriented art form. Widely imitated and expanded by artists ranging from A Tribe Called Quest to Dr. Dre, the rap skit has long since become a hip-hop album ubiquity.

Noteworthy among *Nation*'s tracks is the cautionary anthem "Don't Believe the Hype." Stoked by skeletal funk samples of James Brown and Rufus Thomas, a darting, wounded-bird horn sound-effect, Chuck D.'s serious-as-a-heart-attack proclamations and Flava Flav's "boy-yee" counter-punctuations, the track was catchy *and* ferocious. Additional major statements include the incessantly distorted "Bring the Noise," the powerful anti-draft dissertation "Black Steel in the Hour of Chaos," and the aforementioned Bomb Squad–sound turning point "Rebel Without a Pause." Shrewdly mastering the album at a louder than normal decibel level, the pumped-up volume helped to further distinguish the relentless cuts from their competition.

P.E. managed to top *Nation* with 1990's truculent *Fear of a Black Planet*. Specifically crystallizing the group's "mind terrorism" mission statement was "Welcome to the Terrordome," the Bomb Squad's crowning achievement of dizzying sonic mayhem. "Terrordome" playfully begins with a short staccato horn breakdown, but the party is short-lived, as a paranoiac fuzz-guitar sample (derived from the Temptations' Whitfield-produced "Psychedelic Shack") quickly slices in to ratchet up the apocalyptic tension. Then all hell breaks loose, as Shocklee's kitchen-sink mix gives way to clattering

Ice Cube
AmeriKKKa's
Most Wanted
(1990)

industrial rhythms, Terminator X's propeller-like scratching, a multitude of sampled James Brown grunts, and a deluge of barely recognizable funk snippets from Kool and the Gang and Instant Funk. Finally, Chuck D. enters the scene, bellowing the opening rhyme: "I've got so much trouble on my mind/I refuse to lose/Here's your ticket/Hear the drummer get wicked." Rather than the contemporary practice of relying on one recognizable sample to power a song's hook, Shocklee's segmented sound-effect snippets were specifically designed to mirror, challenge, and catalyze Chuck D.'s flowing, bellicose raps. "Welcome to the Terrordome" is the perfect realization of Public Enemy's "mind terrorism" mission statement.

Cut before costly music publishing clearances were enforced, *Fear of a Black Planet* is an angry sonic tapestry tautly packed with disorienting samples that unpredictably detonate from every cranny of the mix, akin to the Dust Brother's sample-crazed production of the Beastie Boys' *Paul's Boutique*. Honing its sound to razor-sharpness, the Bomb Squad waged its war on ammunition extracted from Afrika Bambaataa, Sade, Eric Clapton, Queen, Roy Ayers, Eddie Murphy, and Sly Stone samples. Tracks like the Flava Flav–led indictment "911 Is a Joke," the frenetic "Power to the People," the scathing "Burn Hollywood Burn," and the all-mighty "Fight the Power" (a crucial component of Spike Lee's racial-tension exploration *Do the Right Thing*), help make the album one of the most sonically devastating and lyrically provocative releases of all-time.

Dr. Dre

Ultimately, Shocklee and the Bomb Squad were victims of their own success. *Fear of a Black Planet* had shattered nearly every rap convention. As a consequence, Shocklee had nowhere left to go with Public Enemy. Breaking from P.E., Shocklee lent his distinctively confrontational sound to Ice Cube's widely heralded 1990 solo debut, *AmeriKKKa's Most Wanted*. An unflinchingly tough album, the archetypal release saw the former N.W.A. member beginning to distance himself from the violent glamorization of West Coast gangsta rap, as he bravely embraced the Bomb Squad's East Coast–centric sound.

In 1998 Shocklee reunited with Public Enemy on *He Got Game*, its solid comeback album/soundtrack for Spike Lee's film of the same name. Underscoring the reunion was the inescapable fact that hip-hop had changed remarkably in the decade since Public Enemy's reign. No longer an underground conduit for protest, hip-hop had largely abandoned the group's sonically militant confrontation in favor of a less controversial, tamer pop-oriented sound. Perhaps no one was more responsible for hip-hop's move towards the platinum-enriched mainstream than another ex–N.W.A. gangsta-rapper, Dr. Dre.

• • • • •

There was a time when Compton was just another neglected inner city, virtually unknown to anybody who didn't live near the conurbation of Los Angeles. It was in this particularly tough urban area that a teenager named Andre Young began to escape his bleak surroundings by immersing himself in music. Amassing an overflowing stack of electro-funk and '60s soul records, Young began to spin his unwieldy collection at early-1980s house parties around Compton. Possessed with an uncanny knack for getting booties bouncing, Dre (as he was nicknamed) had the simple but elusive skill that every successful DJ needs: He could make folks dance. Word of Dre's skills soon led to a regular DJ slot at Eve's After Dark, a popular Compton club where he worked between 1982 and 1985.

A slave to the rhythm, Dre's bedroom doubled as a sound laboratory. After creating the synthetic drum machine beats at home during his days, he would intersperse them into his DJ sets at night. Slyly using his captive club audience as test-marketers, Dre had the benefit of snagging instant feedback for his homespun beats. Consequently, he was able to zero in on what worked and what did not. It was while spinning at After Dark that he struck up a friendship with a fellow DJ known as Yella. Kindred spirits, Dre and Yella began to hole up in one of After Dark's side rooms, cutting raw hip-hop demos together on the club's archaic four-track recording machine.

Trading on their phenomenally popular After Dark sets, Dre and Yella secured their own time slots on L.A.'s KDAY radio station. Hosting a popular mix show modeled on his club formula, Dre's fame spread from Compton throughout the vast L.A. basin. Among the many taking note of his rising star was Lonzo Williams, a wannabe singer and the owner of Eve's After Dark. Williams sensed his top DJ was onto something with his nose for fresh beats and crowd-pleasing instincts and recruited Dre for a new group he was forming called the World Class Wreckin' Cru. Joining Dre were his high school pal Cli-N-Tel, Yella, and Williams himself. The group recorded several Dre-produced songs (often recorded at the After Dark studio) that fused Arthur Baker–style electro-funk, old-school rap and poppy synth-based soul. Cut in the same cloth as other locally based electro-rap acts like the Egyptian Lover and L.A. Dream Team, the Wreckin' Cru enjoyed modest commercial success though the mid-1980s with robotic rump shakers like "Juice" and "Surgery" and the slow-jam classic "Turn Off the Lights."

With his street-tempered profane sensibility and love of hard-edged rap, Dre came to loathe the group's increasingly safe, pop-oriented synth sound. Making matters worse was the laughable Williams-mandated attire that often included fey lace outfits and even lipstick and makeup. Glaringly out of step with his hard-knock Compton reality, Dre finally left the group near the end of the 1980s. Affected by the increasingly heinous gang violence around his neighborhood, rebel icons like sexually explicit comedians Richard Pryor and Rudy Day Moore, and Al Pacino's infamous *Scarface* character, Dre co-wrote the unblinkingly violent street fantasy "Boyz 'N the Hood" with fellow rapper Ice Cube in 1986. Recently, Dre and Cube had joined forces with Ruthless Records, a label that had been financed on drug money accrued by a pint-sized dealer and rapper named Eazy-E.

A keen judge of talent and quality, Eazy-E was thrilled by "Boyz 'N the Hood"'s unflinching street-wise vividness, and he promptly offered the song to one of Ruthless's groups, HBO. Illustrative of the growing stylistic chasm between the left and right coasts, the New York–based HBO dismissed the crude Compton-incubated song as "West Coast Shit."[3] Clearly, there was a distinction emerging between the well-established New York school of rap, typified by Run DMC, Boogie Down Productions, and Public Enemy, and the unrepentant violence-without-consequences themes of the upstart West Coast wing.

Acting on Dre's suggestion, Eazy-E recorded "Boyz 'N the Hood" himself. The song became Ruthless's first release and later the title of an acclaimed 1991 film starring Ice Cube. With their defiant new sound coalescing, Dre and Eazy-E assembled a new group with DJ Yella, Ice Cube, MC Ren, and (briefly) Arabian Prince. Building on the harsh gangbanging and misogynist fantasies introduced in "Boyz 'N the Hood," the group impudently christened itself Niggaz With Attitude, a.k.a. N.W.A.

After recording several unapologetically hedonistic, ultra-raw street anthems like "8 Ball" and "Dopeman," N.W.A. exploded onto the national consciousness with its baleful second album, *Straight Outta Compton* in 1988. Leveraging Public Enemy's extreme sonic assault but ditching their militant message, the Jheri-curled N.W.A. crudely romanticized the nefarious underbelly of ghetto life in all its nihilistic glory. Hip-hop had been strong-armed into the volatile era of "gangsta rap."

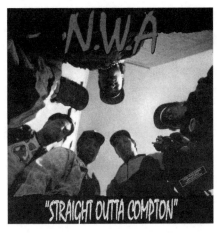

N.W.A.
Straight Outta Compton
(1988)

While MTV and commercial radio remained predictably gun-shy to the group's misanthropic sound, nothing could stop *Straight Outta Compton*, from becoming an instant hip-hop landmark. In contrast to the Bomb Squad's claustrophobic sound collages, Dre ominously kept N.W.A's early sound stark and frighteningly minimal. By punctuating cuts like "Gangsta Gangsta" and "Express Yourself" with sparse drum-machine beats and sporadic, lean funk guitar or horn samples, Dre squarely put the focus on the outlaw group's polarizing themes.

Following the departure of Ice Cube at the end 1989, N.W.A. lost its most vicious and talented rapper. Soldiering on through the next couple of years, the group frequently courted public outrage, most spectacularly with Dre's deceptively funky production of "Fuck the Police." One of the most controversial and debated songs ever recorded, the incendiary anti-anthem ominously portended the rising inner-city tensions that would spectacularly boil over in the 1992 L.A. riots.

With Eazy-E taking on the bulk of the rapping leads, the group's gangsta themes began to verge into self-parody. However, Dre's skills continued to develop at an astounding clip, and his productions became more layered and assured with each ensuing release. With his sound growing more lushly complex and overtly funky, Dre's soaring confidence led him towards courting outside production assignments. In 1989 he helmed N.W.A. associate D.O.C.'s *No One Can Do It Better* and (ex-Wrecking Cru singer) Michel'le's hit R&B single "No More Lies," both of which helped establish his reputation as a main purveyor of the new West Coast hip-hop sound.

In 1992 Dre was at a turning point. Seeking greater autonomy, he left N.W.A. and formed Death Row Records with burly and imposing ex-college football player Marion "Suge" Knight. After cutting his first solo tracks for the movie *Deep Cover*, Dre released his debut, *The Chronic*, in December of 1992. Dre himself was never the most adept rapper; while his productions were sure-handed and uniformly innovative, his rapping delivery was generally stilted and clumsy. Wisely, he turned much of the rapping duties for *The Chronic* over to a lanky newcomer from the Long Beach projects (first featured on *Deep Cover*) who went by the unforgettable moniker Snoop Doggy Dogg.

With Snoop's languid, Mississippi-meets-Cali drawl, the rapper's style was as refreshing as a breezy Santa Ana summer wind. One-hundred-eighty degrees from Chuck D.'s measured, stentorian baritone, Snoop's voice wheezed and irregularly fluttered over Dre's signature combo platter of blunted beats, rotund basslines, cooing female backup singers, and whining keyboards. This was not cramped music for congregating on grimy New York street corners; rather, it was the expansive aural equivalent of slowly rolling down endless stretches of L.A. asphalt, stoned on ultra-potent "chronic" weed. Ultimately, potent *Chronic* hits like "Let Me Ride" and "Ain't Nuthin' but a 'G' Thang" share more in common with the sun-baked So-Cal good-time ideals of the Beach Boys than the politically-charged "Black CNN" directives of P.E.

Liberally indulging in George Clinton's cartoon-colorful Parliament/Funkadelic "P-Funk" sound, Dre ingeniously sidestepped the early 1990s' barrier of paying exorbitant publishing clearances (which would have made Public Enemy and N.W.A.'s sample-heavy late-eighties songs too expensive to release) by "interpolation," a method that involved real musicians and singers re-recording song snippets to be used as samples. In doing so, Dre compensated the song's composer but was not obligated to additionally pay the record label that originally released the song.

Rather than Shocklee's menacing mode of cramming samples together beyond recognition, Dre's "G-Funk" milked singular hooks for all their catchiness, as evidenced on "G Thang" (heavily reliant on the creeping echoed melody of Leon Haywood's "I Wanna Do Something Freaky to You") and "Let Me Ride" (which borrows from Parliament's

Dr. Dre.
The Chronic
(1992)

debauched jubilee "Swing Down, Sweet Chariot" and its cosmic "Mothership Connection"). Brilliantly aiding the album's eight-times-platinum success were Dre's template-setting music videos. Generously featuring scores of scantily clad honies, tricked-out low riders, and 40-ounce-fueled parties, the iconic images helped bring his fun-in-the-Cali-sun G-Funk ideal to weather-beaten MTV viewers everywhere.

Dre continued his slow G-Funk roll with Snoop's monstrous 1993 debut, *Doggystyle*, a release that became the first debut album to enter the charts at Number 1. With Dre refining the glistening West Coast grooves of *The Chronic*, Snoop delivered another round of slow-as-molasses raps on such 1990s-defining hits as "Gin and Juice" and "What's My Name." With his production formula polished, Dre's G-Funk sound was now not only dominating the hip-hop world, but the pop charts at large.

However, all was not well at Death Row. Beset by violence, law-suits, and court cases, the label was beginning to get more headlines for its legal troubles than its music.

Dre's last walk on Death Row came in 1996, when he teamed up with old-school funk pioneer Roger Troutman (of Zapp) for Tupac Shakur's breakthrough hit "California Love." Based on Zapp's robotic classic "More Bounce to the Ounce," the Number 1 smash was an unabashed throwback to Dre's electro-funk roots. Unfortunately, the triumph quickly turned to tragedy when Tupac was gunned down while sitting in Knight's car on the Las Vegas strip. With black clouds gathering over Knight, Dre wisely reprieved himself from Death Row.

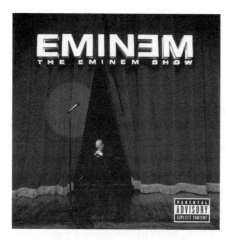

Eminem
The Eminem Show
(2002)

Forming his own Aftermath Records in 1997, a somewhat wearied Dre officially pronounced gangsta rap dead. Always looking to break new talent, he began to produce soundtracks such as *Above the Rim* and *Murder Was the Case*. Craftily using the soundtracks to showcase new discoveries including Warren G., Nate Dogg, Jewell, and Tha Dogg Pound, Dre successfully expanded his empire. By the end of the 1990s Dre was working with a new protégé, Marshall Mathers, a loquacious white rapper who was soon to be better known as Eminem.

The Detroit-bred Mathers originally caught Dre's eye after placing second in the freestyle category of a 1997 Rap Olympics showdown in Los Angeles. Following his ballyhooed performance, Eminem was swooped up by Dre's parent-label, Interscope Records, and the two quickly went into the studio together. Over Dre's signature slow-rolling sound, Enimem unleashed a torrent of sometimes comical, often violent character-driven raps and rhymes. The pairing proved to be commercial and critical magic as Eminem's story-raps captivated imaginations everywhere. After two decades a white rapper had finally been imbued with legitimate street-cred. Catapulted by his astonishingly successful debut, *Slim Shady*, and its similarly constructed Dre-produced follow-ups, *The Marshall Mathers LP* and *The Eminem Show*, Eminem had transcended hip-hop's limitations to become the first true pop phenomenon of the new millennium.

Long pre-occupied with his outside productions, Dre finally got around to releasing *2001*, his long-awaited follow-up to *The Chronic* in 1999. While the album expectedly featured Snoop Dogg, Eminem, and a multiple of funk samples and interpolations, it also introduced new elements to Dre's G-Funk formula including David Axelrod–sampled psychedelic strings ("Next Episode"), jazz ("Still D.R.E."), opera ("What's the Difference"), and smatterings of reggae. By tweaking his sound, Dre's enduring production style continues to hold its own over a new crop of bar-raising production challengers like ethno-beat maven Timbaland (Missy Elliott, Jay-Z, Nas) and modernistic rap-dance remixing duo the Neptunes (Nelly, Ludacris, Air).

• • • • •

After more than two decades since "Rap-O, Clap-O," hip-hop has demonstrated a remarkable resiliency. From its street-corner party roots, to Arthur Baker's pioneering electro-funk club remixes, to Public Enemy's New York mind terrorism, to N.W.A.'s incendiary West Coast gangsta-rap, and from Dr. Dre's pop conscious "G-Funk," to the reign of his new millennium golden-boy Eminem, rap's reach has seeped far beyond its inner-city origins. Stretching from suburban malls to rural trailer parks, from bedrooms in Tokyo to clubs in Rio, its irresistible, bumping beat has thumped across both physical and cultural borders. As its influence continues to expand across genres, elements of hip-hop now reside in bombastic "New Metal" bands, coy indie-rockers, Jamaican Dancehall ragamuffins, electronica technocrats, and glittering pop divas. Originally an underground underdog, it has defied the odds to become perhaps the dominating musical force and the new epicenter of recording innovation.

KEY RECORDINGS
Arthur Baker

Arthur Baker –	"Breakers Revenge" (Atlantic 1984)
	Breakin' (Perfecto 2001)
Arthur Baker and – the Backbeat Disciples	*Merge* (A&M 1989)
	"The Message is Love" (with Al Green) (A&M 1989)
	Give in to Rhythm (RCA 1991)
Afrika Bambaataa & – the Jazzy Five	"Jazzy Sensation" (Tommy Boy 1981)
Afrika Bambaataa – (with Soul Sonic Force)	"Planet Rock" (Tommy Boy 1982)
	"Looking for the Perfect Beat" (Tommy Boy 1983)
	Planet Rock: The Album (Tommy Boy 1986)
Joe Bataan –	"Rap-O, Clap-O" (Salsoul 1979)
Jeff Beck –	*Flash* (Epic 1985)
Black Uhuru –	"Great Train Robbery" (Brutal) (Ras 1986)
Brooklyn Funk – Essentials	*Cool and Steady and Easy* (RCA 1995)
Tevin Campbell –	T.E.V.I.N. (Warner Bros. 1991)
Neneh Cherry –	"Buffalo Stance" (remix) (Virgin 1989)
Criminal Element – Orchestra	"Put the Needle to the Record" (WTG 1989)
	Locked Up (WTG 1989)
Will Downing –	"A Love Supreme" (4th & Broadway 1988)
Bob Dylan –	*Empire Burlesque* (Columbia 1985)
Face to Face –	"10, 9, 8" "Under the Gun" (Face to Face) (Epic 1984)
	Confrontation (Epic 1985)
Fleetwood Mac –	"Big Love" (remix) (Warner Bros. 1987)
Freez –	"I, O, U" (Streetwise 1982)
Glory –	"Can You Guess What Groove This Is?" (Posse 1980)
Hall and Oates –	*Big Bam Boom* (RCA 1984)
Debbie Harry –	"Brite Side" "Sweet and Low" (Def, Dumb and Blonde) (Sire 1989)
Cyndi Lauper –	"Girls Just Want to Have Fun" (remix) (Columbia 1984)
Jack E. Makossa –	"Opera House" (Minimal 1987)
Nona Hendryx –	*The Heat* (RCA 1985)
Nairobi –	"Funky Soul Makossa" (Streetwise 1982)
Naked Eyes –	"(What) In the Name of Love" (EMI 1984)

New Edition –   "Candy Girl" (Streetwise 1982)
                        Candy Girl (Streetwise 1983)

New Order –   "Blue Monday" (Factory 1983)
                        "Confusion" (Factory 1983)
                        "Thieves Like Us" (Factory 1984)
                        "Touched by the Hand of God" (Factory 1987)
                        "1963" (remix) (London 1995)

Northend –   "Happy Days" (Emergency 1981)

Pet Shop Boys –   "In the Night" (remix) (EMI 1986)

Planet Patrol –   "Play at Your Own Risk" (Tommy Boy 1982)
                        "Cheap Thrills" (Tommy Boy 1983)
                        Play at Your Own Risk (Tommy Boy 1983)
                        "I Didn't Know I Loved You (Until I Saw You
                            Rock and Roll)" (Tommy Boy 1984)

John Rocca –   *Best of: I.O.U.* (Hot Productions 1996)

Rockers Revenge –   "Walking on Sunshine" (Streetwise 1981)

Rolling Stones –   "Too Much Blood" (remix) (Warner Bros. 1984)

Bruce Springsteen –   "Dancing in the Dark" (remix) (Columbia 1984)

Tina B. –   *Tina B.* (Elektra 1984)

Wally Jump Jr. and –   "Tighten Up (I Just Can't Stop Dancin')"
    the Criminal Element   (A&M 1987)
    Orchestra

Original Soundtrack –   *Beat Street* (Atlantic 1984)

Various Artists –   *Artists Against Apartheid: Sun City*
                            (Manhattan 1985)

The Bomb Squad

Bell Biv DeVoe –   "B.B.D. (I Thought It Was Me)" (Poison)
                            (MCA 1990)

Peter Gabriel –   "Steam" (remix) (Geffen 1992)

Ice Cube –   *AmeriKKKa's Most Wanted* (Priority 1990)

Chaka Khan –   "Life is a Dance" (The Remix Project)
                            (Warner Bros. 1989)

LL Cool J –   *Walking With a Panther* (Def Jam 1989)

Public Enemy –   "Bring the Noise" (Less Than Zero soundtrack)
                            (Def Jam 1987)
                        Yo! Bum Rush the Show (Def Jam 1987)
                        It Takes a Nation of Millions to Hold Us Back
                            (Def Jam 1988)
                        "Fight the Power" (Motown 1989)

Public Enemy (cont.) –   "Welcome to the Terrordome" (Def Jam/Columbia
           1989)
           "Anti-Nigger Machine" (Def Jam 1990)
           "Brothers Gonna Work It Out" (Def Jam 1990)
           Fear of a Black Planet (Def Jam 1990)
           "Power to the People" (Def Jam 1990)
           Apocalypse 91...the Enemy Strikes Back (executive
           producer) (Def Jam/Columbia 1991)
           Greatest Misses (executive producer)
           (Def Jam 1992)
           He Got Game (Def Jam 1998)

Run-D.M.C. –   "3 in the Head" "Ooh Watcha Gonna Do" "Big
           Willie" (*Down With the King*) (Profile 1993)

Slick Rick –   *The Great Adventures of Slick Rick*
           (Def Jam 1988)

Son of Bazerk –   *Bazerk Bazerk Bazerk* (Soul/MCA 1991)

Terminator X & the –   *Super Bad* (executive producer) (Def Jam 1994)
Godfathers of Threatt

Third Bass –   *The Cactus Album* (Def Jam 1989)

Young Black –   *Young Black Teenagers* (MCA 1991)
   Teenagers   *Dead End Kidz Doin' Lifetime Bidz* (MCA 1993)

Hank Shocklee

GP WU –   *Don't Go Against the Grain* (executive producer)
           (MCA 1998)

Aaron Hall –   *Truth* (produced with Keith Shocklee) (Silas 1993)

Paul Jackson Jr. –   *Out of the Shadows* (Atlantic 1990)

Big Daddy Kane –   *Looks Like a Job for Big Daddy*
           (Cold Chillin' 1993)

Dr. Dre

Above the Law –   "Freedom of Speech" (*Pump Up the Volume*
           soundtrack) (MCA 1990)
           Livin' Like Hustlers (Epic 1990)

Mary J. Blige –   "Family Affair" (*No More Drama*) (MCA 2001)

DJ Quik –   *Under tha Influence* (Ark 21 2002)

The D.O.C. –   *No One Can Do it Better* (Ruthless 1991)

Dr. Dre –   "Deep Cover" (*Deep Cover* soundtrack)
           (Sony 1992)
           The Chronic (Priority/Interscope 1992)

"Let Me Ride" (Death Row 1993)
"Nuthin' But a G Thang" (Death Row 1993)
"Still D.R.E." (Aftermath 1999)
2001 (Aftermath 1999)
"Next Episode (Aftermath 2000)

Eazy-E –   *Eazy Does It* (Priority 1990)
                Eternal E (Ruthless 1995)

Eminem –   *Slim Shady LP* (Interscope 1999)
                "My Name Is" (Interscope 1999)
                Marshall Mathers LP (Interscope 2000)
                "The Real Slim Shady" (Interscope 2000)
                "Stan" (Interscope 2000)
                The Eminem Show (Interscope 2002)
                "Without Me" (Sony 2002)

Eve –   *Scorpion* (Interscope 2000)
                Eve-Olution (Interscope 2002)

50 Cent –   "In da Club" (Shady/Aftermath/Interscope 2003)

The Firm –   *The Firm* (Aftermath 1997)

Warren G. –   *Return of the Regulator* (Uptown/Universal 2001)

Ice Cube –   "Hello" (War & Peace Vol. 2) (Priority 2000)

Jay-Z –   "The Watcher 2" (*Blueprint2: The Gift
                and the Curse*) (Def Jam 2002)

Jewell –   "Harvest for the World" (*Murder Was the
                Case* soundtrack) (Death Row 1994)

Mack 10 –   "Hate in Yo Eyes" (*Bang or Ball*) (Universal 2001)

Michel'le –   "No More Lies" (Ruthless 1990)

N.W.A. –   "8-Ball" (Ruthless 1987)
                "Dope Man" (Ruthless 1987)
                N.W.A and the Posse (Ruthless 1987)
                Straight Outta Compton (Ruthless 1988)
                "Express Yourself" (Ruthless/Priority 1989)
                "Boyz-N'-the-Hood" (Priority 1999)
                100 Miles and Runnin' EP (Ruthless 1990)
                Niggaz4life (Priority 1991)

Nas –   *It Was Written* (Columbia 1996)

Scarface –   "Game Over" (Untouchable) (Rap-A-Lot 1997)

Snoop (Doggy) Dogg –   "What's My Name?" (Death Row 1993)
                Doggystyle (Death Row/Interscope 1993)
                "Gin and Juice" (Interscope 1994)
                "Murder Was the Case" (Death Row 1994)
                "Hennessey n Buddah" "Lay Low"
                      (*Tha Last Meal*) (Priority 2000)

END NOTES

Chapter One

1. Mark Lewisohn, *The Beatles: Recording Sessions*, (New York: Harmony Books, 1988), p. 72.

2. George Martin (with Jeremy Hornsby), *All You Need Is Ears*, (New York: St. Martin's Press, 1979), p. 133.

3. Mark Ribowsky, *He's a Rebel: Phil Spector Rock and Roll's Legendary Producer*, (New York: Cooper Square Press, 1989), p. 132.

4. *The London Evening Standard*, January 24, 1964.

5. Mark Lewisohn, *The Beatles: Recording Sessions*, (New York: Harmony Books, 1988), p. 69.

6. Mark Ribowsky, *He's a Rebel: Phil Spector Rock and Roll's Legendary Producer*, (New York: Cooper Square Press, 1989), p. 198.

7. Harvey Robert Kubernik, "Jack Nitzsche—Phil Spector's Arranger Remembers the Classic Hits," *Goldmine Magazine*, June 17, 1988, Vol. 14, No. 14.

8. Mark Lewisohn, *The Beatles: Recording Sessions*, (New York: Harmony Books, 1988), p. 72.

9. Harvey Robert Kubernik, "Jack Nitzsche—Phil Spector's Arranger Remembers the Classic Hits," *Goldmine Magazine*, June 17, 1988, Vol. 14, No. 14.

10. George Martin (with Jeremy Hornsby), *All You Need Is Ears*, (New York: St. Martin's Press, 1979), p. 200.

11. Ibid.

12. Ibid.

13. Ibid, p. 209.

14. Mark Lewisohn, *The Beatles: Recording Sessions*, (New York: Harmony Books, 1988), p. 96.

15. Ibid, p. 99.

16. Ibid, p. 192.

17. Richard Williams, *Out of His Head: The Sound of Phil Spector*, (New York: Outerbridge & Lazard, 1972).

18. Mark Ribowsky, *He's a Rebel: Phil Spector Rock and Roll's Legendary Producer*, (New York: Cooper Square Press, 1989), p. 255.

19. Ibid, p. 268.

20. Ibid, p. 277.
21. Ibid, p. 278.
22. David Fricke, *Hey Ho Let's Go: Ramones Anthology* liner notes, p. 54, Warner Archives, 1999.

Chapter Two

1. Brian Wilson with Todd Gold, *Wouldn't It Be Nice*, (New York: Harper, Collins, 1991), p. 59.
2. Ibid, p. 64.
3. Ibid, p. 64.
4. Carol Kaye personal interview, 2001
5. Brian Wilson with Todd Gold *Wouldn't It Be Nice* (New York: Harper, Collins, 1991), p. 79.
6. David Leaf, *The Beach Boys and the California Myth*, (New York: Grosset & Dunlap, 1978), p.73.
7. Carol Kaye, personal interview, 2001.
8. Brian Wilson with Todd Gold, *Wouldn't It Be Nice*, (New York: Harper, Collins, 1991), p. 145.
9. Dawn Eden, Sagittarius *Present Tense* liner notes, Sundazed Records, 1997.
10. Ibid.
11. David Bash, The Millennium *Magic Time* liner notes, Sundazed Records, 2001.
12. Dawn Eden, Sagittarius *Present Tense* liner notes, Sundazed Records, 1997.
13. Ibid.
14. Ibid.
15. David Bash, The Millennium *Magic Time* liner notes, Sundazed Records, 2001.
16. Ibid.
17. Ibid.
18. Ibid.
19. Ibid.
20. Ibid.
21. Ibid.
22. Ibid.
23. Joan Didion, *The White Album*, (New York: Simon & Schuster, 1979), p. 41, 47.

Chapter Three

1. All quotes taken from personal interviews conducted with Shel Talmy and David Axelrod, January 2003.

Chapter Four

1. Blair Jackson, "Eddie Kramer: Traffic's 'Dear Mr. Fantasy,'" *Mix Magazine*, February 1, 2003.

2. Richard Buskin, *Inside Tracks*, (New York: Avon Books, 1999), p. 128.

3. Ibid, p. 130.

4. Ibid, p. 129.

5. Ibid.

6. Paul Laurence, "Goats Head Soup—An In-depth Interview with Rolling Stones Producer Jimmy Miller," *Circle Magazine*, 1974.

7. Ibid.

8. Ibid.

9. Richard Buskin, *Inside Tracks*, (New York: Avon Books, 1999), p. 131.

10. Ibid, p. 132.

11. Ibid.

12. Ibid, p. 131.

13. *Rolling Stone*, July 17, 1975.

14. Shel Talmy, personal interview, January 2003.

15. John Tobler and Stuart Grundy, *The Record Producers*, (New York: St. Martin's Press, 1982), p. 147.

16. Richard Buskin, *Inside Tracks*, (New York: Avon Books, 1999), pp. 142–143.

17. John Tobler and Stuart Grundy, *The Record Producers*, (New York: St. Martin's Press, 1982), p. 148.

18. Ibid.

19. Ibid, p. 149.

20. Ibid.

21. Ibid.

22. Ibid.

23. Richard Buskin, *Inside Tracks*, (New York: Avon Books, 1999), p. 131.

24. John Tobler and Stuart Grundy, *The Record Producers*, (New York: St. Martin's Press, 1982), p. 157.

25. Ibid.

26. Richard Buskin, *Inside Tracks*, (New York: Avon Books, 1999), p.145.

27. John Tobler and Stuart Grundy, *The Record Producers*, (New York: St. Martin's Press, 1982), p. 158.

28. Andy Neill and Matt Kent, *Anyway Anyhow Anywhere: The Complete Chronicle of the Who*, (New York: Friedman/Fairfax Books, 2002), p. 199.

29. Ray Coleman, *Rod Stewart: The Biography*, (Pavilion Books: London, 1994), p. 104.

30. Marc Eliot, *To the Limit: The Untold Story of the Eagles*, (New York: Little, Brown and Company, 1998).

Chapter Five:

1. Al Green with Davin Seay, *Al Green: Take Me to the River*, (New York: Harper Entertainment Books, 2000), p. 196.

2. Ibid.

3. Ibid.

4. Ibid, p. 199.

5. James Dickerson, *Goin' Back to Memphis*, (New York: Schirmer Books/Simon & Schuster, 1996), p. 146.

Chapter Six:

1. Arthur Lubow, *People*, 1983.

2. Brian Eno, *Discreet Music* liner notes, Obscure Records, 1975.

3. Dave Marsh, "Her Horses Got Wings, They Can Fly," *Rolling Stone*, January 1, 1976.

4. Ibid.

5. John Cale, personal interview, 1989.

6. Ibid.

7. Andy Gill, "The Oblique Strategist," *Mojo Magazine*, June 1995.

8. Al Wiesel, "John Cale Q&A," *Rolling Stone*, Oct. 17, 1996.

9. Ibid.

10. Clinton Heylin, *From the Velvets to the Voidoids*, (New York: Penguin Books, 1993), p. 192.

11. Dave Marsh, "Her Horses Got Wings, They Can Fly," *Rolling Stone*, January 1, 1976.

12. Andy Gill, "The Oblique Strategist," *Mojo Magazine*, June 1995.

13. Ibid.

14. John Orme, "Eno: The Electric Boogaloo," *Melody Maker*, February 14, 1980.

15. Ibid.

16. Ibid.

Chapter Seven

1. Danny Kelly, "Lee Perry Interview," *New Musical Express*, November 17, 1984.

2. *Grand Royal Magazine*, Issue 2, 1995.

3. Danny Kelly, "Lee Perry Interview," *New Musical Express*, November 17, 1984.

4. Stephen Davis and Simon Peter, *Reggae International*, (New York: Knopf, 1983).

5. Ibid.

6. Doug Wendt, *Lee Perry: Reggae Greats* liner notes, Mango Records, 1984.

7. Bob Mack, "Robert Palmer Interview," *Grand Royal Magazine*, Issue 2, 1995, p. 8.

Chapter Eight

1. John Tobler and Stuart Grundy, *The Record Producers*, (New York: St. Martin's Press, 1982), p. 228.

2. Ibid.

3. Ibid.

4. Ibid.

5. Ibid.

6. Mark Lewisohn, *The Beatles Recording Sessions*, (New York: Harmony Books, 1988), p. 154.

7. John Tobler and Stuart Grundy, *The Record Producers*, (New York: St. Martin's Press, 1982), p. 228.

8. Ibid, p. 228.

9. Ibid, p. 230.

10. Ibid, p. 238.

11. Blair Jackson, "Chris Thomas: Three Decades on the Cutting Edge and the Charts," *Mix Magazine*, January 1, 1999.

12. Ibid.

Chapter Nine

1. Interview with Bernard Sumner, Peter Hook, and Stephen Morris, *New Music Express*, December 13, 1997.

Chapter Ten

1. Arthur Baker biography: *www.arthurbaker.net.*

2. Ibid.

3. Alan Light (editor), *The Vibe History of Rap,* (New York: Three Rivers Press, 1999).

INDEX

295

ABOUT THE AUTHOR

Photo: Jon Strickland

David N. Howard

has been a music journalist for over two decades. In 1986, he co-founded the ground-breaking Los Angeles–based publication *Contrast*. Formerly a contributing editor at *Raygun* and *The Nose,* he also served as managing editor for the online music resource, the Ultimate Band List (UBL.com). He currently lives in Santa Monica, CA. *Sonic Alchemy* is his first book.